BLACK LEADERSHIP IN AMERICA

STUDIES IN MODERN HISTORY

General editors: John Morrill and David Cannadine

This series, intended primarily for students, will tackle significant historical issues in concise volumes which are both stimulating and scholarly. The authors combine a broad approach, explaining the current state of our knowledge in the area, with their own research and judgements: and the topics chosen range widely in subject, period and place.

Titles already published

FRANCE IN THE AGE OF HENRY IV *Mark Greengrass*

VICTORIAN RADICALISM *Paul Adelman*

WHITE SOCIETY IN THE ANTEBELLUM SOUTH *Bruce Collins*

BLACK LEADERSHIP IN AMERICA: FROM BOOKER T. WASHINGTON TO JESSE JACKSON (*2nd Edn*) *John White*

THE TUDOR PARLIAMENTS *Michael A.R. Graves*

LIBERTY AND ORDER IN EARLY MODERN EUROPE *J.H. Shennan*

POPULAR RADICALISM *D.G. Wright*

'PAX BRITANNICA'? BRITISH FOREIGN POLICY 1789–1914 *Muriel E. Chamberlain*

IRELAND SINCE 1800 *K. Theodore Hoppen*

IMPERIAL MERIDIAN: THE BRITISH EMPIRE AND THE WORLD 1780–1830 *C.A. Bayly*

A SYSTEM OF AMBITION? BRITISH FOREIGN POLICY 1660–1793 *Jeremy Black*

BRITANNIA OVERRULED: BRITISH POLICY AND WORLD POWER IN THE 20TH CENTURY *David Reynolds*

POOR CITIZENS: THE STATE AND THE POOR IN TWENTIETH-CENTURY BRITAIN *David Vincent*

THE HOUSE OF LORDS IN BRITISH POLITICS AND SOCIETY 1815–1911 *E.A. Smith*

POLITICS UNDER THE LATER STUARTS: PARTY CONFLICT IN A DIVIDED SOCIETY 1660–1715 *Tim Harris*

BRITAIN AND LATIN AMERICA IN THE NINETEENTH AND TWENTIETH CENTURIES *Rory Miller*

Black Leadership in America: From Booker T. Washington to Jesse Jackson

Second Edition

John White

Longman

London and New York

LONGMAN GROUP UK LIMITED
Longman House, Burnt Mill, Harlow,
Essex CM20 2JE, England
and Associated Companies throughout the world.

Published in the United States of America
by Longman Inc., New York

© Longman Group Limited 1985

This edition © Longman Group UK Limited 1990.

First published 1985
Second edition 1990
Fifth impression 1994

BRITISH LIBRARY CATALOGUING IN PUBLICATION DATA
White, John 1939–
    Black leadership in America : from Booker T. Washington to Jesse Jackson. –
    2nd. ed. – (Studies in modern history (Longman Firm))
    1. United States. Black Communities. Leadership, history
    I. Title
    305.896073

    ISBN 0-582-06372-8

LIBRARY OF CONGRESS CATALOGUING IN PUBLICATION DATA

White, John, 1939–
    Black leadership in America : from Booker T. Washington to Jesse Jackson/
    John White. – 2nd ed.
    p.cm. – (Studies in modern history)
    Includes bibliographical references.
    ISBN 0-582-06372-8 (U.S.)
    1. Afro-American leadership – History. 2. Afro-American – Politics and
    government. 3. Afro-Americans – Biography. 4. Black nationalism – United
    States–History. 5. United States – Race relations. I. Title. II. Series:Studies in
    modern history
    (Longman (Firm))
    E185.61.W59   1990
    973'.0496073022–dc20
    [B]   89-77972
                                                                                 CIP

Set in 10/12pt Times
Printed in Malaysia by VVP

Contents

Contents

Preface to Second Edition

Since the appearance of the first edition of this book (*Black Leadership in America, 1895-1968*) in 1985, there has been a continuing academic and popular interest in the historical (and contemporary) experiences of black Americans. The notable black leaders – Booker T. Washington, W. E. B. Du Bois, Marcus Garvey, Malcolm X, Martin Luther King, Jr, and Jesse Jackson – of the twentieth century continue to receive scholarly attention in books and articles, as well as in the media. In particular, the period of the civil rights struggle in the United States, often dated from the Montgomery, Alabama bus boycott of 1955–56 and the emergence of Martin Luther King, Jr, as a national and international figure, has been subjected to intense examination and assessment. The American PBS award-winning series 'Eyes of the Prize' did much to alert the viewers to the episodes, personalities and achievements of the civil rights coalition, as well as the general outlines of the black experience since Emancipation. This book intends to incorporate some of the more recent scholarship, while retaining an emphasis on the historical context in which successive black leaders functioned. It also attempts to rectify some of the shortcomings of the first edition. The roles of women in black protest movements (and the responses of a male-dominated black leadership class to their involvement) is discussed with particular reference to the post-World War II era. For example, Mrs Jo Ann Robinson, the assertive and active head of the Women's Political Council in Montgomery, Alabama, was instrumental in calling for a boycott of the city's buses unless conditions for the black passengers were significantly improved, nearly eighteen months before the historic arrest of Mrs Rosa Parks on 1 December 1955. Again, within the civil rights coalition, Fannie Lou Hamer emerged as a grass-roots spokesperson for Mississippi's poor black citizens; in Selma, Alabama, Mrs Amelia P. Boynton played a crucial role in bringing SNCC field workers into the state; Ella Baker was a major force in both the SCLC and SNCC (and one of King's most trenchant critics); Septima Clark, a school teacher in Charleston, South Carolina, lost her job for refusing to resign her membership of the NAACP, and subsequently worked for the Highlander Folk School, setting up 'Citizenship Schools' across the South, preparing black adults to read and to vote. Anne Moody, a young black girl who grew up in Mississippi, became a civil rights activist and was increasingly critical of the strategies of the established black leadership.

Indeed, it has now become fashionable to assert that too much attention has been given to black *leaders* in the United States, at the expense of the rank-and-file who, it is claimed, were frequently in advance of those who professed to lead them. And, it has also been argued, the *local* concerns of black communities in America were often not those of the nationally-known protest organizations – the National Association for the Advancement of Coloured People (NAACP), the National Urban League (NUL), Marcus Garvey's Universal Negro Improvement Association (UNIA), or the various elements which comprised the civil rights coalition: the Southern Christian Leadership Conference (SCLC), the Congress of Racial Equality (CORE), the Student Non-Violent Coordinating Committee (SNCC) and the several black nationalist/separatist organizations of the 1960s and 1970s. The present study pays some attention to these contentions, but, again, is more concerned to illustrate the themes of continuity and change, conflict and competition, race and class, theory and ideology as exemplified by the six major leaders selected, and the movements they inspired. In sum, I have tried to give greater attention to the goals of successive black protest movements as perceived by their 'leaders', participants and critics, as well as the interactions between the racial philosophies of the leaders themselves.

On his recent tour of the southern states of America, the Trinidadian novelist and travel writer V. S. Naipaul was informed by an Atlanta journalist that only black Americans had 'leaders', designated as such by the media (and, he might have added, by historians). Naipaul was initially impressed by the observation, since it recalled the attitude of the explorers who traditionally ask of the 'natives' they discover: 'Take me to your leader'. On reflection, however, he:

began to wonder whether – since black politics in the United States were still racial and redemptive and simple – black people in the United States couldn't after all be said to have leaders, people they simply followed. And I wondered if it was possible in these circumstances for black people to stand apart from their leaders, any more than it was possible for people of the Caribbean or Africa to stand apart from the racial or tribal chiefs whom they had created.[1]

No black leader in America has been 'simply followed'. Rather, they have articulated the feelings and the demands of their constituents. When they have been notably in advance of or at variance with their 'people', they have become isolated, 'leaders without followers' or have faced criticisms from contending or aspiring 'leaders'.

Like its predecessor, this book reflects my belief that an examination of those preeminent Negro leaders who have commanded national (and international) attention in the twentieth century will reveal one constant factor: reasoned black reactions to prevalent and frequently unremitting white racism. Primarily a work of synthesis and explication it will, I hope, encourage readers to consult the specialized articles and books which are cited in the Bibliographical Essay. This edition draws on the more recent writings of American and British scholars; it is also informed by the constructive suggestions of students, colleagues and critics in Europe and the United States.

John White
Department of American Studies
University of Hull
October, 1989

REFERENCES

1. V. S. Naipaul, *A Turn in the South* (New York, 1989), p.31.

Acknowledgements

We are grateful to the following for permission to reproduce copyright material:

Authors' Agents (Joan Daves) for extract from speech 'I have a Dream' by Martin Luther King Jr. (c) 1963 by Martin Luther King Jr. 1968 Estate of Martin Luther King Jr; Bobbs Merrill Co Inc for an extract from pxxxvii *Black Protest Thought in the 20th Century* (1971), by Meier, Rudwick & Broderick; Random Century Group/Paul R. Reynolds Inc for extracts from *Malcolm X: Autobiography 1968-80* by Alex Haley.

Introduction: Black Leaders and Limited Options

American Negro history is basically a history of the conflict between integrationist and nationalist forces in politics, economics, and culture, no matter what leaders are involved and what slogans are used.[1]

In the struggle for racial equality, civil and political rights, economic and educational advancements, black Americans, both during and after slavery, responded to the proposals and rhetoric of the leaders drawn from their own ranks. Yet one of the anomalies of Afro-American history is that blacks, as an ethnic group, have had only limited opportunities to select their own leaders. Ironically, it was during slavery that black leaders in the South – like Denmark Vesey, Gabriel Prosser and Nat Turner – planned conspiracies or led revolts aimed at some form of 'freedom', which (for obvious reasons) were not dependent on white sponsorship or support. But Frederick Douglass, an ex-slave and the most famous black abolitionist, was initially thrust into the public gaze by his Northern white supporters. Booker T. Washington, also a former slave, owed his elevation as much to such influential white patrons as his teacher, Samuel Chapman Armstrong, President Theodore Roosevelt, and the industrialist-turned philanthropist, Andrew Carnegie, as to his own remarkable abilities. Similarly, W. E. B. Du Bois, the towering black American intellect of the twentieth-century, became a key figure in the National Association for the Advancement of Coloured People only with the approval and financial support of upper-class white reformers of the Progressive era. Of the male black leaders under consideration, Marcus Garvey, Martin Luther King, Jr, and Jesse Jackson owed their rise to the reception accorded to them by blacks. Yet they were also perceived (if not sanctioned) by whites as leaders of their respective movements. Malcolm X, it can be argued, gained his reputation as much from the distorted publicity he received from the white-controlled media as from the endorsement of his black constituents. Whatever their ideological (or physiological) complexion, then, black American leaders have historically depended on white as well as on Negro recognition of their claims to speak for their race. Like their supporters, black leaders have had to contend with a caste system based on racial discrimination and proscription. For long periods, they were also effectively denied the franchise, entry into the major political parties or access to the centres of power. By definition, black leaders occupied tenuous and vulnerable positions in their own and surrounding white community. They were, initially at least, self-styled exemplars of their race.

Writing in 1944, the Swedish sociologist, Gunnar Myrdal, suggested persuasively that the extreme positions of Negro leadership behaviour on behalf of blacks as a subordinate (and segregated) caste were those of *accommodation* and *protest*. In the Southern states, where the caste system was most rigid and strictly enforced, whites sought alliances and tacit agreements with those 'accommodating' black leaders who could help them to perpetuate the values and practices of white supremacy. For their part, Southern black leaders needed to establish and maintain contact with influential whites which, in turn, provided them with influence and prestige within the black community. As Myrdal observed: 'The Negro leader in this setting serves a "function" to both castes and his influence in both groups is cumulative – prestige in the Negro community being an effect as well as a cause of prestige among whites.'[2] Similarly, in the Northern states, government agencies, political parties and philanthropic organizations made 'contact' with the Negro community through the white-appointed (or approved) black 'leaders'. Much of the competitiveness, rivalry and 'opportunism' of Negro leadership in America has derived from this need to satisfy (or not exceed) the demands of white supporters, while remaining responsive to the desires of black constituents. The black novelist and playwright James Baldwin, writing about Martin Luther King, Jr, observed tartly that:

> ...the problem of Negro leadership... has always been extremely delicate, dangerous and complex. The term itself becomes remarkably difficult to define, the moment one realizes that the real role of the Negro leader, in the eyes of the American Republic, was not to make

the Negro a first-class citizen but to keep him content as a second-class one.[3]

Again, the agitation and goals of black 'radicals' have often served to legitimate the claims of more 'moderate' Negro leaders in the eyes of white Americans. Thus personal as well as ideological rivalries have had positive (as well as dysfunctional) effects in the struggle for racial equality and black freedom. (But as Myrdal noted: 'Since power and prestige are scarce commodities in the Negro community, the struggle for leadership often becomes ruthless.')[4]

'Black leadership' has not been confined or limited to a few individuals – however exceptional or charismatic. In the twentieth century, the rise of national organizations like the NAACP, NUL, SCLC, CORE and SNCC, as well as the powerful influence of the black church and the activities of grass-roots movements at the state and local levels, have constituted a collective form of civil rights protest. The initiatives, concerns and demands of black men and women at particular junctures and in specific places have not always been those recognized by the established black leadership class. In some instances, these 'leaders' have, in effect, been led by their followers. Yet whatever their awareness of grass-roots demands and problems, black leaders have all necessarily operated within the constraints of what has been termed 'a politics of limited options'. Historically, these options often reflected significant differences between the limits of permissible activity in the states north and south of the Mason–Dixon line.

PERSPECTIVES: BLACK PROTEST AND ACCOMMODATION, 1800–1877

The varied responses of black Americans to their subordinate and inferior position in American society date from the establishment of racial slavery in the colonial period. In the years following the American Revolution – which both strengthened the institution of slavery and heightened black aspirations for freedom and equality – these responses persisted and multiplied. Black slaves and 'free people of colour' (in the North and South) resisted or made some kind of accommodation to enslavement and non-citizenship, supported or eschewed proposals for black repatriation or colonization overseas, adapted to or challenged emerging patterns of racial segregation,

3

embraced or rejected notions of their African cultural heritage, favoured or discounted alliances with whites and, from the 1830s, in the Negro Convention and abolitionist movements, attacked all forms of racial proscription. By the mid-1820s the Northern and Southern states of the American Union were clearly distinguishable in their attitudes towards slavery, but not in their attitudes toward and treatment of blacks. Indeed, Alexis de Tocqueville, visiting America in the 1830s, believed that:

> Race prejudice seems stronger in those states that have abolished slavery than in those where it still exists, and nowhere is it more intolerant than in those states where slavery was never known. [5]

Recent studies have confirmed the accuracy of Tocqueville's impressions. Anti-black sentiment and legislation in the states of the North-East and the territories of the West marked the period from the early 1800s down to the Civil War. Nearly every Northern state barred blacks from voting, serving in the militia, or receiving more than a rudimentary education. Racial segregation was evident in all forms of transportation and in hotels, restaurants, prisons, hospitals and cemeteries. Minstrel shows – the most popular form of entertainment in nineteenth century America – conveyed romanticized images of plantation slavery and crude caricatures of the alleged stupidity, fecklessness and gullibility of Northern free blacks. Ironically, free blacks in the North now became frozen on the bottom rungs of the economic ladder as they faced increasing competition from white immigrants. But in one respect at least, Northern blacks possessed – and utilized – an advantage not shared by their Southern counterparts. The expansion of the North's white population (through immigration and natural increase) provided whites with a sense of security unknown to white Southerners. Northern blacks were, therefore, allowed to retain certain basic liberties – the right to petition for the redress of grievances, to publish their own journals and newspapers, and to engage in political protest and activities. In 1827, a group of black New Yorkers founded *Freedom's Journal*, the first black newspaper, edited by John Russwurm and Samuel Cornish. Their paper attacked the thinly-veiled racism of the American Colonization Society, established in 1816, and asserted that its real aim was the strengthening of slavery by the removal of the free black population from the United States. Similarly, Richard Allen, a Philadelphia-born slave who had purchased his freedom in 1777, the year of his conversion to Methodism, experienced and rejected the church's

4

discriminatory treatment of its black members. Allen concluded (in the face of white hostility) that only a separate church, served by black clergy, could meet the spiritual and temporal needs of free blacks. He began to organize and implement a black version of Wesleyanism, became the first black bishop of the African Methodist Episcopal Church, and organized the initial meeting of the National Negro convention movement in 1830. Unable to condone slave violence, Allen provided the organizational structure for black abolitionism, and inspired free blacks in other parts of the North to establish their own churches.

Important in their own right, Allen's career and achievements also provided a notable nineteenth century precedent for black clerical leadership and influence within the Negro community. In 1829, David Walker, Boston agent for *Freedom's Journal*, issued his *Appeal* – in essence, a nineteenth century Black Power manifesto, urging Southern slaves to strike for their freedom, as it excoriated the tortures inflicted on blacks 'by the enlightened Christians of America'. In 1843, Henry Highland Garnet, a former slave, informed delegates to the National Convention of Colored Citizens at Buffalo, New York, that slaves would be fully justified in using violence to gain their freedom. Echoing Walker, Garnet, in his 'Address to the Slaves of the United States of America' exhorted them to 'Strike for your lives and liberties. You cannot be more oppressed than you have been – you cannot suffer greater cruelties than you have already. Rather die free men than live to be slaves. Remember that you are FOUR MILLIONS. Let your motto be resistance! resistance! RESISTANCE!'

Such aggressive and uncompromising sentiments effectively separated black from white abolitionists, most of whom, following the lead of William Lloyd Garrison, declared themselves pacifists, and saw their call for emancipation as an appeal to reason and conscience, as an exercise in moral suasion. Although blacks came to form separate (and more militant) abolitionist organizations, their earlier alliances with white reformers set precedents for interracial cooperation in the cause of civil rights, which were to be revived in the twentieth century by the NAACP, National Urban League and the Congress of Racial Equality.

After 1830, Northern blacks increasingly denounced segregated schools as unequal and inferior, and demanded educational integration. The Negro Convention Movement – confined to the Northern states until after the Civil War – operated sporadically from 1830 to 1860. Early conventions, attended by Negro ministers, lawyers, businessmen and physicians, lodged protests against slavery and the indignities faced by free blacks. Negro delegates with the support of white reformers supported the creation of manual labour schools for both blacks and whites. Just as the white-dominated abolitionist movement became split between its moral suasionist and political activist wings, so too, the Negro Convention Movement became more militant, and endorsed independent black protest against disfranchisement and segregation. The Convention Movement failed to secure mass support for any one strategy – cooperation with whites, independent political action, emigrationism – or to achieve black political or social equality. But it did provide forums, at the state and national levels, for a developing black leadership class.

The outstanding black leader of the nineteenth century was undoubtedly Frederick Douglass (1817–95). Born in Maryland, Douglass was for several years a house slave in Baltimore, where he learned to read and write. In 1838, when he could no longer tolerate his condition, Douglass escaped from slavery, married Anne Murray, a free black, and settled in New Bedford, Massachusetts. After seeing a copy of Garrison's abolitionist journal, *The Liberator*, Douglass became a lecturer for the Massachusetts Anti-Slavery Society, and an avowed Garrisonian. An eloquent and impassioned orator, Douglass quickly became the leading spokesman for abolitionism. When doubts were expressed that he had ever been a slave, Douglass published his *Narrative of the Life of Frederick Douglass* (1845), a graphic and convincing description of his slave experiences, and a landmark in abolitionist (and black American) literature. Fearful for his safety after publication of the *Narrative*, Douglass's friends sent him on a two-year visit to Britain, where he impressed audiences with his high intelligence and withering condemnations of slavery. After his British supporters purchased his freedom, Douglass returned to America, and moved to Rochester, New York, where he published his own weekly newspaper, *The North Star*. As a journalist, essayist and public speaker, Douglass inveighed against the twin evils of racial slavery and racial discrimination. A supporter of the Liberty and Republican parties, Douglass was prominent in the Negro Convention Movement of the 1840s and 1850s. Personal rivalries and ideological differences led to his split with the Garrisonians in 1851. Douglass rejected the Garrisonian slogan of 'No Union With Slaveholders' as an abandonment of the slaves to the not-so-tender mercies of their owners. He also disagreed with Garrison's view that the federal Constitution was a pro-slavery document, and resented Garrison's intemperate attacks on the Northern churches, citing the existence of abolitionist sympathisers in some denominations. Douglass also disliked the patronizing attitudes of many white abolitionists, and believed that to be successful, abolitionists must endorse political activism. Douglass welcomed John Brown's abortive attempt to incite a slave insurrection at Harper's Ferry in Virginia in 1859 (although he had been unaware of Brown's intentions), and applauded Lincoln's issuance of the Emancipation Proclamation in 1863. During the war Douglass pressed for the acceptance of blacks into the Union armed forces, believing that a Northern victory would secure both the permanent abolition of slavery and citizenship rights for the freedman. In addition to the support for the Union cause, Douglass was active in espousing a variety of reforms – women's rights, temperance, and world peace – and opposed capital punishment, lynching and the convict lease system. He was also a notable advocate of 'industrial education' for blacks, and stressed the virtues of self-help, capital accumulation and strict morality. Espousing racial pride and constant protest against all forms of discrimination, endorsing non-violent passive resistance, and looking toward the full integration of blacks into American society, Douglass, in several respects, antedated and anticipated Booker T. Washington's stress on vocational education and self-help, the concerns of twentieth century black nationalists and Martin Luther King's philosophy of non-violent direct action. During Reconstruction, Douglass stood behind Republican attempts to enforce civil rights in the defeated South, and pushed for enactment of the 1875 Civil Rights Act, and the ratification of the Fourteenth and Fifteenth Amendments, with their guarantees of citizenship and voting rights for blacks. As a loyal Republican, Douglass supported the corrupt administration of President Grant, and the compromise of 1877, despite its abandonment of Southern blacks to local white rule.

As a reward for faithful services to the Republican party, Douglass was appointed a United States Marshal, Recorder of Deeds for the District of Columbia, and Ambassador to Haiti. With the worsening of race relations in the post-Reconstruction South, Douglass protested vigorously against disfranchisement, lynching and the spread of segregation, but also advised Southern blacks to make the best of their situation, and to adjust to the reality of white supremacy. Anticipating Booker T. Washington, who delivered his 'Atlanta Compromise' address in 1895 (the year of Douglass's death), he advocated the founding of an Industrial College for blacks, and informed Harriet Beecher Stowe, the celebrated author of *Uncle Tom's Cabin*:

> We need mechanics as well as ministers. We need workers in iron, clay and leather. We have orators, authors and other professional men, but these reach only certain classes, and get respect for our race in certain select circles. We must not only be able to black boots but to make them. [6]

In 1873, Douglass moved to Washington, D.C., where he settled on a fifteen acre estate, a wealthy and respected 'elder statesman' of the first phase of the black protest movement. Following the death of his first wife, his marriage to Helen Pitts, a white woman from a prominent Rochester family, brought a storm of protest, to which Douglass reportedly replied: 'My first wife was the colour of my mother, and the second, the colour of my father.' A European tour in 1886–87, added to his already prodigious international reputation.

Other nineteenth century black spokesmen, however, viewed racial equality as a dream impossible of realization, and advocated the wholesale emigration of Negroes to Africa, Central or South America as the only solution to implacable white racism. During the 1850s Martin R. Delany became the leading black spokesman for black emigrationism. In his best-known work, *The Condition, Elevation, Emigration, and Destiny of the Colored People of the United States* (1852), he declared of American Negroes: 'We are a nation within a nation: as the Poles in Russia, the Hungarians in Austria, the Welsh, Irish and Scotch in the British dominions.' Opposed to black 'repatriation' to Liberia, as proposed by the American Colonization Society, Delany advocated the establishment of an independent black state in East Africa to which black Americans could emigrate.(He later declared his preference for the West Indies, Central and South America as offering better prospects). But with the outbreak of the Civil War, Delany abandoned emigrationism in favour of working for racial equality in America, and was active in the Freedmen's Bureau, the one federal agency created to protect the rights of blacks freed by the Emancipation Proclamation and Confederate defeat.

In the antebellum period, few blacks responded to calls for mass emigration, since they lacked sufficient funds and, more significantly, regarded themselves as more American than African. But in articulating concepts of black separatism, voluntary repatriation and identification with Africa, mid-nineteenth-century spokesmen made their conviction very apparent that racial equality within America was a chimera.

Within the slave states of the South, black resistance to servitude took many forms, ranging from secret conspiracy and open rebellion, malingering, running away, feigned illness and sabotage to the more metaphysical forms of 'resistance' offered by a distinctive Afro-American religion with its selective reading of the scriptures and the culture of the slave quarters – folktales, jokes, rituals, family and kinship bonds – which provided some protection against the power and authority of the master class. 'Leadership' within the slave community was provided by preachers, conjurers, musicians, parents and grandparents. Yet despite attempts by some historians to celebrate (if not romanticize) the autonomy of the 'slave community' in the antebellum South, slaves, by definition, had severely limited options and room for manoeuvre, and signally (but understandably) failed to develop traditions of protest or revolutionary leadership. In at least three dramatic instances, however, black leaders in the slave South demonstrated their resolve and capacity to plan uprisings against a system designed for their permanent subjugation.

In 1800, Gabriel Prosser, a slave in Henrico Country, Virginia, organized a conspiracy among his fellow slaves, aimed at overthrowing slavery and setting up a black state. A small guerilla force of about 200 men was to enter Richmond, capture arms, overcome the white population, and take the governor hostage. Prosser, a skilled blacksmith who was probably literate, was familiar with the scriptures, and with the ideals inspired by the French Revolution. His plan involved the systematic allocation of tasks to various individuals, the calculation of the number of slaves likely to support the coup, and clandestine meetings to formulate strategy and tactics. The conspiracy was betrayed to the Virginia authorities by two of Prosser's slave followers, the incipient slave revolt was crushed, and Prosser, together with thirty of his followers, was executed. But, despite its failure, Prosser's conspiracy helped to rivet the fear of slave revolt (and 'black power') on the mind of the white South.

The other significant slave conspiracy was that inspired and organized by Denmark Vesey, in and around Charleston, South Carolina, in 1822. Vesey, a former slave who had managed to purchase his freedom, was a profoundly religious man, and a leading member of the African Methodist Episcopal Church. Inspired by Old Testament accounts of Jewish enslavement and persecution, Vesey saw himself as a black Moses, destined to lead his people out of bondage. He also hoped to secure external aid from the West Indies and Africa to maintain an independent black state. Again this conspiracy was also betrayed, over 130 of the alleged participants were arrested, and thirty-five, including Vesey, were hanged. Although Vesey does not appear to have had any clear idea as to the form and structure of the state he wished to establish after the overthrow of slavery, his conspiracy, like that of Prosser, demonstrated that slaves and former slaves possessed the capacity for militant leadership, and the ability to attract followers.

Nat Turner, a Virginia slave, was to lead the most bloody nineteenth century slave revolt in Southampton County, Virginia, in 1831 (a year which also marked the appearance of Garrison's *Liberator*). The son of an African-born slave mother, Turner was moved to violence by the events and mystical experiences of his youth. Like Vesey, Turner drew upon an apocalyptic version of Christian doctrine, together with revelations and prophetic dreams and visions to inspire (and later, to justify) his actions. Notwithstanding the fact that he had been kindly treated by his master, Joseph Travis, Turner and his slave followers murdered the Travis family and about fifty other whites before the state militia put down the insurrection. After eluding capture for several weeks, Turner was tried and hanged in November 1831. His revolt terrified the South, prompted the Virginia legislature to discuss the possibility of ending slavery (the motion was defeated) and provided later generations of black militants with an authentic hero and slave leader.

In contrast, the free black caste (itself an anomaly in a racially-based slave system) in the South, although never providing overall leadership for slave rebellion, nevertheless succeeded in gaining a strong sense of collective worth and individual identity through the founding of religious, fraternal and educational institutions. Largely the creation of the era of the American Revolution (when both the British and the colonists offered blacks their freedom as a reward for military service), and of self-purchase and manumission by their owners, Southern free blacks (who exhibited class, colour and denominational divisions), faced increasing repression and discrimination in the decades before the Civil War. Manumission became progressively more difficult from the Upper to the Lower South, and free blacks also faced the danger of being kidnapped and sold as slaves. Generally more skilled, better-educated and lighter-skinned than the mass of slaves, free blacks faced economic competition from both slaves and whites. Although free blacks and slaves had much in common – ancestry, family ties, work experiences and church membership – there were also conflicting pressures which effectively weakened any strong sense of racial unity and precluded a slave/free black alliance for the overthrow of white hegemony. However degraded or uncertain their position, free blacks in the South were aware that their prospects for survival, as well as for any economic advancement, depended on their ability to distinguish themselves, in the eyes of whites, from the mass of slaves. (Wealthy and light-skinned free Negroes shunned the African churches, benevolent and fraternal organizations favoured by darker and poorer free blacks, and formed their own exclusive clubs and organizations). As Ira Berlin has observed, the free blacks of the slave South deferred to whites on all occasions, and in doing so 'satisfied the paternalistic pretensions of upper-class whites' while implicitly renouncing 'their objections to the Southern caste system'.[7]

To a remarkable degree, these strategies continued into the post-Civil War period. Southern black leaders continued to favour the cautious and conciliatory racial policies which they had practised and perfected during slavery, and displayed 'conservative' rather than 'radical' tendencies. Militant proposals (within the context of their time) for effecting racial change came out of the Northern states with their traditions of free speech and political agitation; more cautious, conciliatory and diplomatic proposals for racial improvement continued to impress Southern blacks, aware of the dangers posed by virulent white racism, and the continued existence, after 1865, of various forms of involuntary servitude and coerced labour. Black leaders in the former Confederate states, both during and after Reconstruction, were drawn disproportionately from the ranks of antebellum free people of colour, or were former slaves who had occupied relatively privileged positions. Collectively, they were moderates, aware of the necessity for compromise and/or dissimulation if they were to gain the white patronage necessary to advance both themselves and their communities.

The successful black leader, Myrdal believed, became 'a consummate manipulator', cajoling the white man into doing what the black leader desired. Inevitably, the Negro leader came to derive satisfaction in his manipulative skills in 'flattering, beguiling, and outwitting the white man'. But there was also the real danger that the Southern race leader, living on his wits (and at some personal danger) might become simply a self-seeker, 'having constantly to compromise with his pride and dignity'. Northern race leaders, in contrast, as beneficiaries of a long tradition of sanctioned protest, were both able and expected to produce displays of 'actual opposition' to white racism, and with less danger of retaliation from offended whites. But whether they functioned in a more or less relaxed racial environment, black leaders, Myrdal noted, had historically been engaged in a similar 'keen and destructive personal rivalry'. He was quick to add, however, that 'national Negro leadership is no more corrupt no more ridden with personal envy and rivalry than any other national leaderships.'[8]

FROM BOOKER T. WASHINGTON TO JESSE L. JACKSON

In the twentieth century, six black spokesmen have gained recognition as outstanding advocates and ideologues of strategies and goals of racial advancement. After the death of Frederick Douglass in 1895, Booker T. Washington (1856–1915), as even his most vociferous critics conceded, was the nationally acknowledged leader of black Americans. The most powerful and influential black man of his day, Washington, despite the efforts of numerous biographers, remains a complex, and ambiguous figure. Born a slave, Washington embraced the Protestant ethic of work, godliness and personal hygiene, and urged the building of black character and business enterprise. Well-versed in the racial mores and etiquette of the South, Washington was able to turn white paternalism and patronage to his own advantage, if not to that of his race. As the principal and founder of Tuskegee Institute in Alabama, a vocational school for blacks, Washington demonstrated his gifts as an administrator, educator and leader. He also made Tuskegee into a power base – 'the Tuskegee machine' – and extended its influence into the towns and cities of the United States. Any assessment of the black experience after slavery must reckon with this enigmatic and controversial educator, activist and interracial diplomat.

During the last twelve years of his life, Washington encountered in William Edward Burghardt Du Bois (1868–1963), his most articulate and distinguished black critic. A New Englander by birth, Du Bois gained a Harvard PhD, and became the self-appointed spokesman for the 'Talented Tenth' – the intellectual black élite which, he believed, would provide the vanguard leadership for the race as a whole. Dedicated to the acquisition of civil and political rights for blacks, and initially espousing racial integration, Du Bois joined with Northern black militants like William Monroe Trotter and with liberal whites, to challenge Washington's influence and power. A poet, novelist, sociologist, historian and a founding member of the NAACP (and editor of its publication, *The Crisis*), Du Bois castigated Washington as the witting or unwitting supporter of white supremacy and permanent black inferiority. Battle lines were drawn, and by the early years of the twentieth century, the black protest movement appeared to be polarized between its 'accommodationist/conservative' and 'radical/activist' wings.

While neither Washington nor Du Bois ever commanded a mass following among black Americans, the Jamaican-born Marcus Garvey (1880–1940) achieved that distinction in the course of his short but spectacular American career. A declared disciple of Booker T. Washington, Garvey became the leading black nationalist in the United States in the period during and immediately after the First World War. Pledged to the unrealistic goal of the liberation of Africa from white colonial rule, the inculcation of racial pride in black Americans, and the separation of races in America, Garvey's racial philosophy, his successes and blunders, attracted the ridicule and scorn of Du Bois to an extent that made his earlier differences with Washington appear comparatively innocuous. Garvey returned Du Bois' enmity (and that of other established black leaders) with interest. Where Washington had spoken primarily for a poverty-stricken black peasantry, only recently 'up from slavery', and Du Bois for a growing Northern black urban bourgeoisie, Garvey capitalized on the depressed condition of the growing urban black population, confined within the physical and psychological constraints of the ghetto. Although Garvey's American career was short-lived, it reflected the rise and significance of Harlem, the black ghetto in New York city, as the most important concentration of Afro-Americans in the United States. Garvey's influence persisted into the 1960s and 1970s, with the re-emergence of a militant black nationalism expressed in the emotive slogan 'Black Power', with its connotations of racial assertiveness, separatism, and pride in the alleged African cultural and spiritual heritage of Afro-Americans.

Although the black socialist A. Philip Randolph's March on Washington Movement (MOWM) during World War II, signalled the shift of black strategy toward direct action protest for political, economic and civil rights, it was not until the appearance of the young Negro clergyman, Martin Luther King, Jr (1929–68), during the momentous Montgomery, Alabama bus boycott of 1955–56, that another black American spokesman commanded national – and international – attention. The exponent and practitioner of 'non-violent' direct action and confrontation in the cause of racial integration (and, later, of political and economic rights), Martin Luther King (like Booker T. Washington, a Southerner by birth and allegiance) became the personification and symbol of the civil rights movement which had as its ultimate goal the realization of racial democracy in America. Towards the end of his life, King expanded his vision to project a coalition of the underprivileged, black and white, in America. He also became increasingly critical of the American capitalist system, and of US involvement in Vietnam. Ironically, King delivered his famous 'I Have a Dream' oration, the climax of the 1963 civil rights March on Washington, as Du Bois died in self-imposed exile in Ghana.

Malcolm X (1925–65), born Malcolm Little, was (like Martin Luther King) a preacher and activist and, for a significant period, the leading spokesman for the separatist Nation of Islam (the Black Muslims). Following his break with the Nation, on doctrinal and personal grounds, Malcolm X became the best-known, and certainly the most notorious, ideologue for black militancy and racial separatism. He was also an admirer of Marcus Garvey and a declared disciple of Elijah Muhammad, leader of the Nation of Islam in its classic black separatist phase. Where Martin Luther King espoused a gospel of non-violent protest and the redemptive value of love and suffering, Malcolm X appeared to condone, if not actively promote, racial warfare. The 'Black Power' slogan and the subsequent rise of such extremist groups as the Black Panther Party were offshoots of Malcolm's black nationalism. Like Marcus Garvey, Malcolm X struck a responsive chord among the black underclass of the nation's ghettos; like Martin Luther King, he was to die a violent death, with his attitudes undergoing significant change.

Immediately following the deaths of King and Malcolm X, no black leader approached their stature or influence, as perceived either by whites or blacks. In 1980, the magazine *Black Enterprise* reported after a poll of 5,000 readers that 'over the last ten years, the absence of clear-cut leadership has been the single most noticeable handicap of the black struggle for equality'. The death in 1981 of Roy Wilkins, who had served as executive director of the NAACP for twenty-two years, and the resignation of Vernon

Jordan, president of the National Urban League for the previous ten years, came at a time of increasing demoralization and frustration within an already fragmented civil rights movement. After its successful campaigns to outlaw segregation in public accommodations and transportation, and the gaining of legal guarantees of civil and voting rights, the civil rights coalition (even before the assassination of Martin Luther King), became increasingly concerned with economic issues. By 1980 the average black family income was $15,806, as against $24,939 for whites; unemployment rates for blacks were three times as great as those for whites. And accompanying the economic and educational advances made by a small number of blacks, there was, by the 1980s, a marked decline in the lifestyles and the prospects of millions of Negro Americans. Again, the election of Ronald Reagan to the White House in 1980, signalled the onset of a conservative reaction against the 'affirmative action' programmes instituted by Lyndon Johnson. (In an analysis of the 1980 election returns, one poll revealed that many whites had voted Republican for the first time because – among other reasons – they believed that the Democrats had been too concerned with issues of race relations, poverty and civil rights.) But in 1984 black Americans, for the first time, were able to vote for a serious black contender for the Democratic party's presidential nomination. Its candidate, the Reverend Jesse Jackson, born in 1941, had been a member of the SCLC and was the declared disciple of Martin Luther King, Jr. Jackson failed to gain the party's nomination, but in 1984 and again in 1988, he gained enormous popular (black and white) support for his projected 'Rainbow Coalition' of the underprivileged and as even his critics concede, is now the outstanding black leader in America.

The following chapters attempt to summarize and to evaluate the contributions of Booker T. Washington, W. E. B. Du Bois, Marcus Garvey, Malcolm X, Martin Luther King and Jesse Jackson to the black protest movement in America, as perceived by themselves, their contemporaries and subsequent commentators. By placing their racial philosophies and leadership strategies in historical context, it is hoped to illustrate the themes of change and continuity in black leadership agendas and demands from the late nineteenth century to the present. Essentially, continuity will be seen to lie in persistent black protest against the inequities of a caste system in a democratic society pledged to the principles enshrined in the Declaration of Independence and the Constitution. Change will be evident in the varying connotations of such concepts as 'integration', 'separatism', 'accommodation', 'conservatism', 'radicalism', and 'equality' at significant junctures in the black American experience. In short, the intention is to provide, within short compass, both individual and interrelated biographies of major Afro-American leaders – and the reponses of those whom they professed to lead.

REFERENCES

1. Cruse, H., *The Crisis of the Negro Intellectual: From its Origins to the Present* (New York, 1967), p.564.
2. Myrdal, G., *An American Dilemma* (New York, 1964), pp.722–3.
3. James Baldwin, 'The dangerous road before Martin Luther King', in C. E. Lincoln (ed.), *Martin Luther King Jr: A Profile* (New York, 1970), pp.106–7.
4. Myrdal, G., *An American Dilemma*, op. cit., p.775.
5. Alexis de Tocqueville, *Democracy in America*, ed. J. P. Mayer & Max Lerner (New York, 1966), Vol. I, p.426.
6. Douglass, Frederick, letter to Harriet Beecher Stowe, 8 March, 1863, in Douglass, *Life and Times of Frederick Douglass* (London, 1884), p. 251.
7. Berlin, I., *Slaves Without Masters: The Free Negro in the Antebellum South* (New York, 1974), p.340.
8. Myrdal, G., *An American Dilemma*, op. cit., pp.773, 778–9.

CHAPTER TWO

Booker T. Washington: Black Enigma

Booker T. Washington was not an easy person to know. He never expressed himself frankly or clearly until he knew exactly to whom he was talking and just what their wishes and desires were.

[W. E. B. DU BOIS] [1]

I wanna tell yuh young people ef yuh take de mind and de heart uv Booker Washington, a real race leader, yuh will nevah think yo'self above nobody else....Booker Washington wuz a great man come down frum Heaven wid a great cane in his han en laid hold de ol' dragon.... Dat dragon...wuz prejudice....One reason I luv Booker Washington wuz dat he wuz no 'spector uv pussons. He loved evahbody. Do' Booker Washington wuz a mulatto he wuz not color struck. He wuz sich a great man.

[HENRY BAKER][2]

They gived that man piles of money to run this school business here in the state of Alabama. But I wouldn't boost Booker Washington today up to everything that was industrious and right....He didn't feel for and respect his race of people to go rock bottom with 'em. He leaned too much to the white people that controlled the money...he had a political pull any way he turned and he was pullin' for Booker Washington.

[NATE SHAW][3]

PERSPECTIVES: SEPARATE BUT UNEQUAL: SOUTHERN RACE RELATIONS, 1865–1895

In 1865 the Confederate States of America finally lost their bid for independence. The South was defeated on the battlefields, but fought a successful campaign in the post-war period against 'Yankee' occupation and the imposition of direct rule from Washington, DC. Although slavery had been destroyed by the war, the white South was determined that its pattern of race relations would not undergo fundamental change. The withdrawal of the last remaining troops from the South in 1877 marked the formal end of Reconstruction – the attempt by Northern Republicans to impose measures of civil and political equality for freedmen in the former Confederate states. The Thirteenth, Fourteenth and Fifteenth 'Civil War' amendments to the Constitution, reforms embodied in the new Southern state constitutions, provision of education for blacks, and attempts to suppress such white supremacist organizations as the Ku Klux Klan, had been the notable achievements of Reconstruction. More significantly, Southern blacks voted in state and local elections, held political offices, moved into urban areas and attempted to exercise their economic rights in a free labour system. In short, they exercised a wide range of choices that had been effectively closed under slavery. But by the terms of the Compromise of 1877, the Republican Rutherford B. Hayes gained the presidency over the rival claims of his Democratic opponent, Samuel J. Tilden, and, as part of the bargain, Northern Republicans abandoned the freedmen to the Democratic 'Redeemer' Southern state governments. Unable to resurrect the slave system in name, Southern whites soon devised legal and extra-legal measures which deprived blacks of the franchise, the right to hold public office, or to engage in political activities. The 'Black Codes', adopted during president Andrew Johnson's direction of the Reconstruction process, were designed to keep Negroes as a landless and closely controlled labour force. Although they were voided by Congressional Reconstruction, the Black Codes were to reappear in the form of various labour laws enacted by Southern state legislatures in the 1870s and 1880s. Vagrancy laws, enticement acts, contract enforcement statutes, and the criminal surety system, were all designed to replace slavery by forms of involuntary servitude for blacks. Staple crop production was resumed on Southern farms and plantations under the sharecropping system, whereby planters and merchants kept black tenant farmers in a state of peonage, unable to clear themselves of debt, and required by law to work indefinitely for their owner–employers. In the urban labour market, freedmen and women found employment in tobacco factories and flour mills and in the extractive industries, but throughout the South, cotton mills were reserved for whites only.

Socially, Southern race relations, both during and after Reconstruction, were marked by the increasing separation of the races – in public accommodations, hospitals, prisons, schools and places of entertainment. Historians have disagreed as to when segregation first appeared in the post-war South – whether it was before, during or at some period after Reconstruction – but point to its full-blown operation in both law and custom in towns and cities throughout the South by the 1890s, with a rigidly separated caste system as the substitute for slavery. Yet, whenever it occurred, segregation (the enforced separation of the races), marked a decisive change from the South's earlier and almost total exclusion of blacks from medical, welfare, educational and other facilities.[4]

Thus, one of the achievements of Radical or Congressional Reconstruction was to secure segregated facilities for blacks where, previously, they had faced exclusion. Moreover, the Republican state governments in the South, while effecting some progressive reforms, never pushed for racial integration as either a desirable or even a possible goal. With the piecemeal ending of Reconstruction, the 'Redeemer' governments simply continued and extended segregationist practices. The best that blacks could hope for were separate accommodations and facilities equal to those provided for whites. Where idealistic Northern Republicans may have hoped that accommodations and services for the two races might be identical, the Redeemer Democrats had no such expectations or intentions. Again, black resistance in the South to increasing racial discrimination may have prompted the final step in the resort of the South to *de facto* segregation.

One response to the restoration of white supremacy in the South was a renewed call for black emigration. Henry McNeal Turner, a black preacher in the African Methodist Episcopal Church, had been expelled from the Georgia state legislature, following the return of the Democrats to power. Turner roundly denounced both Republicans and Democrats for their betrayal of the freedman and, from 1870, began to advocate the emigration to Africa of a select group of blacks with the skills and resources to build a new state. In 1891 Turner visited West Africa for the first time, sent back enthusiastic reports, and returned to America determined to launch an intensive campaign to promote black emigration. A fiery black nationalist, Turner condemned the failings of American society, and tried to get the federal government to pay reparations to blacks for their years in slavery – anticipating the later nationalist-separatism of the Garvey movement and the Nation of Islam.

From 1894, with the aid of white entrepreneurs, who had organized the International Migration Society in Alabama, Turner began to recruit emigrants and sell passages on the Afro-American Steamship Company, founded, with his support, for transportation to Liberia. In March, 1895, twenty-two blacks from various Southern states, recruited by black representatives of the IMS, sailed for Africa. The following year, 325 blacks left for Liberia. During his third visit to West Africa, Turner reported that the settlers were making steady progress. In fact, IMS officials had not provided them with promised food and help, and many of the emigrants died from malaria, while those who survived asked to return to America. Turner's emigrationist campaign appealed only to a small and desperate segment of the Southern black population. But Turner continued to advocate the 'limited option' of black emigration for the remainder of his life (he died in the same year as Booker T. Washington), and can be considered as the immediate ideological forerunner of Marcus Garvey.

During and after Reconstruction, most Southern blacks rejected emigrationism, and placed their hopes in the securing of better schools and welfare facilities, rather than in gaining racial integration. Aware of their precarious position in a society pledged to the restoration and maintenance of white supremacy, those black delegates who attended the first freedmen's conventions held in the South immediately after the Civil War, were careful not to offend white sensibilities by demanding political or social rights and privileges. Instead, they stressed their *Southern* identity and the common interests of whites and blacks. And, disavowing the need for government action and initiative to protect the interests of Negro agricultural workers, blacks in the convention movement, like most black newspapers of the time, espoused the gospel of self-help, group advancement and laissez-faire.

For a time, it appeared that the Populist movement or People's Party – the climax of the agrarian discontent of the 1880s and 1890s – with its critique of both Republicans and Democrats as the creatures of Northern business interests, might produce a bi-racial alliance of Southern black and white farmers in a united protest. In the South, Populist leaders like Tom Watson of Georgia, appealed for black support, arguing that economic distress did not recognize the colour line. In 1892 the Arkansas Populist platform included a resolution submitted by a black delegate, that it was 'the object of the People's Party to elevate the downtrodden, irrespective of race or colour'. Across the South, Populist platforms denounced lynchings and supported the restoration of political rights for blacks. But these expressions of concern for the Negro were essentially rhetorical devices, rooted in expediency rather than in idealism. When Southern planters and merchants used their influence to ensure that black tenants voted the Democratic ticket, Southern Populists, alarmed at the prospect of white competition for the black vote, reversed earlier ostensibly pro-black pronouncements, and joined with their political rivals in espousing black disfranchisement and racial separation. By the 1890s, then, Southern whites of all political persuasions and socio-economic groupings began to unite under the 'banner of white supremacy. The 'Solid South' was not simply the South of Democratic dominance, it was also, and increasingly, a section in which blacks were systematically reduced to positions of dependency, poverty and severely restricted aspirations in a bifurcated social order. Growing up in Mississippi in the first decade of the century, the novelist, Richard Wright, the son of a black sharecropper, quickly learned that:

> Among the topics that Southern white men did not like to discuss with Negroes were the following: American white women; the Ku Klux Klan....Jack Johnson; the entire northern part of the United States; the Civil War; Abraham Lincoln; U. S. Grant; General Sherman; Catholics; the Pope; Jews; the Republican party; slavery; social equality; Communism; Socialism; the 13th, 14th and 15th Amendments to the Constitution; or any topic calling for positive knowledge of manly self-assertion on the part of the Negro. The most accepted topics were sex and religion.[5]

In the North, the radical impulse which had initiated Congressional Reconstruction, began to wane with the deaths or retirement from office of the old Radical Republican leadership. The election of President Grant in 1868, and the subsequent rise of factionalism within the Republican party, with Liberal Republicans favouring an end to military rule in the South and sectional reconciliation, all pointed to the imminent abandonment of the freedman in the cause of sectional harmony. By the early 1870s, Northern business interests were demanding an end to Reconstruction because it was discouraging investment and commercial enterprise in the South.

The United States Supreme Court, in a series of decisions, aided the segregation impulse in rulings which declared that the provisions of the Fourteenth Amendment did not affect segregation by state law if the facilities offered were 'separate but equal'. Mississippi in 1890, and South Carolina in 1895, were the first former Confederate states to amend their constitutions effectively to disfranchise nearly all blacks. Mississippi's racist governor, James K. Vardaman, declared openly: 'There is no use to equivocate.... Mississippi's constitutional convention of 1890 was held for no other purpose than to eliminate the nigger from politics.' Between 1896 and 1915, all Southern states enacted legislation that permitted the Democratic party to declare only whites eligible for voting in primary elections. During the 1880s and 1890s, there were on average one hundred and fifty lynchings of blacks a year – an appalling index of racial tensions in the South. As Neil R. McMillen observes, during these decades, 'mob executions of blacks were so common that they excited interest only in the black community'.[6] Not surprisingly, Southern blacks, although they retained their traditional loyalty to the Republican party, exercised little actual power or influence in the solidly Democratic South. Yet black protest was not entirely extinguished. From 1904 to 1908 Southern Negroes organized a series of unsuccessful boycotts of segregated street cars in such cities as Atlanta, Houston, New Orleans and Mobile. More significantly, increasing numbers of blacks 'voted with their feet' by leaving the section for a new life in the industrialized states of the North – even before the mass exodus of the World War I era. Given the helplessness in black Southerners in the face of white hostility and violence, there is a certain intended irony in C. Vann Woodward's observation that: 'It was an ex-slave who eventually framed the *modus vivendi* of race relations in the New South.'[7]

BOOKER T. WASHINGTON: EARLY LIFE

Booker Taliaferro Washington was born a slave in 1856, on James Burroughs' 207-acre farm in Franklin County, Virginia. The son of a house slave and an unknown white father, Washington later recalled:

> I was born in a typical log cabin, about fourteen by sixteen feet square. In this cabin I lived with my mother, a brother and sister till

after the Civil War, when we were all declared free. Of my ancestry, I knew nothing.[8]

Washington spent nine years in slavery – the last four during the Civil War. By his own account, he was poorly clothed, inadequately fed and denied any opportunities for education, apart from tantalizing glimpses into the schoolroom attended by his young white 'mistress'. His plantation duties involved taking water to slaves working in the fields, carrying corn for grinding to the local mill, and operating a set of fans at the Burroughs' dinner table. Reflecting on this period of his life, Washington castigated slavery for having caused physical labour to be regarded 'as a badge of degradation, of inferiority' by both whites and blacks. As for the 'greatest injury' that slavery inflicted on blacks, Washington later declared that it was:

> ...to deprive them of that executive power, that sense of self-dependence which are the glory and the distinction of the Anglo-Saxon race. For 250 years we were taught to depend on some one else for food, clothing, shelter and every move in life.[9]

In 1865, Washington went with his family to join his stepfather, Washington Ferguson, who had fled to Malden, West Virginia, during the war. In Malden, the reunited family lived in a shanty town, and Washington worked for a time in the salt mines and later as a coal miner – experiences which may partly explain his adult addiction to the rituals of personal hygiene. 'An intense longing to read' was among Washington's earliest memories, and he began to acquire the rudiments of literacy from a copy of Noah Webster's spelling book, a traditional text in American primary schools. He also began to attend a local school started by Negro parents, after completing a 5.00 a.m. to 9.00 a.m. shift at the salt works, with a further two hours shift after the end of afternoon classes. (In his later career, Washington was a strong advocate of the night school.) At some point during his Malden years, Washington heard about the existence of a school for freedmen – the Hampton Normal and Agricultural Institute in Virginia – where blacks could receive academic training while working for their room and board. He recalled:

> I resolved at once to go to that school, although I had no idea where it was, or how many miles away, or how I was going to reach it....I was on fire constantly with one ambition, and that was to go to Hampton.[10]

Hampton Institute had been founded in 1868 by Samuel Chapman Armstrong, the son of Hawaiian missionaries, and a former brigadier general in the Union army. The views of European educators stressing the value of industrial schools had been given a receptive hearing in America before the Civil War, and Frederick Douglass, as has been seen, was a notable black advocate of the idea. Armstrong was impressed with education for the freedman as the best means of smoothing the transition from slavery to freedom. (During Reconstruction, the Freedmen's Bureau had also supported the cause of industrial/agricultural education, in an attempt to improve the condition of Southern blacks.) Armstrong believed also that such a programme, in addition to elevating 'dependent' and 'backward' races, might also provide a strategic ground of compromise between Southern whites, Northern whites and blacks. He was convinced that the freedmen should remain in the South, among their 'best friends' – the Southern whites – engaged primarily in agriculture and programmes of individual and collective self-help. (Bishop Henry M. Turner, on a visit to Hampton in 1878, accused it of inculcating black inferiority.) Armstrong's pedagogic ideas, grounded in the belief that education as a moral and conservative force, appealed to Southern planters and Northern capitalists, united in their wish to have a tractable and trained labour force in the post-war South.

Washington's desire to attend Hampton was intensified during his eighteen-month service as a houseboy in the home of General Lewis Ruffner, owner of the Malden salt works and a coal mine. His stay with the Ruffner family marked the beginning of Washington's life-long association with (and affection for) upper-class whites. It was from Mrs Viola Ruffner (a New Englander) that he also began to imbibe Puritan notions of thrift, cleanliness and hard work which were to form the basis of his social thought. Mrs Ruffner also encouraged Washington's persistent efforts to acquire an education, and allowed him to attend school for an hour a day during the winter.

In 1872, Washington, aged sixteen, set out from Malden to cover the five hundred miles to Hampton – a journey that was to test his mental, physical and financial resources. At the first night's stage-coach stop, Washington, the only black passenger, was excluded from 'a common, unpainted house called a hotel', and refused a meal. When his meagre funds ran out in Northern Virginia, Washington walked and begged rides until he reached Richmond, about eighty miles from Hampton, tired, hungry and completely out of money. Working at odd jobs in Richmond, he finally accumulated sufficient funds to undertake the last stage of his journey; he reached Hampton with fifty cents to spare. The head teacher at Hampton, Miss Mary F. Mackie (like Mrs Ruffner, a New Englander), was visibly unimpressed by the tramp-like figure who presented himself for admission. After some deliberation, she ordered him to sweep out the recitation room, a chore which Washington correctly surmised was his entrance examination. Thanks to Mrs Ruffner's training and his own unflagging enthusiasm, Washington passed the test. After a thorough inspection of the room, Mrs Mackie informed him: 'I guess you will do to enter this institution.'

Washington's three years in Hampton were to be the shaping experience of his life. He later said (and without irony) that Hampton had given him a better education than he could have gained at Harvard or Yale. Working as a janitor for his room and board, and with his clothing and tuition provided by Northern benefactors, Washington gained the rudiments of a liberal education, acquired trade skills, and was fully indoctrinated in the Hampton Christian work-and-cleanliness ethic. He also displayed promise as a student debater and orator. In General Armstrong, Washington found a surrogate father, guide and mentor. He was to model his attitudes, precepts and racial philosophy after Armstrong's example. From 1875 to 1878 he spent a year at Wayland Seminary, a small Baptist theological school in Washington, DC, but disliked both the atmosphere of the capital and the absence of moral and practical training in the Wayland curriculum. In particular, he was critical of the frivolities and pretensions of the city's black population, and the insensitivity of Wayland's black graduates to the needs of the rural black peasantry. After a brief period studying law, Washington gratefully accepted Armstrong's invitation to return of Hampton as a teacher in 1879, where he administered the first night school class for preparatory students unable to afford part-time study during the day. Washington nicknamed them 'The Plucky Class' and under his driving force, the experiment was a success, confirming his belief that poverty was no excuse for ignorance.

TUSKEGEE

In May 1881 General Armstrong received a letter from the state commissioners of a Negro normal school in Tuskegee in the black-belt county of Macon, Alabama, asking him to recommend its first principal. Their assumption was that Armstrong would recommend a white teacher for the post. The 'school' in question consisted only of a dilapidated shack and an old church – both on loan – without teachers or pupils. But the founding of the school owed its origin to the persistence of the black vote in the Deep South in the period immediately after the end of Reconstruction. In the autumn elections of 1880 Colonel Wilbur F. Foster, a Confederate veteran, and a former slaveholder, was a Democratic candidate for the Alabama state senate. Foster approached a black tinsmith, Lewis Adams, a former slave and the leading black citizen of Tuskegee. Foster promised that if Adams would deliver the black vote in the election (Macon County's population was 75 per cent Negro), he could expect to be rewarded. Adams, formerly a Republican but now shrewdly decided on a course of political self-interest for the black community, secured Foster's promise to sponsor and aid passage of a bill for a Negro normal school in Tuskegee. The Democrats won an overwhelming victory in 1880, and Foster fulfilled his part of the bargain: the Alabama legislature approved the project, named a Board of Commissioners, and appropriated $2,000 for teachers' salaries. As R. J. Norrell observes, Alabama's white conservatives, having regained political control, no longer felt fearful of blacks and: 'benevolent paternalism toward blacks made whites feel good about themselves'.[11]

Armstrong recommended Washington for the Tuskegee position, and characterized him as 'a very competent capable mulatto, clear-headed, modest , sensible, polite and a thorough teacher and a superior man'.[12] The Tuskegee Commissioners accepted the nomination, Washington (aware of the local situation), went to Tuskegee determined to put into practice the lessons he had learned (and taught) at Hampton. From the outset, Washington demonstrated his talents as an interracial diplomat.

Cultivating influential whites in the Tuskegee area, including one of the Commissioners, George W. Campbell, a former slaveholder, merchant and banker and Charles W. Thompson, the local Democratic leader – when President McKinley visited Tuskegee in 1898, Washington arranged for him to stay at Thompson's home and also helped his brother to secure the Tuskegee postmastership –

Washington persuaded and cajoled the white community into supporting the new school. He also travelled through Macon County, advertising the school to blacks, and soliciting whatever financial or other help they could offer. On the symbolically chosen 4th of July 1881 Washington formally opened the school, with an intake of thirty students and one teacher – himself. Within a year, he had moved the school to a new site, an abandoned slave plantation which he purchased for $500, half of which was borrowed from General James Marshall, treasurer of Hampton, with a promise to repay the other half within twelve months: both debts were repaid within five months.

With the help of his first assistant, Olivia Davidson, who was to become his first wife, and the labours of the Tuskegee students, the school grew in size and scope. The student body erected buildings and built furniture and, in the process, learned skilled trades. After several failures, Tuskegee produced its own bricks; cabinet and mattress making shops were opened in 1887, and two years later, blacksmith operations, wagon-making and wheel-wrights' work were added to the school 'catalogue'. In particular Washington concentrated the school's efforts on devising and teaching modern agricultural techniques, training skilled artisans and preparing female students to be good housekeepers. New appointments to the Tuskegee staff included George Washington Carver, like Washington a former slave, who had become an agricultural chemist, and was to be a pioneer ecologist. The regime at Tuskegee, modelled on that of Hampton, was even stricter and more Spartan. As principal, Washington ruled as a not-so-benevolent despot, alert to any infraction of the school rules by either staff or students. Although Tuskegee was a nonsectarian school – and Washington always displayed a low regard for the moral and educational standards of black ministers – religious training, in the form of daily attendance at chapel and weekly Sunday evening talks by the principal himself, ensured that Tuskegee graduates would equate education with Christian precepts. Washington also steadily increased the influence of Tuskegee into the surrounding community, with extension courses and, after 1892, annual conferences for farmers which emphasized not only innovative agricultural techniques, but also the personal and moral qualities necessary for success. Even before he emerged as a national black leader, Washington, in speeches and letters to the Northern and Southern press, constantly stressed that great benefits would come to the South – and to the entire nation – if the Tuskegee experiment proved successful. Certainly, Southern white conservatives could only be reassured by Washington's pronouncements on race relations. He informed a meeting of the National Educational Association in Madison, in 1884, that:

> Any movement for the elevation of the Southern Negro in order to be successful, must have to a certain extent the cooperation of the Southern whites. They control the government and own the property – whatever benefits the black man benefits the white man....In spite of all talk of exodus, the Negro's home is permanently in the South: for coming to the bread-and-meat side of the question, the white man needs the Negro, and the Negro needs the white man.[13]

Again, he could inform the editor of the Tuskegee *Macon Mail* in the same year that: 'The race will grow in proportion as we learn to help ourselves in matters of education'. In an address to the Alabama State Teachers' Association in 1882, Washington made an artful plea for the industrial education of blacks – one calculated to reassure and impress his white audience:

> Two hundred years of forced labour taught the coloured man that there was no dignity in labour but rather a disgrace. The child of the ex-slave, naturally influenced by his parents' example, grows up believing that he sees what he thinks is the curse of work. To remove this idea is one of the great missions of the industrial school. The school teacher must be taught that it will not disgrace him to work with his hands when he cannot get a school.[14]

As Washington's fame grew, he was frequently absent from Tuskegee, often on fund-raising drives in the Northern states, where he impressed such millionaire industrial-philanthropists as John D. Rockefeller, Andrew Carnegie, George Eastman and Henry C. Rogers with his own business-oriented and essentially conservative social philosophy. Washington (who also had unstinted admiration for the success symbolized by the possession of great wealth) directed the financial support of Northern philanthropists not only to Tuskegee – which, by 1915, had an endowment of $1,945,000 – but to other black schools and colleges in the South.

Washington, was then, the outstanding black educator of his day, and Tuskegee remains his great (but now sadly decaying) monument. It also became his power base and the headquarters for the 'Tuskegee Machine' (Washington's intricate network of organizations, spies and informers, which derived its power from his control of large sections of the black press, fraternal, business, and religious bodies, and his disbursement of political patronage and philanthropic funds). An influential figure in the post-

Reconstruction South, Washington, after delivering a speech in 1895, was catapulted into national prominence

THE ATLANTA COMPROMISE ADDRESS

In 1895, Washington was invited to speak at the Cotton States and International Exposition held in Atlanta, Georgia. Replying to the invitation, Washington assured his white sponsors: 'It will be my aim to make my remarks of service to the Exposition – especially to the coloured department – and to both races in the South', in a speech designed to 'cement the friendship of the races and bring about hearty cooperation between them'. Although there was nothing new in the address that Washington delivered on 18 September 1895, in Atlanta, the timing and circumstances of his speech ensured that it would reach (and impress) a national audience. Washington's purpose was to announce a pragmatic compromise that would resolve the antagonisms between Southern whites, Northern whites, and the Negro. In a period of worsening race relations, Washington at Atlanta (as he had before) urged blacks to remain in the South, work at 'the common occupations of life', and accept the fact of white supremacy. He deprecated blacks' performances as voters and legislators during Reconstruction, reminded them that they were to live (and prosper) by manual labour, and (to whites) stressed the loyalty and fidelity of Southern Negroes – 'the most patient, faithful, law-abiding and unresentful people in the world. ' He also stressed that blacks had absolutely no interest in securing social equality, and in an arresting metaphor declared: 'In all things that are purely social we can be as separate as the five fingers, yet one as the hánd in all things essential to human progress.' Reduced to their most obvious terms, his proposals to the South were for economic cooperation and social separation (or segregation). But Washington went even further, and assured whites that they had nothing to fear – and everything to gain from trusting blacks.

> As we have proved our loyalty to you in the past, in nursing your children, watching by the sick bed of your mothers and fathers, and often following them with tear-dimmed eyes to their graves, so in the future, in our humble way, we shall stand by you with a devotion that no foreigner can approach, ready to lay down our lives, if need be, in defence of yours.

Turning to blacks in the audience, Washington informed and admonished them that:

> Our greatest danger is that in the great leap from slavery to freedom we may overlook the fact that we shall prosper in proportion as we learn to dignify and glorify common labour. No race can prosper till it learns that there is as much dignity in tilling a field as in writing a poem. No race that has anything to contribute to the markets of the world is long in any degree ostracized. It is important and right that all the privileges of the law be ours, but it is vastly more important that we be prepared for the exercise of these vast privileges. The opportunity to earn a dollar in a factory just now is worth infinitely more than the opportunity to spend a dollar in an opera house.

In conclusion, Washington assured white Southerners that in their efforts to resolve the race problem 'which God had laid at the doors of the South', they would 'have at all times the patient, sympathetic help of my race.'[15] In effect, Washington's most famous speech was a reiteration and adaptation of the optimistic late nineteenth-century ideology of the 'New South', as espoused by Southern publicists anxious to assure Northern business interests and politicians (and themselves) that the trauma of Confederate defeat was over, that the section was ready and able to transform itself into an agriculturally diversified and increasingly industrialized society. Prerequisites for this transformation were Northern capital, and the attraction of skilled white labour – possibly from Europe. But New South spokesmen like Henry W. Grady were resolved that in racial matters, the South would continue to practise self-determination. Grady was a convinced advocate of racial segregation, and contended that the two races had an instinctive desire for separation. Social equality (which blacks did not enjoy anywhere in the United States), was out of the question. To New South ideologues, the concept involved (and offered) more than industrial progress, it would also underwrite the new social order, with blacks as an integral part of the labour force. As Henry Watterson, a New South enthusiast for industrialization and urbanization, declared: 'Under the old system we paid our debts and walloped our niggers. Under the new system we pay our niggers and wallop our debts.'[16]

Washington would have rejected Watterson's terminology, but he implicitly endorsed his sentiments and those of Grady. Significantly, Washington also contributed to the New South contention that the grosser forms of racial injustice were rapidly disappearing. Five years before the Atlanta Address, Washington had informed a Northern audience that although 'the practice of lynching coloured people is one of the curses of the South...usually resorted to when there is a charge of rape', it was being criticized by the Southern press 'and we are sure that a healthy change in public sentiment is being wrought'.[17]

Washington's 'Atlanta Compromise' address caused a sensation at the time and has been variously interpreted by commentators ever since. Not surprisingly, the Southern press heartily endorsed the sentiments it believed Washington had expressed. The *Atlanta Constitution* termed the speech 'the most remarkable address delivered by a coloured man in America', and called Washington a 'sensible and progressive Negro educator'. A South Carolina newspaper acclaimed him as 'one of the great men of the South', and added that 'his skin may be coloured, but his head is sound and his heart is in the right place'. Northern opinion (with only a few dissenting black voices) was equally enthusiastic. A Chicago newspaper, in an editorial widely reprinted in the South, declared that Washington's remarks at Atlanta and his personal example as an educator:

> has done more for the improvement for the negro in the South than has been accomplished by all the political agitators. The possession of a vote does not always ensure respect, but the possession of a good character, a good home, and a little money reserve always ensure respect. If every Southern state had such an institution as that at Tuskegee, Alabama, presided over by such a man as Professor Washington, the race question will settle itself in ten years.[18]

The correspondent of the New York *World* asserted that nothing since Henry W. Grady's address to the New England Society of New York had demonstrated so graphically 'the spirit of the New South'. On all counts – his own rise to eminence from slavery, his deprecation of political activity by blacks and stress on economic advancement, his distrust of labour unions and 'foreigners', and his generally conservative position on social issues – Washington stood revealed as the black defender of the New South creed.

Most estimates of Washington's Atlanta Address have viewed it as an abject surrender of black civil and political rights to the forces of white racism. It is, however, also possible to view it as a masterly exercise in dissimulation or, rather, in racial diplomacy. Writing from Wilberforce University, the young black scholar, W. E. B. Du Bois, congratulated Washington on his 'phenomenal success at Atlanta – it was a word fitly spoken'. A close reading of the text of the Atlanta Address, reveals that it included ultimate goals which white Southerners could not support. There were futuristic implications and nuances in Washington's address. Reading between the lines, as August Meier perceptively remarks, Washington, although he asserted that blacks must begin at the bottom:

> surely...believed that eventually they would arrive at the top...his Negro supporters emphasized the future implication of his remarks... the dominant whites were impressed by his conciliatory phraseology, confused his means for his ends, and were satisfied with the immediate programme he enunciated. [19]

Whatever the nuances, the Atlanta Address made Washington an acclaimed black leader. James Weldon Johnson, national organizer and executive secretary for the NAACP, reflecting on Washington's rise to fame, attributed it to his 'epochal' Atlanta speech, as a direct consequence of which:

> he had at a stroke gained the sanction and support of both the South and the North – the South, in general, construing the speech to imply the Negro's abdication of his claim to full and equal citizenship rights, and his acceptance of the status of a contented and industrious peasantry; the North feeling that the opportunity had arisen to rid its conscience of a disturbing question and shift it over to the South. The great body of Negroes, discouraged, bewildered, and leaderless, hailed Mr Washington as a Moses. This was indeed a remarkable feat – his holding of the South in one hand, the North in the other, and at the same time carrying a major portion of his race along with him. [20]

For his part, Washington regarded himself as the successor to, if not the strict disciple of Frederick Douglass. In *The Story of My Life and Work* (1910), intended primarily for a black readership, Washington asserted:

> Mr Douglass had the same idea concerning the importance and value of industrial education that I have tried to emphasize. He also held the same ideas I do in regard to the emigration of the Negro to Africa, and was opposed to the diffusion and dissemination of the Negro throughout the North and Northwest, believing as I do that the Southern section of the country where the Negro now resides is the best place for him.[21]

But Washington also believed that the issues which Douglass had agitated were not relevant to the 'New South'. In his biography of Douglass, Washington noted that his career fell 'almost wholly within the period of revolution and liberation'. But:

> that period is now closed. We are at present in the period of construction and readjustment. Many of the animosities engendered by the conflicts and controversies of half a century ago still survive....But changes are rapidly coming about that will remove, or at least greatly modify, these lingering animosities.[22]

It is unlikely that Douglass would have endorsed these Washingtonian sentiments and comparisons. In the last year of his life, asked by a student what advice he would give to the younger black generation, Douglass reportedly replied: 'Agitate! Agitate! Agitate!' When the same student posed the identical question to Booker T. Washington in 1899, he received the answer: 'Work! Work! Work! Be patient and win by superior service.'[23]

UP FROM SLAVERY

From 1895 until his death in 1915, Washington's determination, power and influence made him a force to be reckoned with. He continued to act as the seemingly omnipotent and autocratic principal of Tuskegee, but also embarked on extensive fund-raising and lecturing tours. His message, with few exceptions, was a restatement of the Atlanta Address: blacks should eschew politics, cultivate habits of thrift, economy, sobriety and honesty, and concentrate on the acquisition of Christian character, property and industrial skills. Urged by his admirers to write an (inspirational) account of his remarkable career, Washington collaborated with a ghostwriter to produce *The Story of My Life and Work* (1900). Poorly produced, and replete with grammatical and typographical errors, the book sold about 15,000 copies within a year of publication, but received luke-warm reviews in the press. His second autobiography, *Up From Slavery* (1901), which first appeared in serial form, was a more fully-planned and executed project. Max Bennett Thrasher, a white journalist, a teacher, and a regular visitor to Tuskegee (and employed by Washington as the school's public relations man), acted as ghostwriter for the book. *Up From Slavery* presented Washington as a black Horatio Alger, who had succeeded because of his internalization and application of the Puritan work ethic, instilled in him by successive white mentors. An immediate publishing success, the book appealed to a foreign readership as well, and was quickly translated into more foreign languages than any other American book of its time. Several of Tuskegee's most generous benefactors became converts to Washington's philosophy of race relations after reading his autobiography. Andrew Carnegie, who had earlier refused to meet Washington, felt that *Up From Slavery* exemplified his own brand of Social Darwinism, and donated a library building to Tuskegee as well as $600,000 in

United States Steel bonds (from which Washington personally gained an income). White readers of the autobiography welcomed not only its retailing of familiar maxims of self-help and perseverence in the face of adversity, but also its sanguine portrayal of black life (both during and after slavery). In effect, *Up From Slavery* complemented the Atlanta Compromise address (which was also included in the text). It presented the 'authorized' view of race relations in the South during the period of Congressional Reconstruction that had been such an affront to Southern whites. Black involvement in this phase of Reconstruction was also sternly deprecated by Washington:

> In many cases it seemed to me that the ignorance of my race was being used as a tool with which to help white men into office, and that there was an element in the North which wanted to punish the Southern white men by forcing the Negro into positions over the heads of Southern whites....Besides, the general political agitation drew the attention of our people away from the more fundamental matters of perfecting themselves in the industries at their doors and at securing properties. I saw coloured men who were members of the state legislatures, and country officers, who, in some cases, could not read or write, and whose morals were as weak as their education....Many of the Southern whites have the feeling that, if the Negro is permitted to exercise his political rights now to any degree, the mistakes of the Reconstruction period will repeat themselves. I do not think that this will be true, because the Negro...is fast learning the lesson that he cannot afford to act in a manner that will alienate his Southern white neighbors from him. [24]

Most obviously, however, *Up From Slavery* was an extended song of praise – a series of 'advertisements for myself' – to Booker T. Washington. As one literary critic has aptly remarked, the book 'reads like a saint's life written by a saint'. And:

> Like Dickens' virtuous co-narratress in *Bleak House*, Washington is forced into the artless ruse of quoting everyone's praises of him so as not to be praising himself directly all the time. He does no wrong, has no enemies, suffers hardships willingly, is universally beloved, and is, for it all (as he confesses) quite humble.[25]

Washington's former teacher at Hampton, Mrs Mary F. Mackie, was inordinately proud of her pupil, and declared (without noting the irony) that the book 'sets off more graphically than any article I have read, the transition from slavery to freedom. It reads like a romance.'[26]

BLACK LEADER

In the last twenty years of his life, Washington had a dual career as educator and race leader. During the administrations of Theodore Roosevelt and William Howard Taft, Washington dispensed the limited federal patronage for blacks, strengthened the intricate network of the 'Tuskegee Machine' and, with the help of his devoted secretary, Emmett J. Scott, monitored the activities of his Negro critics. In 1900, putting one of his favourite precepts into practice, Washington founded the National Negro Business League to promote black entrepreneurship and advertise the economic success some blacks had achieved. The League not only reflected Washington's belief that black advancement lay in economic progress, but also provided him with a cadre of loyal supporters in the major cities of the North. In the South, Washington, hypersensitively aware of the precarious position of blacks, ingratiated himself with successive governors of Alabama, promoted health measures for Negroes, and promoted such economic ventures as black owned-and-operated cotton mills and land purchase schemes.

By 1901, Washington was at the height of his fame, and received the presidential seal of approval when Theodore Roosevelt invited him to dinner at the White House. The episode angered Southern whites, who felt he had breached the unwritten rules of racial etiquette. One 'prominent Southerner' wrote to a Chicago newspaper that:

> Every Southern man of intelligence honors Booker T. Washington, but no Southern gentleman would sit at table with him under any consideration whatever. We are willing to pay him homage for his good works, but we cannot admit him to social equality, because that involves a principle which is vital to the preservation of the Southern white race from the evils of intermarriage with blacks.

The American historian, James Ford Rhodes, reported the reaction of one white man from Tuskegee to Washington's White House dinner: 'Now when I meet the man who has done all this, I can't call him Booker like I call any ordinary nigger, but by thunder, I can't call a nigger *mister*, so I just say professor!'[27] But, as even his black critics reluctantly conceded, the White House episode had greatly enhanced Washington's national reputation. Henry M. Turner informed him that: 'You are about to be the great representative and hero of the Negro race, notwithstanding you have been very conservative'.[28]

Yet, although he had the ear of presidents and philanthropists,

Washington was unable to halt, let alone improve, the deteriorating racial situation of the Progressive era. In 1896, the Supreme Court's decision in *Plessy versus Ferguson*, appeared to give judicial sanction to the 'separate but equal' doctrine, apparently already endorsed by Washington at Atlanta. Again, while he helped to deliver the black vote to the Republicans in state and national elections, Washington seemed powerless when Theodore Roosevelt, in a blatantly racist act, summarily dismissed three companies of black troops in Brownsville, Texas, after they had forcibly resisted a white mob. Similarly, Taft's policy of removing Southern black officeholders indicated the very real limits of Washington's political influence.

On numerous occasions, Washington himself was made painfully aware of the virulence of white racism. When a white chambermaid in an Indianapolis hotel was reported to have refused to make up Washington's bed and to have lost her job in consequence, a Texas newspaper solicited funds 'For a Self-Respecting Girl'. Washington also discovered that segregation, imposed by whites on blacks, had produced accommodations that were certainly separate but decidedly unequal. He once confessed that: 'The mere thought of a trip on a railroad brings to me a feeling of intense dread and I never enter a railroad coach unless compelled to do so.'[29] But Washington also worked to end the more blatant forms of racial discrimination. He secretly sponsored legal suits against the exclusion of blacks from jury service, the various ingenious devices employed to deny black suffrage, and the persistence of coerced labour in the South. In his last years – possibly because of his failures to prevent presidents Roosevelt, Taft and Woodrow Wilson from giving executive approval to racial segregation – Washington became more outspoken against Jim Crow. He criticized conditions in the cars and waiting rooms of Southern railroads, the persistence of lynching, a Congressional proposal to exclude African immigrants, and the blatant racism of D. W. Griffith's epic motion picture *Birth of a Nation*, with its romantic portrayal of the Ku Klux Klan. But Washington's strongest protest against discrimination did not appear until after his death, in a posthumously published article, 'My View of the Segregation Laws'. Racial segregation, Washington asserted, was 'ill-advised' in that it was both unjust and productive of further injustices. It was also 'unnecessary', and resented by 'every thoughtful Negro'. Again, segregation was 'inconsistent' since 'the negro is separated from his white neighbor, but the white businessmen are not prevented from doing business in Negro neighborhoods'. Finally, segregation was harmful to both its victims and its sponsors – 'Wherever a form of segregation exists, it will be found that it has been administered in such a way as to embitter the Negro and harms more or less the moral fibre of the white man'. That blacks did not openly express their detestation of the system was no proof that they did not resent it.[30]

Washington travelled extensively at home and abroad, and had a world-wide following. Tuskegee was regularly visited by Africans, West Indians, Asians, European missionaries and white colonialists. On his three trips to Europe, Washington had tea with Queen Victoria, and met the Danish royal family. He stayed with – and impressed – H. G. Wells, who compared Washington favourably with W. E. B. Du Bois, a man who 'conceals his passionate resentment too thinly', whereas Washington 'looks before and after and keeps his council with the scope and range of a statesman...his is a mind that can grasp the situation and destinies of a people'.[31] On his 1910 visit to Denmark, Germany, Austria-Hungary, Italy and England, Washington concluded that despite handicaps, the American Negro was better off than 'the man farthest down' in Europe, in that he enjoyed a better standard of living, educational, economic and political opportunities. When Washington told a meeting of the London Anti-Slavery Society in 1910 that American race relations were improving, he drew an angry retort from John E. Milholland of the NAACP, who was also in England. W. E. B. Du Bois, informed of the incident, published an 'Appeal to Europe' which appeared in the British and American press. Du Bois accused Washington of relating only selected items to European audiences because of his dependence on white support, and stressed instead widespread discrimination, lynching, and the failure of the courts to protect blacks as the less sanguine side of the contemporary American racial scene.

Despite his foreign travels, Washington did not alter his fundamental outlook which was essentially that of a provincial Southerner. He never visited Africa, Asia or the West Indies, and before he sailed to Europe in 1910, resolved not to enter a single art gallery, museum or palace. Washington also had little awareness of or interest in the African heritage of African-Americans. He was, however, quite prepared to advise the European colonial powers in Africa to the extent of supplying Tuskegee staff or graduates to promote programmes of industrial education (within the existing political order) among African peoples in Togo, Nigeria, the Belgian

37

Congo, South Africa and Liberia. He also urged that Africans be taught English in order to give them a *lingua franca*, and promote their Western acculturation. Although he endorsed German colonialism in Africa, toward the end of his life, Washington criticized white imperialist oppression in the Congo and South Africa – not because of any Pan-Africanist sentiments, but rather to highlight the impracticality of black emigration to Africa as a solution to the American race problem. (In a letter of 1893, protesting against Henry M. Turner's promotion of African emigration, Washington asserted: 'This talk of any appreciable number of our people going to Africa is the merest nonsense... It does no good, but...does a great deal of harm among the ignorant of our people, especially in the far South.')[32]

In 1915, on a speaking engagement in New York, Washington collapsed from nervous exhaustion, arteriosclerosis and kidney failure (an initial diagnosis of syphilis was withdrawn after protests from Washington's personal physician). Informed that he had only a short time to live, he asked to be taken back to Tuskegee: 'I was born in the South, I have lived and laboured in the South, and I expect to be buried in the South'.[33] He died at Tuskegee on 14 November, 1915. Washington's statue on the Tuskegee campus expresses his life in the form of a parable. He is depicted lifting 'the veil of ignorance' from the kneeling figure of a young black man, holding on his knees an open book and agricultural and industrial tools. Washington's critics, in his lifetime and after, suggested another reading of the tableau: rather than lifting, Washington was lowering a 'veil of ignorance' over the eyes of his people.

WASHINGTON AND HIS BLACK CRITICS

Opposition to Washington's ideas and to his white-sanctioned position as race leader, came from a relatively small group of mainly Northern blacks – journalists, lawyers, clergymen and educators. Initially united only by their dislike of various elements of Washington's programme, his contemporary black critics accused him of a range of offences, miscalculations and misdemeanours. He was faulted for deprecating political action on the part of blacks while at the same time functioning as a 'boss', condemned for attempting to impose a partisan and regional strategy for racial advancement on the country as a whole, castigated for his control of the Negro press and his friendships with white editors, with the resultant suppression of criticism. Washington's policies of industrial education were pronounced anachronistic, and his portrayals of harmonious race relations as travesties of the truth. In a letter published in an Atlanta journal, only three months after the Atlanta Address, a black correspondent expressed alarm at Washington's overnight elevation to the position of race leader, and rejected as unseemly any comparisons between Washington and Frederick Douglass:

> Every race must make its own heroes... If another race selects our heroes, puts them upon pedestals, and tells us to bow down to them and serve them, woe be unto us. It is supreme folly to speak of Mr Washington as the Moses of the race. If we are where Mr Washington's Atlanta speech placed us, what need have we of a Moses? Who brought us from Egypt, through the wilderness to these happy conditions? Let us pray that the race will never have a leader, but leaders. Who is the leader of the white race in America? It has no leader, but leaders. So with us.[34]

The Cleveland *Gazette* reported a black Atlanta journal as stating:

> Prof. B. T. or Bad Taste Wash. has made a speech....The white press style Prof. Bad Taste the new Negro, but if there is anything in him except the most servile type of the old Negro, we fail to find it in any of his last acts....let the race labor and pray that no more new Negroes such as Prof. Bad Taste will bob up.[35]

As black migration to the North continued, and with the growth of a professional black élite, attacks on Washington became sharper and more concerted. Julius F. Taylor, Negro editor of the *Chicago Broad Ax* was an ardent Democrat, and resented Washington's involvement in Republican patronage politics. Taylor typified Washington as 'the Great Beggar of Tuskegee' and 'the greatest white man's nigger in the world', and warned in 1899:

> The time is not far distant when Booker T. Washington will be repudiated as the leader of our race, for he believes that only mealy-mouthed Negroes like himself should be involved in politics.[36]

William Monroe Trotter, the fiery editor of the *Boston Guardian*, was an early and bitter critic of Washington. When Andrew Carnegie donated $600,000 to Tuskegee, Trotter expressed the hope that Washington would no longer need to engage in fund-raising tours, and asserted:

This man, whatever good he may do, has injured and is injuring the race more than he can aid it by his school. Let us hope that Booker Washington will remain mouth-closed at Tuskegee. If he will do this, all his former sins will be forgiven.

Taking issue with Washington's reported statement that the revised constitutions of the Southern states had placed 'a premium on intelligence, ownership of property, thrift and character', Trotter accused him of self-deception and asked rhetorically:

What man is a worse enemy to the race than a leader who looks with equanimity on the disfranchisement of his race in a country where other races have universal suffrage, by constitutions that make one rule for his race and another for the dominant race?

Trotter deplored Washington's rise to fame, and charged him with being the 'Benedict Arnold' of the black race. He appealed for a 'black Patrick Henry' who would save his people from the dangers into which Washington had led them, one who would inspire them rather with the words 'Give Me Liberty or Give Me Death'.[37]

But the most searching, reasoned and influential critique of Washington's precepts and policies was produced by W. E. B. Du Bois (see Chapter 3), in his seminal essay 'Of Mr Booker T. Washington and Others', a chapter of *The Souls of Black Folk* (1903). Although he began by conceding that: 'Easily the most striking thing in the history of the American Negro since 1876 is the ascendency of Mr Booker T. Washington' Du Bois charged that Washington's leadership had resulted in (if it had not directly encouraged) black disfranchisement, the creation of an inferior civil status for blacks, and the withdrawal of funds from institutions of higher training for Negroes. Washington, he suggested, faced a 'triple paradox' in that:

1. He is striving to make Negroes artisans, businessmen and property owners; but it is utterly impossible under modern competitive methods, for workingmen and property owners to defend their rights and exist without the right of suffrage.

2. He insists on thrift and self-respect, but at the same time counsels a silent submission to civic inferiority such as is bound to sap the manhood of any race in the long-run.

3. He advocates common school and industrial training, and deprecates institutions of higher learning; but neither the Negro common schools, nor Tuskegee itself, could remain open one day were it not for teachers trained in Negro colleges, or trained by their graduates.

Although he paid tribute to Washington's achievements in placating the white South, and in shrewdly appealing to the spirit of commercialism in the North, Du Bois pronounced Washington's vision narrow, crass and pessimistic. Washington, he concluded, represented 'in Negro thought the old attitude of adjustment and submission'.[38] James Weldon Johnson recalled that Du Bois' critique provided a rallying point for blacks opposed to Washington 'and made them articulate, thereby creating a split of the race into two contending camps'.[39] The Niagara Movement of 1905, and its successor, the NAACP (see Chapter 3) were to institutionalize opposition to Washington. Washington's responses to his black critics consisted of a few half-hearted (and abortive) attempts at reconciliation and cooperation, together with unremitting efforts to influence, infiltrate or sabotage their organizations. In 1904 he persuaded the Du Bois-led faction to attend a secret meeting to iron out their differences. This New York conference (held in Carnegie Hall) was marked by mutual suspicions, and failure to achieve a truce or agreement between the Washington and Du Bois forces. With the support of such benefactors as Andrew Carnegie, Washington controlled the proceedings, outmanoeuvered his opponents, and secured the election of loyal followers to a Committee of Twelve for the Advancement of the Negro Race, a purely advisory body which, during its brief existence, reported directly back to Tuskegee.

Washington keenly resented any challenges to his leadership. As Du Bois later confirmed, their conflict was essentially a power struggle, couched in terms of differences in educational and political ideology. With some real justification, Washington argued that his Northern-based black critics had no real appreciation of racial conditions in the South. In a revealing letter, written in 1911, Washington summarized what he regarded as the outstanding differences between himself and Du Bois.

> I believe that the Negro race is making progress...that it is better for
> the race to emphasize its opportunities than to lay over-much stress on
> its disadvantages. He believes the Negro race is making little progress.
> I believe that we should cultivate an ever manly, straightforward
> manner and friendly relations between white people and black people.
> Du Bois pursues this policy of stirring up strife between white and
> black people...he fails to realize that it is a work of construction that
> is before us now and not a work of destruction.[40]

For his part, Du Bois, during his long life, continually revised his estimates of Washington, presenting him in a more sympathetic light, and stressing the significant differences in their background and education. But it was his essay 'Of Mr Booker T. Washington' that propelled Du Bois into the position of a rival black leader.

ASSESSMENT

In the circumstances of his time and place, Washington evolved a programme and strategy designed to secure the acquiescence of Southern and Northern whites in the educational and economic elevation of a rural black peasantry (recently 'up from slavery'), and an aspiring urban black bourgeoisie. Aware that slavery had brought physical labour into disrepute, Washington – in tune with his age – preached a gospel of hard-work, self-help and self-reliance. His advocacy of industrial education reflected this belief, as it also reconciled Southern whites to the idea of *any* form of education for blacks. Tuskegee Institute, the Tuskegee Machine, and the carefully-crafted phrase of the 'Atlanta Compromise' and other addresses, made Washington's position as the most visible black leader of his day virtually impregnable. Above all, Washington was a master tactician, interracial diplomat and archetypal 'trickster'. In many respects, he bears an unfortunate (but intentional) resemblance to Dr A. Herbert Bledsoe, the black college principal in Ralph Ellison's novel, *Invisible Man*. Describing his methods and rise to power in the South to the ingenuous narrator, Bledsoe could well have been retailing Washington's personal success formula:

> Negroes don't control this school or much of anything else. True they support it, but I control it. I's big and black and I say 'Yes, suh', as loudly as any burrhead, when its convenient....The only ones I even *pretend* to please are big white folk, and even those I control more than they control me. I tell them; that's my life, telling white folks how to think about the things I know about....It's a nasty deal and I don't like it myself. But I didn't make it and I know that I can't change it. I had to be strong and purposeful to get where I am. I had to wait and lick around. I had to act the nigger. I don't even insist that it was worth it, but now I'm here and I mean to stay – after you win the game you take the prize and keep it and protect it; there's nothing else to do.[41]

Despite repeated invitations to move North, Washington realized that his work lay in the South, although the growing criticism from Northern black critics forced him, in later years, to sharpen his portrayals of persisting racial inequalities. In a period of worsening race relations, Washington continued to build up the resources and reputation of Tuskegee, and secured philanthropic funding for other Southern black schools and colleges. Unable to prevent the erosion of black voting rights, escalating racial violence and economic exploitation, Washington attempted (both publicly and privately) to hold the line. As Myrdal noted, Washington, his critics to the contrary, was never a totally 'accommodating' race leader, and looked to complete equality as the 'ultimate goal' of black leadership. Dependent on the support of Northern sympathizers and Southern white paternalists, Washington balanced on a precarious tight-rope. Myrdal concluded that:

> For his time, and for the region where he worked and where the nine-tenths of all Negroes lived, his policy of abstaining from talks of rights and of 'casting down your buckets where you are' was entirely realistic.[42]

Washington's faults were glaring – his astigmatism on the intensity and prevalence of white racial prejudice, his unquestioning acceptance of the normative values of white America, his unabashed materialism and philistinism, his tendency to blame blacks for their condition, his paranoid jealousy of other black spokespersons. Yet he also promoted public health measures for blacks and supported black enterprises – notably, the National Negro Business League, which anticipated later forms of economic black nationalism. Moreover, the National Urban League (see Chapter 4), grew out of organizations that subscribed to Washington's advice to Southern rural blacks. In its emphasis on training, the NUL echoed and amplified one of Washington's favourite themes, while his obsession with the tooth-brush foreshadowed the League's efforts to instruct black migrants in the rudimentary practices of urban life.

Most importantly, during the years of Washington's ascendancy (which coincided with increasing hardships, proscriptions and dangers for Negroes), militant black protest and agitation in the South was not simply unrealistic, but might have proved a warrant for genocide. The last black leader to emerge from slavery, Washington lived dangerously, forced in Langston Hughes' phrase to spend most of his life with his head 'in the lion's mouth'. Not only was Washington attacked by black 'radicals', he also failed to mollify Southern black extremists. Addressing the Peace Jubilee in Chicago, celebrating the end of the Spanish-American War, Washington (unguardedly) declared that racial hatred, especially in the South, was a 'cancer' that would one day destroy the nation. Southern whites were displeased – but Washington's assertion that the victims of lynching in the South 'are invariably vagrants, men without property and standing', more than made amends for such slips of the tongue. Thomas Dixon, Jr, author of *The Clansman: An Historical Romance of the Ku Klux Klan* (1905), alleged that Washington, precisely because of his skill in disguising his real aims, was quietly preparing the way for the amalgamation of the races, or (and equally dangerous), the building of a separate Negro nation. Even Washington's endorsement of industrial training for blacks was subversive, since 'if there is one thing a Southern white cannot endure it is an educated negro'. By the same token, Washington's efforts to make the Negro into a potential competitor in the market-place with the white man could only end in bloodshed.[43]

Booker T. Washington, one of his biographers contends, has not been accorded a fair evaluation 'partly because his methods were too compromising and unheroic to win him a place in the black pantheon, but also because he was too complex and enigmatic for historians to know what to make of him'.[44]

Yet, as J. R. Pole suggests, Washington's role-playing (which certainly exacted a price in nervous tension and exhaustion), although devious, was not unique:

> In many ways he emerges as a type remarkable for its familiarity among the operators of American interest groups – that familiarity being disguised by skin pigmentation. He worked assiduously within the system, to whose economic and political conventions he faithfully subscribed; he took conservative views of larger social causes while showing great tactical skill in maintaining his own personal power base.[45]

Throughout the South, in the era of Jim Crow, local black leaders, in the main, followed policies of racial conservatism, stressing economic opportunity over social equality, and espousing a Washingtonian gospel of black progress through thrift, material accumulation and industrial training. And, as N. R. McMillen states of black leaders in Mississippi in the late nineteenth and early twentieth centuries, they (and their counterparts elsewhere) 'conceded nothing to whites that had not already been taken by force'.[46] Although there is no scholarly consensus on Booker T. Washington's achievement (or limitations) as a black leader, he certainly should not be blamed for the failure of black Americans to secure racial equality, however defined, in his own lifetime or afterwards. He has been blamed for too much anyway.

As Martin Luther King judiciously observed, Washington should not be dismissed simply as 'an Uncle Tom who compromised for the sake of keeping the peace'. His sincerely-held belief was that 'if the South was not pushed too far ... it would voluntarily rally to the Negro's cause'. But his faith was misplaced and reviled.

Washington's error was that he underestimated the structures of evil; as a consequence, his philosophy of pressureless persuasion only served as a springboard for racist Southerners to dive into deeper and more ruthless oppression of the Negro.[47]

REFERENCES

1. Du Bois, W. E. B., *Dusk of Dawn*, (New York, 1940), pp.78–9.
2. Baker, Henry, born 1854, Alabama, interviewed, 1938, in John W. Blassingame (ed.), *Slave Testimony: Two Centuries of Letters, Speeches, Interviews, and Autobiographies* (Louisiana State UP, 1977), p.675.
3. Rosengarten, T., *All God's Dangers: The Life of Nate Shaw* (New York, 1974), pp.568–9.
4. Rabinowitz, H. N., *Race Relations in the Urban South, 1865–1890* (Oxford UP, New York, 1978).
5. Wright, Richard, *Black Boy* (London, 1947), pp.253–4.
6. McMillen, N. R., *Dark Journey: Black Mississippians in the Age of Jim Crow* (University of Illinois Press,1989), p.228.
7. Woodward, C. Vann, *Origins of the New South* (Louisiana State UP, 1951), p.356.
8. Harlan, L. R. *et al.* (eds), *The Booker T. Washington Papers: Vol I* (University of Illinois Press, 1972), p.215. (cited hereafter as Papers).
9. *Papers, Vol. IV* (1975), p.92.
10. *Papers, Vol. I* (1972), p.236.
11. Norrell, R. J., *Reaping the Whirlwind: The Civil Rights Movement in Tuskegee* (New York, 1985), p.14.
12. Harlan, L. R., *Booker T. Washington: The Making of a Black Leader, 1865–1901* (Oxford U.P., New York, 1972), p.110.
13. *Papers, Vol. II* (1972), p.256,p.258.
14. *Ibid.*, p.194.
15. The entire Atlanta Address is reproduced in *Up From Slavery* (various editions) and in *Papers, Vol. I*.
16. Gaston, P. M., *The New South Creed: A Study in Southern Mythmaking* (Louisiana State U.P., 1970), p.147.
17. *Papers, Vol. III* (1971), p.29.
18. Logan, R. W., *The Betrayal of the Negro: From Rutherford B. Hayes*

to *Woodrow Wilson* (London, 1965), p.285.

19. Meier, A., *Negro Thought in America, 1880–1915* (University of Michigan Press, 1963), p.101.
20. Johnson, J. W., *Black Manhattan* (New York, 1930), pp.131–2.
21. *Papers, Vol. I* (1972), p.56.
22. Washington, Booker T., *Frederick Douglass* (London, 1906), pp.3–4.
23. Foner, P. S. (ed.), *The Life and Writings of Frederick Douglass* (New York, 1950), Vol. IV, pp.149–50.
24. *Papers, Vol. I* (1972), pp.258–9.
25. Littlejohn, D., *Black on White: A Critical Survey of Writing by American Negroes*, (New York, 1966), p.30.
26. Harlan, *Making of a Black Leader, op. cit.*, p.248.
27. Thornbrough, E. L., 'Booker T. Washington As Seen By His White Contemporaries', *Journal of Negro History*, 53 (1968), p.172.
28. Harlan, L. R., *Booker T. Washington: The Wizard of Tuskegee, 1901–1915* (Oxford U. P., New York, 1983), p.5.
29. *Papers, Vol. II* (1972), p.271.
30. Washington, Booker T., *New Republic*, 4 December 1915.
31. Harlan, *Wizard of Tuskegee, op. cit.*, p.284.
32. *Papers, Vol. III* (1974), p.377.
33. Harlan, *Wizard of Tuskegee, op. cit.*, p.424.
34. Foner, P. S., 'Is Booker T. Washington's Idea Correct?', *Journal of Negro History*, 55 (1970), p.344.
35. Harlan, *Making of a Black Leader, op. cit.*, p.226.
36. Nielson, D. G., *Black Ethos: Northern Urban Negro Life & Thought, 1890–1930* (London, 1977), pp.199–200.
37. Meier, A., E. Rudwick & F. L. Broderick (eds), *Black Protest Thought in the Twentieth Century* (2nd edn, New York, 1971), pp.32-35.
38. Du Bois, W. E. B., *The Souls of Black Folk* (New York, 1968 edn.), pp.48–9.
39. Johnson, *Black Manhattan, op. cit.*, p.134.
40. *Papers, Vol. X*, (1981), pp.608–9.
41. Ellison, Ralph, *Invisible Man* (Penguin, Harmondsworth, 1952), p.119.
42. Myrdal, *An American Dilemma* (New York, 1944), p.741.
43. Thornbrough, 'Booker T. Washington As Seen By His White Contemporaries', *op. cit.*, p.180.
44. Harlan, *Making of a Black Leader, op. cit.*, p.vii.
45. Pole, J. R., 'Of Mr Booker T. Washington and Others,' in *Paths to the American Past* (Oxford U.P., 1979), pp.184–5.
46. McMillen, *Dark Journey, op. cit.*, p.300
47. King, M. L., *Where Do We Go From Here?: Chaos or Community?* (New York, 1967), p. 129.

CHAPTER THREE

W. E. B. Du Bois: Talented Propagandist

My first clear memory of Dr Du Bois was my pride in his recognized scholarship and his authority in many fields of work and writing. We Negro students joined the NAACP which Dr Du Bois helped to organize and build; we read religiously *Crisis* of which he was editor for so many years, and in which he wrote clearly, constructively and militantly on the complex problems of the American scene, on the Negro question, on Africa, on world affairs.   [PAUL ROBESON][1]

I first read Du Bois' *The Souls of Black Folk* in my home and his novel *The Quest of the Silver Fleece*. He writes, my father would say, but he doesn't lead anybody.[2]

PERSPECTIVES: NORTHERN BLACKS ORGANIZE FOR PROTEST, 1890–1910

The late nineteenth century saw several attempts at the formation of Negro movements to protest against racial discrimination and Washingtonian accommodationism. In 1890, delegates met in Chicago at the call of T. Thomas Fortune, editor of the *New York Age*, and the most able black journalist of his day. Three years earlier, Fortune had appealed to blacks to organize a National Afro-American League which would agitate for the removal of six principal grievances: the suppression of voting rights in the South, which had the effect of denying blacks political participation in the states where they were most numerous; the prevalence of mob rule and lynching in the South; the inequitable distribution of funds between black and white schools; the degrading prison system in the South; discrimination and segregation on Southern railroads, and the denial of accommodations to blacks in public places. Writing from Tuskegee, Booker T. Washington supported these proposals, and the Chicago convention adopted a constitution along the lines recommended by Fortune – the desired goals to be secured by appeals to public opinion, litigation and non-violent demonstrations. By 1893, however, Fortune announced that the League was defunct because of lack of funds and inadequate support. In 1898, at a meeting in Rochester, New York, the League was revived as the National Afro-American Council, with a statement of objectives similar to those of the original League platform. Conceived as a comprehensive civil rights organization, the Council during its ten year existence was largely ineffectual, and rent by factionalism. Washington did not hold any office in the Council, but through his friendship with Fortune became a dominant influence in its activities. Inevitably, black responses to the Council reflected, to a large extent, approval for or opposition to Washington's policies. When W. E. B. Du Bois, a young professor at Atlanta University, was made director of a Negro business scheme promoted by the Council, Washington sensed a challenge to his leadership and formed the National Negro Business League – with the help of a list of black businessmen provided for him by Du Bois.

While the Afro-American Council continued to be dominated by Washingtonians, a group of twenty-nine black 'radicals', responding to an appeal by Du Bois, met on the Canadian side of the Niagara Falls, in July 1905, to form an organization opposed to Washington and the influence of the Tuskegee Machine. The Niagara Movement, which resulted from this meeting, placed responsibility for the racial problem squarely on whites. Its demands included: freedom of speech and criticism – an oblique reference to the Tuskegee Machine; manhood suffrage for all black Americans; the eradication of caste distinctions based on colour; universal common school education (to include federal aid and the chance of higher education for all blacks); equal employment opportunities and constant agitation as the strategy to secure Negro rights.

In many respects, the Niagara Movement reflected the aspirations of the college-educated black élite and its determination to effect profound changes in American race relations through direct action. The white journalist, Ray Stannard Baker, surveying American race relations in the early twentieth century, noted of the Niagara Movement: 'The party led by Dr Du Bois is a party of protest which endeavours to prevent Negro separation and discrimination against

Negroes by political agitation and political influence.'[3] Predictably, Booker T. Washington was opposed to the Niagara Movement from its inception, and his obstructionist tactics and ubiquitous influence undermined the organization, which was never able to gain white support. It was also unable to gain an appreciable following among the masses of blacks, and went down to short-term defeat as a protest movement. But the Niagara Movement was further evidence of the growing dissatisfaction of Northern blacks with Washington's Southern-style leadership and claim to be regarded as spokesman of the race. Ray Stannard Baker characterized Washington as 'an opportunist and optimist who 'teaches that if the Negro wins by real worth a strong economic position in this country, other rights and privileges will come to him naturally'. And, Baker added, 'many highly educated Negroes, especially in the North, dislike and oppose him [Washington]'.[4] To Myrdal, writing in the 1940s, the Niagara Movement signified:

> the first organized attempt to raise the Negro protest against the great reaction after the Reconstruction. Its main importance was that it brought to open conflict and wide public debate two types of Negro strategy – one stressing accommodation and the other raising the Negro protest. Booker T. Washington and W. E. B. Du Bois became national symbols for these two main streams of Negro thought.[5]

By 1903, the Niagara Movement had ceased to be an effective organization, but had laid the foundation for the National Association for the Advancement of Coloured People (NAACP), a bi-racial coalition of black radicals and white liberals, pledged to advance black civil and political rights – and a more serious challenge to Washington's hegemony.

In the summer of 1908, a race riot in Springfield, Illinois, home of Abraham Lincoln, resulted in the deaths of eight Negroes, fifty injured people, and a mass exodus of blacks from the city. William E. Walling, a white Kentuckian, socialist and social worker, reporting the incident in an article entitled 'The Race War in the North', issued an appeal for a revival of the spirit of the abolitionist crusade, and urged the formation of a national organization of whites and blacks to work for social justice. Among those responding to Walling's appeal were Mary White Ovington, a wealthy Northerner from an abolitionist background, who had just completed the study of blacks in New York City, and Henry Moskowitz, a Jewish social worker. At their suggestion, Oswald Garrison Villard, grandson of William Lloyd Garrison, and editor of the New York *Post*, issued a 'call' on the centennial of Lincoln's birth, for a national conference to debate 'the renewal of the struggle for civil and political liberty'. Those responding to the call included such leading white Progressive reformers as Jane Addams, Rabbi Stephen S. Wise, and the 'muckraking' journalists Ray Stannard Baker and Lincoln Steffens. Black respondents included Du Bois, the militant educationalist Ida Wells Barnett (who had earlier been active in the formation of the first national organization for Negro women), and Bishop Alexander Walters, who had served in the National Afro-American League and its successor, the Afro-American Council. The conference was held in the spring of 1909, as the National Negro Committee Conference. Booker T. Washington declined an invitation to attend on the grounds that did not wish to jeopardize his work in the South, and was interested only in 'progressive, constructive' work for the race, and not in 'agitation and criticism'. In his address to the Conference, Du Bois emphasized the interrelatedness of politics and economics, but avoided attacking (or naming) Washington directly. Resolutions were adopted condemning the repression of blacks, appealing to the federal government to compel the Southern states to honour the 14th and 15th amendments, and demanding that black children receive a proportional share of educational appropriations. Although the Conference organizers were anxious not to alienate Booker T. Washington, black delegates rejected a proposal inviting him to join the steering committee, and forced through a resolution which clearly indicated opposition to his policies:

> We fully agree with the prevailing opinion that the transformation of the unskilled coloured labourers in industry and agriculture into skilled workers is of vital importance to the race and to the nation, but we demand for the Negroes as for all others a free and complete education, whether by city, state, or nation, a grammar school and industrial training for all, and technical, professional and academic education for the most gifted.[6]

Although Villard attempted to prevent the Committee from taking an anti-Washingtonian stance, Washington stated that he would have no association with the body unless guarantees were given that neither Du Bois nor William Monroe Trotter would formulate its policies. In 1910 the National Negro Committee changed its name to the National Association for the Advancement of Coloured People, with the white lawyer and Progressive reformer Moorfield Storey, as president. The announced aim of the new organization was 'to make 11,000,000 Americans physically free from peonage, mentally free from ignorance, politically free from disfranchisement, and socially free from insult'.

From its inception, the NAACP put its emphasis on effecting

change by lobbying for corrective legislation, educating public opinion, and securing favourable court decisions. Its first judicial victory came in 1915, when it secured a Supreme Court ruling that Oklahoma's 'grandfather clause', designed to withhold the ballot from blacks, was unconstitutional. By 1914, there were thirteen blacks on the Association's Board of Directors, most of whom had earlier belonged to the Niagara Movement, and the NAACP had 6,000 members in fifty branches, and a circulation of over 31,000 for its magazine *Crisis*. Washington declared his opposition to the NAACP, and expressed concern that white delegates to the 1910 meeting had gulled blacks into believing that they could achieve progress 'by merely making demands, passing resolutions and cursing somebody'.[7] When Du Bois accepted an invitation to take up the post of Director of Publications and research for the NAACP, any hope of a rapprochement between the organization and the Tuskegee Machine was lost. Already perceived as Washington's most formidable black critic, Du Bois, as editor of *Crisis*, consolidated his reputation as the most gifted propagandist of the black protest impulse.

W. E. B. DU BOIS: CURRICULUM VITAE

William Edward Burghardt Du Bois was born in Great Barrington, Massachusetts in 1868, the year of president Andrew Johnson's impeachment; he died in Ghana in 1963, in self-imposed exile, at the time of the civil rights March on Washington. A poet, novelist, historian, sociologist and essayist, Du Bois occupies a towering position in Afro-American letters. An outstanding scholar and teacher, Du Bois also became a political activist, founding member of the NAACP and editor of its journal *Crisis* – in all of these roles, he was consistently the champion of racial justice. At various points of his long career, Du Bois was the declared opponent of Booker T. Washington and Marcus Garvey – yet had more in common with them than he cared to admit. Du Bois was also a socialist and Communist, an integrationist and advocate of a form of voluntary segregation, a black nationalist and a pioneering Pan-Africanist. A supporter of black American participation in World War I, he became a pacifist and a Soviet/Chinese sympathizer during the Cold War of the 1950s. An élitist who singularly lacked the common touch and championed the cause of the 'Talented Tenth', Du Bois was aloof, arrogant and visionary. During the 1930s he was to alienate the black bourgeoisie and intelligentsia who had earlier supported his integrationist 'radicalism'. Despite claims by some admirers to the contrary, Du Bois' intellectual biography is marked by ambivalence, inconsistency and change. An ardent admirer of Western cultural values and achievements, he was also the impassioned spokesman for racial pride and consciousness as the prerequisites for black advancement. Du Bois expressed his fundamental ambivalence concerning racial and national identity in his essay 'Of Our Spiritual Strivings' in *The Souls of Black Folk.*

> One ever feels his two-ness – an American, a Negro; two souls, two thoughts, two unreconciled strivings; two warring ideas in one dark body, whose dogged strength alone keeps it from being torn asunder. The history of the American Negro is the history of this Strife – this longing to attain self-conscious manhood, to merge his double self into a better and truer self. In this merging he wishes neither of the old selves to be lost. He would not Africanize America, for America has too much to teach the world and Africa. He would not bleach his soul in a flood of white Americanism, for he knows that Negro blood has a message to teach the world.[8]

To no black American is this statement more applicable than to Du Bois himself.

Of French Huguenot, Dutch and Negro ancestry, Du Bois described his racial background as consisting of 'a flood of Negro blood, a strain of French, a bit of Dutch, but thank God! no 'Anglo-Saxon''.[9] Although his father deserted his family soon after Du Bois was born, his childhood in Great Barrington, a town of about 5,000 with only a few Negroes, was apparently a happy one. It was only when he and his classmates decided to exchange visiting cards, and one girl refused to accept his, that Du Bois, already conscious of his darker complexion, felt a 'vast veil' had shut him off from his white companions.

An exceptional high school student, Du Bois, at the age of fifteen, contributed literary, political and social essays to the New York *Globe* and the New York *Freeman.* In these early pieces, he urged blacks to join the local temperance movement, to form a literary society, and to take a greater interest in politics. In 1885, he won a scholarship to attend Fisk University, a black college in Tennessee, where he first encountered extreme racism and, simultaneously, began to cultivate his identity as an Afro-American.

> No one but a Negro going into the South without previous experience of colour caste can have any conception of its barbarism...I was thrilled to be for the first time among so many people of my own colour or rather of such extraordinary colours, which I had only glimpsed before, but who it seemed were bound to me by new and exciting eternal ties....Into this world I leapt with enthusiasm: henceforward I was a Negro.[10]

At Fisk, Du Bois also encountered rural poverty and ignorance at first hand, when for two summers he taught in black schools in Tennessee. The experience confirmed his growing belief in the power of education and reason to resolve racial conflict and secure black advancement. Simultaneously, it also increased his awareness of the enormous intellectual gulf between himself and the generality of the black people.

Graduating from Fisk in 1888, Du Bois entered Harvard, where he was greatly influenced by the philosophers William James, Josiah Royce and George Santayana, gained a BA degree in 1890, and an MS in the following year. As a graduate student in history at Harvard, Du Bois left for Europe in 1892, on a scholarship from the Slater Fund, to study abroad. He enrolled at the University of Berlin for courses in history, economics and sociology, where he studied under the economist Gustav Schmoller and the historian Heinrich von Treitschke, having already decided to take a PhD in social science. A declared admirer of Bismarck, who had created the German state through the force of his will and personality, Du Bois' later Pan-Africanism was undoubtedly influenced by his exposure to the rise of German national consciousness. His stay in Germany also acquainted him with socialist theory and practice.

On his return to America in 1894, Du Bois had also arrived at his basic intellectual and ideological convictions. The Negro race, Du Bois believed, could only advance through its own self-help and the assistance by whites of good will. Black leadership must be provided by the race's intellectuals – the 'Talented Tenth' – who would inspire their own people while seeking aid and stimulation from whites. At Harvard, he claimed to have 'conceived the idea of applying philosophy to an historical interpretation of race relations', and saw the discipline of sociology 'as the science of human action'.[11] In his PhD dissertation *The Suppression of the African Slave Trade to the United States of America, 1638–1870*, Du Bois argued that moral cowardice encouraged by greed, had seen the continuation of the trade after it had been prohibited by law; its suppression had resulted from a mixture of humanitarian, economic and political pressures. His original and provocative thesis was published in 1896 as the first volume in the Harvard Historical Series, and Du Bois seemed destined for an academic career.

From 1894–96 he was a professor of Latin and Greek at Wilberforce University, a black college in Ohio – having rejected an offer from Booker T. Washington to teach mathematics at Tuskegee. (In the first autobiography, Du Bois notes wryly: 'It would be interesting to speculate just what would have happened if I had accepted the ...offer at Tuskegee instead of that at Wilberforce.'[12] Repelled by the religious fervour which frequently erupted at Wilberforce in the form of spiritual revivals, Du Bois gratefully accepted an invitation from the University of Pennsylvania to carry out a study of the black population of Philadelphia. *The Philadelphia Negro* (1899), was a sociological work which criticized the city's blacks for their immorality, criminality, neglect of education, failure to organize for social betterment, and the inattention of the Negro middle class to its potential for leadership. White Philadelphians were judged guilty of racist attitudes, and were urged to cooperate with 'better' Negroes by recognizing class and status distinctions within the black community. Widely regarded as a model study of an urban black community, *The Philadelphia Negro* established Du Bois' academic reputation. Research for the book also broadened his racial outlook, and he later confessed: 'I became painfully that merely being born in a group, does not necessarily make one possessed of complete knowledge concerning it. I had learned far more from Philadelphia Negroes than I taught them concerning the Negro problem.'[13]

From 1897 to 1910, Du Bois was Professor of Sociology and History at Atlanta University, where he directed the preparation and publication of a series of studies which documented the existence of segregation in every area of American life – in labour unions, prisons, business and industry. But significantly, in view of his controversial proposal for 'voluntary segregation' in the 1930s, the Atlanta Studies also acknowledged segregation as a unifying force in black life. In this period also, Du Bois refined and amplified his con- ception of blackness and the meaning of the Afro-American experience. 'The Conservation of Races', an address delivered to the newly-formed American Negro Academy in 1897, and published as a pamphlet, was Du Bois' most detailed statement on the nature of racial prejudice and discrimination, and included a call for the black community to maintain a separate racial identity. Discounting the existence of meaningful physical differences between the races, Du Bois claimed that there were 'spiritual and physical differences' between them. Where the English had bestowed on the world ideas of constitutional liberty and commercial freedom, and the Germans, discoveries in science and philosophy, black people still had to reveal their gifts and qualities. These gifts, celebrated by Du Bois in *The Souls of Black Folk*, were those of 'pathos and humour', folk tales and artistic and musical abilities. He advised the American Negro Academy to seek 'to comprise something of the best thought, the most unselfish striving and the highest ideals'.[14]

During the early 1900s Du Bois, although deeply engaged in scholarship, was increasingly convinced that the worsening racial situation required more direct confrontation. The publication of *The Souls of Black Folk*, with its critique of Washington, his own activities as an organizer of the Niagara Movement and author of its Manifesto in 1905, and his response to the call which saw the founding of the NAACP, completed Du Bois' transition from academician to propagandist. Opposed to Washington's accommodationism, Negro allegiance to the Republican party, and the complete assimilation of blacks into the white American way of life, Du Bois, as editor of *Crisis*, offered his alternative visions of the present condition and future prospects of Afro-Americans.

CRISIS EDITOR

The first issue of *Crisis* appeared in November 1910, with a circulation of 1,000 copies; within a year, it was selling 16,000 copies monthly. As editor of the magazine from 1910 to 1934, Du Bois acknowledged that during this period:

> The span of my life...is chiefly the story of *The Crisis* under my editorship....I determined from the beginning to make my work with the Association not that of executive secretary but editor of its official organ....With this organ of propaganda and defence we were able to organize one of the most effective assaults of liberalism upon reaction that the modern world has seen....If...*The Crisis* had not been in a sense a personal organ and expression of myself, it could not possibly have attained its popularity and effectiveness.[15]

Certainly, some of Du Bois' finest (and most polemical) prose appeared in his monthly editorials. Determined from the outset that the journal would reflect his own ideas (even when they ran counter to those of the NAACP leadership), Du Bois aimed his editorial shafts at the literate, middle class black public. He regularly criticized the South for its inhuman treatment of blacks, as evidenced by segregation, white primaries, the convict lease system and lynching. Early issues also featured editorials and articles on 'Coloured High Schools', 'The Coloured College Athlete', and 'Women's Clubs', and repeated assertions that blacks possessed a superior spiritual sense and beauty that made them a chosen people. Du Bois called for resistance to attempts being made outside the South to institute segregated schools, attacked the black churches for their racial conservatism, and defended the rights of women – in particular, their right to vote. Anticipating later theorists, Du Bois stressed the links between Afro-American and women's political liberation:

> Every argument for Negro suffrage is an argument for women's suffrage; every argument for women's suffrage is an argument for Negro suffrage; both are great movements in democracy.

He was, however, also concerned about the racism in the contemporary white women's movement, and predicted that 'the women's vote, particularly in the South, will be cast almost unanimously, at first, for every reactionary Negro-hating piece of legislation'. Aware of the double oppression – racial and sexual – suffered by black American women, Du Bois stated in *Darkwater: Voices From Within The Veil* (1920) that although he could forgive the South for slavery and its attempt to destroy the American Union, he could not forgive 'its wanton and continued and persistent insulting of the black womanhood it sought and seeks to prostitute to its lust'.[16]

The third issue of *Crisis* carried Du Bois' avowal: 'I am resolved to be...law-abiding, but refuse to cringe in body and soul, to resent deliberate insult, and to assert my just rights in the face of wanton aggression' and he recommended black self-defence against white vigilante mobs.

Employing an array of techniques and literary devices, Du Bois wrote in a clear, direct style, and used savage invective and sardonic humour to depict racial indignities and atrocities. In 1911, he dramatically described a lynching in Pennsylvania:

> Ah, the splendour of that Sunday night dance. The flames curled and beat against the moonlight sky. The church bells chimed. The scorched and crooked thing, self-wounded and chained to his cot, crawled to the edge of the ash with a stifled groan, but the brave and sturdy farmers pricked him back with the bloody pitchforks until the deed was done. Let the eagle scream! Civilization is again safe![17]

In 1914, Du Bois published a letter of an anonymous witness to the lynching of Samuel Petty, accused of having killed a Deputy Sheriff in Leland, Mississippi:

> The man who had killed the officer submitted to arrest by the mob, which...numbered about 400. Placing a rope around his neck he was led to the centre of the town and in the presence of women and children they proceeded to hold a conference as to the kind of death that should be meted out to him. Some yelled to hang him; some to burn him alive. It was decided in a few minutes. Willing hands brought a large dry-goods box, placed it in the centre of the street; in it was straw on which was

poured a tub of oil; then the man was lifted with a rope around his neck and placed in this box head down, and then another tub of oil was poured over him. A man from the crowd deliberately lit a match and set fire to the living man....the poor creature managed to lift himself out of the box, a mass of flames, and...attempted to run. The crowd allowed him to run to the length of the rope....until he reached a distance of about twenty feet; then a yell went up...to shoot. In an instant there were several hundred shots and the creature fell in his tracks....Not a voice was heard in the defence of the man....I looked into the faces of men whom I knew to be officers to the town lending a willing hand in the burning of this man.[18]

In 1919, after an intensive investigation, the NAACP published *Thirty Years of Lynching in the United States, 1889–1918*, which estimated that 3,224 black men and women had been lynched during this period. In only 19 per cent of these cases had rape or other forms of sexual assault been alleged – despite the South's repeated contention that lynching was 'necessary' as a means of protecting its white women from black ravishment. During the First World War, *The Crisis* publicized the rising incidence of lynch law, most dramatically in a 1916 account (published as an eight-page supplement) of the seizure and lynching of Jesse Washington, a mentally retarded adolescent, sentenced to death for the murder of a white woman in Waco, Texas. 'The Waco Horror', a report of the episode, complete with photographic evidence, was used as the opening move in an NAACP campaign for an Anti-Lynching Fund. Distributed to 42,000 *Crisis* subscribers, 52 Negro weeklies and 700 white newspapers, it was also sent to all members of Congress and to a list of 500 'moneyed men' in New York, who were asked to subscribe to the appeal. The 'Waco Horror' included the information that:

Washington...was dragged through the streets, stabbed, mutilated and finally burned to death in the presence of a crowd of 10,000. After the death what was left of his body was dragged through the streets and parts of it sold as souvenirs. His teeth brought $5 a piece and the chain that bound him 25 cents a link. He was lowered into the fire several times by means of the chain around his neck.[19]

In *Dusk of Dawn*, Du Bois attributed the increase in lynching during this period partly to the influence of the motion picture 'The Birth of a Nation', which, he asserted:

fed to the youth of the nation and to the unthinking masses...a story which twisted the emancipation and enfranchisement of the slave in a great effort toward universal democracy, into an orgy of theft and degradation and rape of white women.[20]

Du Bois' editorship was marked by almost constant friction between himself and the NAACP board. At issue was usually disagreement over the relationship between the journal and the Association. Without consulting the board, Du Bois attacked large sections of the black press, asserting that they did not publish the true facts about the racial situation, or consistently support the cause of civil rights. Irritated black editors responded sharply to such attacks and in 1914, at its annual convention, the NAACP passed a resolution praising the Negro press and, indirectly, rebuking Du Bois. In response, Du Bois charged that some of his white critics within the Association were racists, and argued that the 'Negro problem' could not be separated from other humanitarian and social concerns of the day. In these, as in other views, his editorial statements often diverged from agreed NAACP policy.

On Booker T. Washington's death in 1915, Du Bois paid him a critical tribute in *The Crisis*. Washington was, he conceded, 'the greatest Negro leader since Frederick Douglass, and the most distinguished man, white or black, who has come out of the South since the Civil War'. He had correctly directed the attention of blacks to economic development, and stressed the desirability of 'technical education', and the securing of property. Although he had induced white Southerners to 'at least think of the Negro as a possible man', Du Bois concluded that Washington must also bear 'a heavy responsibility for the consummation of Negro disfranchisement, the decline of the Negro college and school, and the firmer establishment of colour caste in this land'.[21]

In 1916 Du Bois, with other leading blacks, attended a meeting called by Joel Springran, a white member of the NAACP, at his home in Amenia, New York. The 'Amenia Conference', in a series of conciliatory resolutions, attempted to bridge the differences between the Washingtonians and their opponents. All forms of education were declared desirable for blacks; political rights were to be secured through the cooperation of all black leaders, and 'antiquated subjects of controversy...and factional alignments' were to be eliminated. Nine years later, Du Bois, recalling the Amenia Conference, professed that:

> It not only marked the end of the old things and the old thoughts...and ways of attacking the race problem...in addition to this it was the beginning of new things.[22]

Yet it was Du Bois himself who soon violated the Amenia principle of cooperative and concerted black protest. As *Crisis* editor, he continued to attack the principle of industrial education, advised blacks to leave the South and castigated Southern black leaders for their timidity. The most controversial editorial ever published in *The Crisis* was Du Bois' 'Close Ranks' plea of July 1918 which declared:

> Let us, while this war lasts, forget our special grievances and close ranks
> shoulder to shoulder with our fellow citizens and the allied nations who
> are fighting for democracy. We make no ordinary sacrifice, but we make it
> gladly with our eyes lifted to the hills.[23]

Although he viewed World War I as the consequence of imperial
rivalry between the European powers in Africa, Du Bois supported
American intervention on the side of the Allies. He believed that
participation by American blacks would lead to a lessening of racism
(in the event of an Allied victory), and that the war would promote the
independence of former German colonies. Both assumptions proved
wrong, but, as he remembered in *Dusk of Dawn*:

> I was , in principle, opposed to the war. Everyone is. I pointed out in the
> *Atlantic Monthly* in 1915 how the partition of Africa was the cause of
> conflict. Through my knowledge of Germany, I wished to see her
> militarism defeated and for that reason when America entered the War I
> believed we would in reality fight for democracy including the coloured
> folk and not merely for war investments.[24]

(Du Bois had earlier supported president Woodrow Wilson who
was to take America into the war, under the mistaken impression that
he would support Negro rights.) Black radicals denounced the
sentiments expressed in 'Close Ranks', and argued that agitation for
civil rights should not be suspended, despite the emergency created by
American involvement in the war.

A. Philip Randolph, the leading black socialist (and later leader of
the Brotherhood of Sleeping Car Porters) asserted that 'Close Ranks'
was as shameful as Washington's Atlanta Compromise, and castigated
Du Bois as a sycophant. When Du Bois was offered a commission in
the Intelligence branch of the United States Army, his black critics
accused him of having been bribed to support the policies of the
Wilson administration. In the event, the army withdrew the offer, but
Du Bois' behaviour in the affair, which included the demand that he
should receive $1,000 a year from the NAACP to supplement his army
pay, called into question his judgement and commitment to black
protest. If, as his critics maintained, Du Bois had been an
accommodationist in time of war, his optimism about black advances
was short-lived. He was angered by continued racial discrimination by
the American Federation of Labour (AFL), and appalled at the race
riots in the 'Red Summer' of 1919 that greeted returning black
veterans. Again, the reemergence of the Ku Klux Klan after 1915, and
its rapid growth in American cities exacerbated an already volatile
racial situation. Du Bois' response to these events was his editorial
'Returning Soldiers' of May 1919, which advised blacks to 'return

fighting' in the struggle at home against racism. America, victorious over German imperialism, was still a 'shameful land':

> It *lynches*. And lynching is barbarism of a degree of contemptible nastiness unparalleled in human history. Yet for fifty years we have lynched two Negroes a week. It *disfranchises* its own citizens....It *insults* us....we are cowards and jackasses if now that the war is over we do not marshal every ounce of our brain and brawn to conquer a sterner, longer, more unbending battle against the forces of hell in our own land. We *return*. We *return from fighting*. We *return fighting*. Make way for Democracy![25]

'Returning Soldiers' prompted the United States Department of Justice to investigate *The Crisis* and other black journals. It published a condemnatory report, 'Radicalism and Sedition Among Negroes As Reflected in Their Publications', but did not prosecute.

Between 1918 and 1928 Du Bois, (who had earlier made three trips to Europe), visited France, England, Belgium, Switzerland, Portugal, Germany, Russia and Africa. These journeys, he later wrote, 'gave me a depth of knowledge and a breadth of view which was of incalculable value for realizing and judging modern conditions and, above all, the problem of race in America and the world'.[26] While America's racial conflicts continued to engage most of his attention, Du Bois came to believe that they must be set in the context of the universal problem of the 'colour line'. During the 1920s he directed a *Crisis* campaign against black colleges and universities which did not have representative numbers of Negroes on their faculties or in administrative positions. In 1924 he suggested that the NAACP, the AFL and the railroad brotherhoods should organize an interracial commission, with the objective of creating integrated labour unions. But the NAACP leadership, primarily concerned with issues of political and civil rights, did not consider the promotion of unionism among blacks as a cause it could officially support. Du Bois himself was soon to abandon his earlier tolerant attitude toward organized labour in the face of increasing discrimination within the labour movement, and his growing conviction that blacks could not expect white support or good will.

Although he agreed with other militants that economic considerations were of fundamental importance to the black masses, Du Bois, during the 1930s and 1940s, no longer considered a black/white alliance of the disadvantaged to be a possibility, given the intensity of American racism. Accordingly he proposed the formation of black economic cooperative enterprises based on socialist principles and the notions of self-help and cultural nationalism. His assumption was that

past
1920

as consumers, blacks could (and would) provide a foundation for this form of collective economic enterprise. In the financially ailing *Crisis*, he proposed that blacks should develop this separate economy, and to the consternation of the NAACP (and many black radicals), advocated racial 'self-segregation' as the road to ultimate black political and economic power. While he welcomed the expansion of government activities under Franklin Roosevelt's New Deal, Du Bois did not expect the administration's policies to effect any sea-change in black-white relations. And although he conceded that blacks had undoubtedly gained from New Deal welfare and public works programmes, Du Bois did not want them to remain dependent on a supposedly benevolent president. Rather, they should accept the persistence of racial prejudice, including the reality of enforced segregation, and develop their own institutions. In presenting the case for black economic separatism, Du Bois attempted to reassure *Crisis* readers that his ideas did not conflict with NAACP objectives and policies. The Association's traditional opposition to segregation, he argued, had been in fact opposition to discrimination, and the two were not necessarily synonymous. Since the NAACP had long supported such 'segregated' institutions as churches, schools and newspapers, a self-segregated black economy was simply another step in the formation of institutions which would bolster black pride and morale. In essence, Du Bois urged blacks (and the NAACP) to face the fact of enforced segregation and turn it to advantage. Members of the 'Talented Tenth' should become planners of producer and consumer cooperatives which would form 'a Negro nation within a nation'. Blacks should patronize Negro-owned stores and use the services of the black professional classes.

> With the use of their political power, their power as consumers, and their brain power, added to that of personal appeal which proximity and neighbourhood always give to human beings, Negroes can develop in the United States as an economic nation within a nation, able to work through inner cooperation, to fund its own institutions, to educate its genius, and at the same time...to keep in helpful touch with the mass of the nation. This has happened more often than most people realize, in the case of groups not so obviously separated from the mass of people as are the American Negroes. It must happen in our case, or there is no hope for the Negro in America.[27]

Walter White (who had succeeded James Weldon Johnson as executive secretary of the NAACP), claimed that Du Bois' editorial on 'voluntary segregation' had been used by agencies in Washington, DC, to freeze relief projects for blacks, and reasserted the

Association's position was that 'to accept the status of separateness means inferior accommodations...and spiritual atrophy for the group segregated'.[28] When the NAACP passed a resolution condemning 'enforced segregation', Du Bois launched a campaign to reorganize the Association along more 'progressive' lines.

But, in advocating black economic self-sufficiency, and in appearing to condone – if not actively encourage – racial segregation, Du Bois was running against the tide of dominant black thought. To his critics, 'a Negro nation within a nation' smacked of Booker T. Washington's accommodationism and petty capitalism. Francis Grimke, a black minister who had participated in the founding of the NAACP, asserted that Du Bois' apparent acceptance of Jim Crow signalled the end of his role as a race leader. A Chicago black newspaper mourned the passing of a 'race champion' and over a picture of Booker T. Washington placed the caption 'Was He Right After All?'; above Du Bois' picture it asked 'Is He A Quitter?'

Du Bois denied that his proposals bore any resemblance to Washington's National Negro Business League, which sought to develop a black economy on the basis of free competition and private profit, since his own recommendations called for the organization of an economy based on producers' and consumers' cooperatives. When the NAACP resolved that no official could criticize the Association in *Crisis* without prior approval, Du Bois ignored the ruling, and continued to regard the journal as his own personal medium. Black newspaper editors now expressed concern over the rift in the NAACP, and sided with the Association against Du Bois. Walter White charged Du Bois with having compromised with Jim Crow and undermined the Association's integrationist ideals. On 26 June 1934, Du Bois resigned from the NAACP and returned to Atlanta University. Accepting his resignation, and noting that it could 'not subscribe to some of his criticism of the Association and its officials', the NAACP leadership paid him a generous (and deserved) tribute. Through *The Crisis*, he had:

> created what never existed before, a Negro intelligentsia, and many who have never read a word of his writings are his spiritual disciples and descendants. We shall be the poorer for his loss, in intellectual stimulus, and in searching analysis of the vital problems of the American Negro; no one in the Association can fill his place with the same intellectual grasp.[29]

If Du Bois' call for a separate black community failed to win either élite or majority support, his Pan-African enthusiasms also failed to communicate themselves to the NAACP and most readers of *The Crisis*.

PAN-AFRICANISM

As a young child, Du Bois heard his grandmother singing a 'heathen melody' to her children, and, like Alex Haley, sixty years later, instinctively felt that the strange-sounding words spoke to his African 'roots'.

Do ba-na co-ba, ge-ne me, ge-ne me!
Ben d'nu-li, nu-li, nu-li, bend' le

These lines were handed down orally in the Du Bois family, and 'we sing it to our children, knowing as little as our fathers what its words may mean, but knowing well the meaning of its music. This was African music....the voice of exile.'[30] After his rejection by the white children in Great Barrington, and his experiences at Fisk, Du Bois discovered his 'African racial feeling' and felt himself to be both African by 'race' and 'an integral member of the group of dark Americans who are called Negroes'.[31]

Concern with Africa, the ancestry and culture of African-Americans, and the deliverance of the African continent from the European colonizing powers, became central themes of Du Bois' thoughts and writings. Yet whether as a scholar, propagandist, or the organizer of four Pan-African Congresses between 1919 and 1927 (a fifth was held in Manchester, England, in 1945), Du Bois' conception of Africa was that of a romantic racialist. It ignored cultural differences and conflicts between Africans themselves, and gave American blacks an inspirational role which they (and most Africans) found faintly ridiculous. Reporting on his first experiences of Africa in 1923, when he attended the inauguration of the president of Liberia, Du Bois apprised *Crisis* readers:

> The spell of Africa is upon me. The ancient witchery of her medicine is burning my drowsy, dreary blood. This is not a country, it is a world, a universe of itself and for itself, a thing Different, Menacing, Alluring. It is a great black bosom where the spirit longs to die. Things move – black shiny bodies, bodies of sleek and unearthly poise and beauty.[32]

Idyllic pictures of African village and tribal life, with 'well-bred and courteous children, playing happily and never sniffing or whining' (anticipating the depiction of West African tribal life in the TV serial 'Roots'), were intended to awaken in black Americans pride in Africa and, by implication, pride in themselves. Although he was to ridicule Marcus Garvey's glorification of blackness, Du Bois was himself a racial chauvinist, holding for all of his life a near-obsession with colour.

His active interest in Africa began in 1900, when he attended the first Pan-African Congress held in London, and attended by delegates from Ethiopia, the Gold Coast, Sierra Leone, Liberia, the Caribbean and the United States. As chairman of the Committee of the Address to the Nations of the World, Du Bois issued a call to action:

> Let the Nations of the World respect the integrity and independence of the free Negro states of Abyssinia (properly Ethiopia), Liberia, Haiti, etc. and let the inhabitants of these states, the independent tribes of Africa, the Negroes (people of African descent) of the West Indies and America, and the black subjects of all Nations take courage, strive ceaselessly, and fight bravely, that they may prove to the world their incontestable right to be counted among the great brotherhood of mankind.[33]

The Second Pan-African Congress, organized by Du Bois, and held in Paris in 1919, was attended by 59 delegates from 15 countries. They resolved that Germany's African colonies should be turned over to an international organization, and that a code of laws be drawn up for the protection of Africans. At the Third Pan-African Congress, held in London, Brussels and Paris in 1921, a committee headed by Du Bois was sent to petition the League of Nations on behalf of the African colonies. The Fourth Pan-African Congress, which met in Paris and Lisbon in 1923, issued a set of eight demands seeking equality for black people throughout the world. At the Fifth Congress, held in New York in 1927, the major resolutions adopted by the delegates, in addition to demanding 'the development of Africa for the Africans and not merely for the profit of the Europeans' asked for independence for India, China and Egypt. Du Bois either organized or played a leading role in each of these Congresses yet, as he was to admit, black Americans (not to mention the European powers) were not inspired by his Pan-Africanist visions. One of Du Bois' biographers suggests that in many respects, the Pan-African Congresses echoed the Niagara Movement:

> a handful of self-appointed spokesmen challenged a staggering problem by passing resolutions....periodic conferences to recodify the platform, refresh personal contacts, and exchange enthusiasm and information, and the manifestos designed to rally coloured support and to convert white opinion. In the end, the Congresses accomplished, if anything, less than Niagara.[34]

Such a judgement is not entirely fair. Just as the Niagara Movement was a forerunner of organized black protest in twentieth-century America, the Pan-African Congresses pointed to the later course of political independence in Africa and the Third World. African nationalists like Kwame Nkrumah and Jomo Kenyatta were to acknowledge Du Bois as a founding father of Pan-Africanism. In the United States, such ideologically divergent leaders as Martin Luther King and Malcolm X were also to pay tribute to Du Bois' African dream. And for all his romanticization of Africa, Du Bois never advocated the 'return' of African-Americans to their ancestral homeland, but rather equated Pan-Africanism with Zionism, while his celebrations of African primitivism and the sensuousness of its arts, was in tune with the dominant mood of much of the writing and concerns of the Harlem Renaissance. At the height of the Garvey Movement in America, Du Bois cautioned:

> Africa belongs to the Africans. They have not the slightest intention of giving it up to foreigners, white or black....They resent the attitude that other folk of any colour are coming in to take and rule their land. Liberia is not going to allow American Negroes to assume control and direct her government. Liberia, in her mind, is for Liberians.[35]

Du Bois himself blamed the failure of Pan-Africanism in the short term on the opposition of the colonial powers, the patronizing and selfish attitudes of whites to Africa, and the indifference of black Americans to the plight of their African contemporaries. Ironically, Marcus Garvey's flamboyant and fantastic notion of uniting all the Negroes of the world into one great organization was to eclipse Du Bois' Pan-Africanism, just as it also underlined his inability to reach a mass audience.

'A LEADER WITHOUT FOLLOWERS', 1934–1963

The most prolific and gifted of all Afro-American scholars and intellectuals, Du Bois was never a successful leader or organizer. After his resignation from NAACP in 1934, at the age of sixty-six, he became, more than ever, isolated and increasingly bitter – in F. L. Broderick's phrase, 'a leader without followers'. His romantic faith in Africa, contempt for capitalist values and attraction to world socialism, left Du Bois remote from the everyday concerns of the majority of black Americans. From the time of his return to Atlanta University until his death in Ghana in 1963, Du Bois remained estranged from the Talented Tenth because of their opposition to socialism and voluntary segregation, and their support for integration and increased opportunity within the capitalist system. His rejection of interracial cooperation, insistence that racial prejudice was on the increase, and separatist proposals were also out of step with the liberal reformism of the New Deal.

Shortly after his return to Atlanta, Du Bois published two major works. *Black Reconstruction in America: An Essay Toward A History Of The Part Which Black Folk Played In The Attempt To Reconstruct Democracy In America, 1860-1880* (1935) offered a Marxist-derived interpretation of the role played by blacks in securing Confederate defeat. Southern slaves, Du Bois argued, had engaged in a 'general strike' when they fled from the plantations to join the invading Union armies. More realistically, *Black Reconstruction* stressed the problems faced by and the achievements of blacks during the Reconstruction era, and anticipated 1960s 'revisionism' of the subject. *Dusk of Dawn*, which appeared in 1940, was subtitled 'An Autobiography of a Race Concept' and presented Du Bois' account – and defence – of his dual careers as an African-American and Pan-African propagandist. 'My life,' he declared:

> had its significance and its only deep significance because it was part of a Problem; but that Problem was...the central problem of the world's democracies and so the Problem of the future world...of which the concept of race is today one of the most unyielding and threatening.[36]

The central theme of *Dusk of Dawn* is the author's search for meaning and harmony in a troubled and racially-divided world. He reiterated his belief in voluntary self-segregation as the only means of ensuring black progress in America, expressed a favourable view of the Marxist interpretation of history because of its stress on the economic foundations of culture (although Du Bois denied that he was a Communist), and reviewed the famous controversy with Booker T. Washington – with Du Bois' presentation of himself as the injured party:

> I was in my imagination a scientist, and neither a leader nor an agitator; I had nothing but the greatest admiration for Mr Washington and Tuskegee, and I had applied at both Tuskegee and Hampton for work.

There had, Du Bois conceded, been significant differences between himself and Washington. Where Washington had placed his faith in industrial education and 'common labour', 'I believed in the higher education of a Talented Tenth who through their knowledge of modern culture could guide the American Negro into a higher civilization'. These theories, Du Bois maintained, were not necessarily opposed, and indeed could have been complementary. But the striking feature of Washington's leadership was 'that whatever he...believed in or wanted must be subordinated to common public opinion and that opinion deferred to and cajoled until it allowed a deviation toward better ways'. But the roots of the controversy lay in the 'discrepancies and paradoxes' of Washington's influence and leadership:

> It did not seem fair...that on the one hand Mr Washington should decry political activities among Negroes, and on the other dictate Negro political objectives from Tuskegee. At a time when Negro civil rights called for organized and aggressive defence, he broke down that defence by advising acquiescence or at least no open agitation.

Above all, Du Bois remembered, the power of the Tuskegee Machine – which reached out to governors, congressmen, philanthropists and presidents – had had to be resisted.

> Contrary to most opinion, the controversy as it developed was not entirely against Mr Washington's ideas, but became the insistence upon the right of other Negroes to have and express their ideas. I was greatly disturbed at this time, not because I was in absolute opposition to the things that Mr Washington was advocating, but because I was strongly in favour of more open agitation against wrongs and above all I resented the practical buying up of the Negro press and choking off even mild and reasonable opposition to Mr Washington in both the Negro press and the white.[37]

(Surprisingly, in view of their deep enmity, Du Bois devoted only a few lines of *Dusk of Dawn* to his later disagreements with Marcus Garvey.)

At the end of his life, living in Ghana, Du Bois was to admit a greater respect for (if not approval of) Washington's leadership. Connor Cruise O'Brien reported the following response when, at the dinner table, 'someone mentioned Washington in a context that implied he had been a stooge for the bosses':

> Du Bois strongly demurred. He said he had in his youth spoken slightingly of Washington and had been memorably reprimanded by his aunts, who told him that it ill became one who had been born free to speak disrespectfully of a man whose back bore the marks of the lash. He went on to say that in the circumstances of the South in Washington's time, he could not have done anything effective in any other way. He – Du Bois – with his Northern and relatively privileged background – had been able to take a different stance and had been obliged to enter into public controversy with Washington. He did not want that controversy to obscure the merits what Washington had achieved. He spoke with evident deep feeling, and all of us who heard him were impressed.[38]

Du Bois' other scholarly publications (after a brief return to the NAACP in 1945), included *Colour and Democracy: Colonies and Peace* (1945), in which he attempted to link the future of Africa with that of the rest of the world, align African nationalism with socialist thought, and condemned the United Nations for its tacit approval of colonialism. (Du Bois served as an associate consultant to the American delegation at the founding session of the United Nations in San Francisco.) By this time, Du Bois (who had been more critical of the European colonial powers than of Hitler but came to regard World War II as another opportunity for the self-determination of oppressed people), was firmly identified with international peace movements against the 'Cold War', with socialism and the representation of African colonial peoples in the United Nations. His expressed sympathies for the Soviet Union, condemnation of the Korean conflict as a capitalist war, an (abortive) attempt to become the American Labour party's representative for New York in the US Senate in 1950 (when he received less than four per cent of the vote), and his chairmanship of the Peace Information Centre which circulated the 1951 'Stockholm Peace Appeal', a Soviet-inspired nuclear disarmament proposal, were all indications of Du Bois' radical stances and activities. When he refused to comply with a US Department of Justice order to register as the agent of a 'foreign principal', Du Bois was indicted by a federal grand jury, but was acquitted. Excoriated in the United States at the height of the McCarthy communist witch-hunting era (when he was prominent in the defence of the Rosenbergs, accused of spying for the Soviet Union), Du Bois was fêted in the Communist world on visits to China and Russia. In 1953, he was awarded the communist-sponsored World Peace Prize and, ten years later, the Lenin Prize. On his ninety-first birthday in Peking, Du Bois informed a large and responsive audience that 'in my own country for nearly a century I have been nothing but a "nigger"'.[39]

Although he welcomed the Supreme Court's 1954 school desegregation decision, applauded the action of 'black workers' in the Montgomery, Alabama bus boycott, and student involvement in the lunch-counter 'sit-ins' of the 1960s, Du Bois remained aloof from the black/white civil rights coalition. He characterized Martin Luther King, Jr as an American 'Gandhi', but also maintained that Southern racists would not be moved simply by logical arguments and moral suasion, and argued that proponents of desegregation should consider the next stage of their campaigns. (In an article published in 1957, Du Bois also reflected that 'it is possible any day' that non-violent leaders like King might be killed.)[40] In 1946, Du Bois, sensing the heightened aspirations of the post-war generation of black Americans, had informed an audience in Columbia, South Carolina:

> The future of the American Negro is in the South....This is the firing line not simply for the emancipation of the American Negro but for the emancipation of the African Negro and the Negroes of the West Indies;

for the emancipation of the coloured races; and for the emancipation of the white slaves of modern capitalistic monopoly.[41]

Reviewing Samuel R. Spencer's biography *Booker T. Washington and the Negro's Place in American Life* (1955), Du Bois strongly dissented from Spencer's view that Washington anticipated the civil rights movement of the 1950s, but in his own day 'did what was possible, given the time and place in which he lived, and did it to the utmost'. Noting that Spencer, a white Southerner, was bound to reach a favourable verdict on Washington, Du Bois repeated his contention that if the Negro, contrary to Washington's advice and example, had not struggled to retain voting and civil rights and 'for the education of his gifted children, for a place among modern men, their situation today would have been disastrous'. Southern whites had dishonoured the terms of the compromise offered by Washington at Atlanta, yet he had been 'treated with extraordinary respect by his fellow Negroes, even when they believed he was bartering their rights for a mess of pottage'. Here, Du Bois was not simply restating his differences with Washington but was also, by implication, linking the militant protest of the NAACP in the early years and his own editorship of *The Crisis* in particular, with the post-World War II civil rights coalition.[42] (On an even more personal note, Du Bois could hardly approve of a book in which he was accused of having had 'delusions of grandeur' when he dared to challenge the Tuskegee Machine, or of the description of himself as 'imperious, egocentric, aloof'.)

In 1961, Du Bois applied for membership of the American Communist Party, having come to the conclusion that:

> Capitalism cannot reform itself; it is doomed to self-destruction. No universal selfishness can bring social good to all. Communism – the effort to give all men what they need and to ask of each the best they can contribute – this is the only way of human life.[43]

Before the announcement of his application was made public, Du Bois, at the urging of President Nkrumah, went to Ghana (where in 1960 he had begun work on preparation of an *Encyclopedia Africana*, a project he had already attempted in 1909 and in 1934), and became a Ghanaian citizen in the last months of his life. If he had lived three more years, Du Bois would have seen Nkrumah ousted by a military coup, and a new regime which suppressed socialism, the doctrine of Pan-Africanism, and aborted the scheme for the *Encyclopedia Africana*. Despite his self-exile and disappointments, Du Bois, as one of his last letters revealed, also preserved an optimistic view of his life and labours:

> I have loved my work. I have loved people and my play, but always I have
> been uplifted by the thought that what I have done will live long and
> justify my life; that what I have done ill or never finished can now be
> handed on to others for endless days to be finished, perhaps better than I
> could have done.[44]

ASSESSMENT

Du Bois, through all his ideological shifts and turns, attempted to
resolve what he regarded (and personally experienced) as being the
fundamental dilemma of the Afro-American – 'one ever feels his two-
ness'. Unlike Booker T. Washington, Du Bois always felt himself
apart from the mass of Negroes and, for significant periods of his life
was definitely out of step with orthodox black responses to such issues
as socialism, Marxism, and Pan-Africanism. An inferior (and
disinterested) administrator, Du Bois, as editor of *Crisis*, was the
outstanding agitator and propagandist of the protest movement which
arose partly as a reaction against Washington's power and policies.
Essentially a man of letters, Du Bois, more than any other black
leader, influenced the Negro intelligentsia (the Talented Tenth), and
contributed to the formation of that black consciousness which had its
flowering in the Harlem Renaissance. Du Bois himself admired but
was rejected by white society, and out of this rejection came his
reasoned but impassioned hatred of racial discrimination and injustice.

From the formation of the Niagara Movement until his resignation
from the NAACP in 1934, Du Bois (who would have preferred a life
of historical and sociological research serving the cause of black
advancement) was the singularly gifted spokesman for black
economic and political rights. With Washington's death in 1915, the
continuing black exodus from the South, and the rising expectations of
an educated black middle class, Du Bois achieved leadership of the
Talented Tenth. Simultaneously, he also waged a bitter internal
campaign against what he regarded as the élitism, conservatism and
narrowness of the organization which had elected him as its major
propagandist. The NAACP rejected Du Bois' call for voluntary
segregation (which he had first articulated in the 1890s), and did not
share his collectivist or Pan-African enthusiasms. Yet, on the eve of
his departure from the NAACP, Du Bois was firmly opposed to any
deprivation of any political, civil or social rights, and to enforced
segregation. As one of his biographers suggests, Du Bois made *The
Crisis* 'a record of Negro achievement' and:

In this context, even Du Bois' aloofness became an asset; it removed him in Negro eyes from everyday life and, by giving him a transcendent quality, it raised the goal of aspiration.[45]

Throughout his long and eventful life, Du Bois was inspired by a vision of reasoned, ordered and dynamic social change. This vision was perhaps best expressed in the 'Postlude' to his second autobiography, subtitled 'A Soliloquy on Viewing My Life from the Last Decade of Its First Century', (1968):

This is a beautiful world. This is a wonderful America, which the founding fathers dreamed until their sons drowned it in the blood of slavery and devoured it in greed. Our children must rebuild it. Let then the Dreams of the Dead rebuke the Blind who think that what is will be forever and teach them that what is worth living for must live again.[46]

Du Bois' vision was flawed – his call to 'Close Ranks' during World War I, although implicitly recognizing that blacks *were* pressing for equality, too readily assumed that they would be prepared to suspend their agitation. His plan for segregated cooperatives of consumers and producers was unrealistic. He viewed Africa through a haze of romanticism, yet also inspired African nationalists. His politics alternated between a radical optimism and a gloomy conservatism, and, at the end of his life embraced the tenets of totalitarian regimes. But through all his ideological searchings, Du Bois was the keeper of America's moral conscience on the question of race and racial inequality. Martin Luther King, Jr, in the last major address before his assassination, delivered a fitting tribute to Du Bois, marking the centennial of his birth:

Dr. Du Bois was a tireless explorer and a gifted discoverer of social truths. His singular greatness lay in his quest for the truth about his own people....Whatever else he was, with his multitude of careers and professional titles, he was first and always a black man....Some people would like to ignore the fact that he was a communist in his later years....It is time to cease muting the fact that Dr. Du Bois was a genius and chose to be a communist. Our irrational obsessive anticommunism has led us into too many quagmires to be retained as if it were a mode of scientific thinking....Dr. Du Bois's greatest virtue was his committed empathy with all the oppressed and his divine dissatisfaction with all forms of injustice.[47]

REFERENCES

1. Robeson, Paul, 'The Legacy of W. E. B. Du Bois', in P. S. Foner (ed.), *Paul Robeson Speaks: Writings, Speeches and Interviews, 1918-1974* (New York, 1978), pp.474–5.
2. Isaacs, H. R., *The New World of Negro Americans* (London, 1963), p.195.
3. Baker, R. S., *Following the Colour Line: American Negro Citizenship in the Progressive Era* (New York, 1964), p.224.
4. Ibid., p.222.
5. Myrdal, *An American Dilemma* op. cit., p.743.
6. Rudwick, E. M., *W. E. B. Du Bois: Propagandist of the Negro Protest* (New York, 1969), p.216.
7. Ibid., p.131
8. Du Bois, W. E. B., *The Souls of Black Folk* (New York, 1968 edn.), p.17.
9. Du Bois, W. E. B., *Darkwater: Voices From Within The Veil* (New York, 1969 edn.), p.9.
10. Du Bois, W. E. B., *The Autobiography of W. E. B. Du Bois: A Soliloquy on Viewing My Life from the Last Decade of Its First Century* (New York, 1968), pp.107-8, 133.
11. Ibid., pp.168, 148.
12. Du Bois, W. E. B., *Dusk of Dawn: An Essay Toward An Autobiography of a Race Concept* (New York, 1940), p.49.
13. Marable, M., *W. E. B. Du Bois: Black Radical Democrat* (Boston, 1986), p.27.
14. Du Bois, W. E. B., 'The Conservation of Races', *American Negro Academy, Occasional Papers 2* (Washington, D.C., 1897), p.13.
15. Du Bois, *Autobiography*, op. cit., pp.258, 260–1.
16. Marable, op. cit., pp.85–6.
17. *Crisis* II (September, 1911).
18. *Crisis* VIII (May, 1914).
19. Hughes, Langston, *Fight For Freedom: The Story of the NAACP* (New York, 1962), p.34.
20. Du Bois, *Dusk of Dawn*, op. cit., p.240.
21. *Crisis* XI (1915–16), p.82.
22. Rudwick, op. cit., p.186.
23. *Crisis* XVI (1918), p.111.
24. Du Bois, *Dusk of Dawn*, op. cit., pp.252–3.
25. *Crisis* XVIII (May, 1919), pp.13-14.
26. Du Bois, *Dusk of Dawn*, op. cit., p.267.
27. Lester, J. (ed.), *The Seventh Son: The Thought and Writings of W. E. B.*

Du Bois, Vol. II (New York, 1971), p.405.

28. Marable, op. cit., p.140.
29. Du Bois, *Dusk of Dawn*, op. cit., pp.314–15.
30. Du Bois, *The Souls of Black Folk*, op. cit., p.184.
31. Du Bois, *Dusk of Dawn*, op. cit., pp.114–15.
32. *Crisis* XXVII (April, 1924), pp.273–4.
33. Clarke, J. H. *et al.*, *Black Titan: W. E. B. Du Bois, An Anthology by the Editors of Freedomways* (Boston, 1970), pp.191–2.
34. Broderick, F. L., *W. E. B. Du Bois: Negro Leader in a Time of Crisis* (Stanford, California, 1959), p.130.
35. *Crisis* (July, 1924), p.106.
36. Du Bois, *Dusk of Dawn*, pp.2–3.
37. Ibid., pp.69–77.
38. Genovese, E. D., *In Red and Black: Marxian Explorations in Southern and Afro-American History* (Vintage Books, New York, 1971), p.154.
39. Rudwick, *Propagandist of the Negro Protest* op. cit., p.293.
40. Marable, op. cit., pp.200–201.
41. Stuckey, S., *Slave Culture: Nationalist Theory and the Foundations of Black America* (Oxford University Press, New York, 1987), p.301.
42. *Science & Society*, 20 (1959), pp.183–5.
43. Marable, op. cit., p.212.
44. Brewer, W. H., 'Some Memories of Dr. W. E. B. Du Bois', *Journal of Negro History*, 53 (1968), p.348.
45. Broderick, op. cit., pp.230–31.
46. Du Bois, *Autobiography*, op. cit., pp.422–3.
47. Foner, P. S. (ed.), *W. E. B. Du Bois Speaks: Speeches and Addresses 1890-1919* (New York, 1970), pp.13–19.

CHAPTER FOUR

Marcus Garvey: Jamaican Messiah

As a kid I heard about Marcus Garvey. We used to sing a song ridiculing him. 'Marcus Garvey is a big monkey man. Marcus Garvey will catch you if he can. All you black folks get in line. Buy your tickets on the Black Star Line.'[1]

Since the death of Booker T. Washington there was no one with a positive and practical uplift programme for the masses – North or South. Said a coloured woman after she had joined the organization: 'Garvey is giving my people backbones where they had wish-bones.'[2]

PERSPECTIVES: THE NORTHERN BLACK GHETTO, 1900-1920

Even before the end of the Civil War, Southern blacks began to move from rural areas to the cities of the South, and, increasingly, to those of the North. A series of economic crises and natural disasters (the ravages of the boll weevil and catastrophic floods in Mississippi and Alabama), the gradual mechanization of Southern agriculture, the adoption of disfranchisement techniques, racial violence and the spread of Jim Crow legislation and practices, combined to drive blacks from the land to urban centres. In 1879, thousands of black tenant farmers, victims of a vicious credit system that kept them in unending poverty, and of returning Democratic 'Redeemer' governments which stripped them of the civil and political rights gained during Reconstruction, left the states of Tennessee, Texas, Mississippi and Louisiana, and headed for Kansas. These black

75

'Exodusters' were the advance wave of the 'Great Migration' of Southern blacks, attracted by the prospect of greater opportunities in the cities of the North-East, Middle West, and the Pacific coast. Between 1890 and 1910 the black population of Chicago increased from 1.3 to 2.00 per cent; in Philadelphia, from 3.8 to 5.5 per cent; in Pittsburgh, from 3.3 to 4.8 per cent, and in Los Angeles, the Negro population was 2.5 per cent of the total population in 1890. In New York City, between 1890 and 1920, the black population increased from less than 70,000 to over 152,000, the majority Southern-born, but with a significant influx from the West Indies. In this same period, one area of New York City – Harlem – was transformed from an all-white, upper-class and fashionable section into a black residential section.

Although there were important differences in the urban experiences of Negroes, reflecting the nature of race relations, the origins and composition of the black population, economic opportunities and the structure of the black leadership class, there was also a marked similarity in the forces which together produced all-black residential areas in the major cities. In all cases, the black ghetto was both the product of white racism, which generally confined blacks to the less-desirable areas of settlement, and of black entrepreneurship, adaptability and community spirit. (Even in the mid-nineteenth century, blacks were more segregated than were white immigrant groups in Northern cities.) In Harlem, this entrepreneurial spirit was evident in the formation in 1904 of the Afro-American Realty Company, which originated in a partnership of ten blacks, organized by Philip A. Payton, a friend and admirer of Booker T. Washington, who saw possibilities of exploiting the section's depressed property market. The Afro-American Realty Company specialized in acquiring five-year leases on property owned by whites, and then renting it to blacks. Charles W. Anderson, the leading New York Republican, and Thomas T. Fortune, editor of the New York *Age*, supported Payton's enterprises. All were proteges of Washington, and members of his National Negro Business League. Ironically, Washington, despite his anti-urban bias, can be considered a founding father of one black ghetto which, by the 1920s had become, in the words of James Weldon Johnson 'the intellectual and artistic capital of the Negro world'.[3]

The black churches were the largest property-owners in Harlem, investing heavily in real estate and building new places of worship. St Mark's Methodist Episcopal Church purchased an apartment house on Lenox Avenue, between 140th and 141st streets, while St Philip's Protestant Episcopal Church (attended by more affluent members of the Negro community), was reported to own or control twenty six-storey buildings on West 135th Street in 1911. By 1918, it was estimated that blacks owned $20 million in Harlem properties. Other black institutions – fraternal orders, social service agencies (including the local offices of the NAACP and the National Urban League), foreign and missionary societies and two weekly newspapers – the *New York News* and the *Amsterdam News* – also established themselves in Harlem, contributing to its fame and growing population. In 1914, blacks inhabited 1,100 different houses within a twenty-three block area of Harlem, and in the same year, an Urban League survey estimated the section's black population at approximately 200,000, of whom 55,000 had been born in the West Indies. By this date, Harlem, initially an elegant, tree-lined area, was becoming a gigantic slum as housing and welfare facilities deteriorated under the sheer weight of numbers.

The National Urban League was one organization which attempted to secure better accommodations for blacks. Founded in 1911, the League grew out of two earlier organizations, the National League for the Protection of Coloured Women, and the Committee for Improving the Industrial Conditions of Negroes in New York. Concerned to offer for recently-arrived rural blacks the kinds of welfare and employment services already available to native and foreign-born whites through settlement houses, charities and immigrant-aid societies, the National Urban League was a bi-racial coalition of progressive whites and professional blacks. Considerably to the right of the NAACP, the NUL reflected Washingtonian policies of moral and economic progress, vocational training, and the de-emphasis of civil and political rights. It attempted to secure employment and homes for migrants, and offered advice on the etiquette and sanitary standards of city life. The League also conducted surveys among urban blacks, issued reports and (unsuccessfully) lobbied the American Federation of Labour to outlaw 'lily-white' union practices. Echoing Booker T. Washington, the League urged blacks to make free use of the toothbrush, the comb, soap and water. In 1911, the NUL and the NAACP agreed to adhere to their respective goals and strategies of racial advancement, but neither organization was able to avoid the charges of black militants like A. Philip Randolph that they were basically middle-class and white-dominated agencies, heavily dependent on philanthropic support, and pledged to the perpetuation of the capitalist system.

American involvement in World War I encouraged further black migration from the South, as northern industries supplied the needs of the allies and, with European immigration closed off, called for skilled and unskilled labour. After the United States Supreme Court, in a decision in 1917, declared municipal segregation ordinances unconstitutional, 'white improvement associations' utilized restricted covenants – agreements among property holders not to sell housing in specified areas to Negroes. As urban conditions worsened, earlier black migrants blamed newcomers for the increasing discrimination with which all Northern blacks had to contend.

In Harlem, tensions between American blacks and West Indian immigrants resulted from fears of economic competition, and jealousy of the business acumen and social mores of the growing West Indian community. Afro-Americans asserted that West Indians were too clannish, overly-ambitious – always prepared to work for lower wages than native-born blacks – and arrogant. West Indians were charged with disregarding the norms of American racial customs, while also standing aloof from black protest organizations. In particular, Afro-Americans were disturbed by the reluctance of West Indian immigrants to become naturalized citizens, failure to assimilate with the black host community and their formation of exclusive fraternal and benevolent associations.

These tensions, together with the generally worsening racial situation after 1918, produced an intensified racial awareness and militancy among black Americans. W. E. B. Du Bois and A. Philip Randolph advocated black resistance to white mobs, and the united action of white and black workers against predatory capitalists. In literature, the arts and music, the Harlem Renaissance signified the advent of the 'New Negro' – assertive, racially proud and in search of a positive Afro-American identity. Into this climate, soon to be overladen by the effects of the Great Depression, a West Indian agitator and visionary injected a compelling appeal to urban blacks who were, for all practical purposes, already living in a social environment which resembled that of an all-black and separatist 'nation'. Moreover, as his fellow West Indian, the poet and novelist Claude McKay observed, Marcus Garvey came to the United States 'as a humble disciple of the late Booker T. Washington, founder of Tuskegee Institute'.[4]

MARCUS GARVEY: BLACK JAMAICAN

Marcus Mosiah Garvey was born in St Ann's Bay, Jamaica, the youngest of eleven children. His parents were of unmixed Negro stock and descended from Maroons – African slaves who had successfully defied the Jamaican slave regime and formed virtually independent black communities in the island's mountains from 1664 to 1765. Because of this Maroon heritage, Garvey was fiercely proud of his blackness, and came to display an almost pathological distrust of light-skinned Negroes. In a 'chapter of autobiography' published in 1925, Garvey recalled:

> My parents were black Negroes. My father was a man of brilliant intellect and dashing courage. He once had a fortune; he died poor. My mother was a sober and conscientious Christian; too soft and good for the time in which she lived.[5]

Garvey's father, a skilled stone-mason, was also literate, possessed a private library, and acted as a local lawyer. After a few years of elementary education, Garvey, already apprenticed to a printer, left school at the age of fourteen. As a child, Garvey (like Du Bois) maintained friendly relations with the white children in his neighbourhood. He played with the children of a Wesleyan minister whose church his family attended, and was especially attached to one of the minister's daughters. But when she was fourteen, her parents separated her from Garvey, and the shock was traumatic.

> They sent her and another sister to Edinburgh, Scotland, and told her that she was never to write or try to get in touch with me, for I was a 'nigger'. It was then that I found that there was some difference in humanity, and that there were different races, each having its own separate and distinct social life. After my first lesson in race distinction, I never thought of playing with white girls anymore.[6]

Moving to Kingston, where he hoped to continue his education, Garvey was forced to work in a printing shop owned by his godfather. By the age of twenty, he became the youngest foreman printer in Kingston, at a time when British and Canadian immigrants were generally taking such jobs. When the printer's union went on strike for higher wages, Garvey was elected leader. The strike failed when the printer imported new machinery and immigrant labour, and the treasurer absconded with the union's funds. Garvey was fired and blacklisted. He became sceptical of the value of the labour movement and of socialism, and went to work for the government printing office.Increasingly conscious of the related issues of race and politics – 'I started to take an interest in the politics of my country, and then I saw the injustice done to my race because it was black' – Garvey also began to oppose British colonial rule in Jamaica.[7]

In 1910 Garvey published his first newspaper, *Garvey's Watchman*, a weekly with a circulation of about 3,000 copies. The venture was short-lived, and Garvey went to Costa Rica, where he worked as a timekeeper on a United Fruit Company banana plantation. He observed the exploitation of West Indian immigrant workers, and founded his second paper, *La Nacion*, in which he attacked the British consul for his indifference to the situation. Garvey then moved on to Panama and was appalled by the depressed condition of Jamaican labourers on the Panama Canal, and produced another newspaper, *La Prensa*. Moving on through Ecuador, Nicaragua, Honduras, Colombia and Venezuela, he discovered essentially similar conditions, and in each case attempted to organize black labour forces. Then, according to his second wife, Garvey, already ill with fever and

> sick at heart over appeals from his people to help on their behalf...decided to return to Jamaica in 1911, and try with the Government there, as well as to awaken Jamaicans at home, to the true conditions on the Spanish mainland.[8]

Unable to interest the authorities in the terrible conditions faced by Jamaican workers abroad, Garvey travelled through Europe, and settled for a time in London, where he met and worked with the Egyptian nationalist Duse Mohammad Ali, an admirer of Booker T. Washington, and publisher of the *African Times and Orient Review*. From Ali, Garvey learned of the subjugation of blacks throughout Africa, and increased his knowledge of African history and cultures. In London, Garvey also first read Washington's *Up From Slavery*, and later remembered: 'I read of conditions in America...and then my doom – if I may so call it – of being a race leader dawned upon me.'[9]

In 1914, Garvey returned to Jamaica with the plan of forming an international black organization which would set up an independent state. On 1 August 1914, he established the Universal Negro Improvement and Conservation Association and African Communities League (the UNIA). As defined by Garvey, the UNIA's grandiose objectives were:

> To establish a Universal Confraternity among the race; to promote the spirit of pride and love; to reclaim the fallen; to administer to and to assist the needy; to assist in civilizing the backward tribes of Africa; to assist in the development of independent Negro Nations and communities; to establish a central nation for the race, where they will be given the opportunity to develop themselves; to establish Commissaries and Agencies in the principal countries and cities of the world for the representation of all Negroes; to promote a conscientious spiritual worship among the native tribes of Africa; to establish Universities, Colleges and Academies and Schools for racial education and culture of the people; to improve the general condition of Negroes everywhere.[10]

The motto of the new organization was 'One God! One Aim! One Destiny!' – similar to the phrase, 'One God, one law, one element', in Tennyson's poem (admired by Garvey) *In Memoriam*. Garvey later said of the UNIA motto that: 'Like the great Church of Rome, Negroes the world over MUST PRACTICE ONE FAITH, that of Confidence in themselves, with One God! One Aim! One Destiny!'[11] In a pamphlet published in Jamaica in 1914, Garvey, styling himself as 'President' of the new movement, addressed the issue of 'The Negro Race and Its Problems', and argued that:

> Representative and educated Negroes have made the mistake of drawing and keeping themselves away from the race, thinking it is degrading and ignominious to identify themselves with the masses of people who are still ignorant and backward; but we are crying out for true and conscientious leadership.

Echoing Booker T. Washington, Garvey declared that although the Negro was 'handicapped by circumstances...no one is keeping him back. He is keeping himself back, and because of this, the other races refuse to notice or raise him'.[12] Washington's influence and example was also evident in Garvey's plan to establish educational and industrial colleges for Jamaican blacks (although West Indian students and staff at Tuskegee had earlier asked a visiting Jamaican delegation to set up a school similar to Tuskegee in the British West Indies). Planning to visit America in 1915, on a fund-raising tour, Garvey (who had been invited by Washington to visit Tuskegee), informed him in a letter that: 'I need not reacquaint you of the horrible conditions prevailing among our people in the West Indies as you are so well informed of happenings all over Negrodom'.[13] Garvey also enclosed a copy of the UNIA manifesto, which included among its objectives, the establishment of industrial schools. Washington, in reply, wished Garvey every success, yet failed to appreciate the heroic aims of the UNIA, and simply informed his Jamaican admirer:

> This is the age of 'getting together', and everywhere we look we see evidence of that constructive accomplishment which are [sic] the result of friendly cooperation and mutual helpfulness. Such, I am sure, is the object of your Association, and I am only sorry that I cannot afford the time just now to give more careful study to your plans so outlined.[14]

At this stage, Garvey viewed himself as a Washingtonian, but never met his mentor, who died before Garvey reached America in 1916. At a UNIA Memorial Meeting for Washington, held in Jamaica, Garvey was reported as having said:

> We can only acclaim him as the greatest hero sprung from the stock of scattered Ethiopia. Washington has raised the dignity and manhood of his race to midway, and it is now left to those with fine ideals who have felt his influence to lead the race on to the highest height in the adopted civilization of the age. He was the man for America. Without the presence of such a man the dominant race would have long ago obliterated the existence of the American Negro as a living force even as the Indians were outdone....Every true Negro mourns the loss of Dr. Booker T. Washington, scholar, orator, educator, race leader and philanthropist.[15]

Throughout his life, Garvey expressed admiration – although often qualified – for Washington. After his second visit to Tuskegee in 1923, Garvey wrote that 'language fails to express my high appreciation for the service Dr. Washington has rendered to us as a people', he was 'an originator and builder who, out of nothing, constructed the greatest educational and industrial institution of the race in modern times'.[16] Garvey also expressed his enthusiasm for Washington's emphasis on self-help, race pride, and his hostility to social equality. But in a later appraisal of Washington's leadership, Garvey voiced a reservation:

> The world held up the great Sage of Tuskegee...as the only leader for the race. They looked forward to him and his teachings as the leadership for all times, not calculating that the industrially educated Negro would himself evolve a new ideal.

Reiterating one of Du Bois' criticisms of Washington, Garvey asserted that:

> If Washington had lived he would have had to change his programme. No leader can successfully lead this race of ours without giving an interpretation of the awakened spirit of the New Negro, who does not seek industrial opportunity alone, but a political voice.[17]

At the height of his power in the United States, Garvey could argue that whereas Washington had looked for concessions from whites, the true race leader must be more aggressive and demanding. Revising an earlier estimate, Garvey concluded that:

> Booker T. Washington was not a leader of the Negro race. We did not look to Tuskegee. The world has recognized him as a leader. We are going to make demands.[18]

When Washington's successor at Tuskegee, R. R. Moton, failed to provide the kind of leadership which Garvey believed a changed situation demanded, he was denounced as the captive of 'white philanthropists' and therefore unfit to speak for the Negro race.

In Jamaica, the UNIA failed to attract the mulatto group of islanders, while the use of the term 'Negro' in its title was resented by many native Jamicans who preferred the term 'coloured'. One Jamaican critic wrote of Garvey's new 'Society with the long name and its big aims'.[19] After a year, the movement had only about one hundred members. Reflecting bitterly on this period, Garvey declared:

> I really never knew there was so much colour prejudice in Jamaica until I started the work of the UNIA. I had just returned from a successful trip to Europe, which was an exceptional achievement for a black man. The daily press wrote me up with big headlines and told of my movement. But nobody wanted to be a Negro. Men and women as black as I or even more so, had believed themselves white under the West Indian order of society...yet everyone beneath his breath was calling the black man a nigger. I had to decide whether to please my friends and be one of the 'black–whites' of Jamaica, and be reasonably prosperous, or come out openly, and defend and help and improve and protect the integrity of black millions and suffer. I decided to do the latter, hence my offence against the 'coloured–black–white' society in the colonies and America...in the opinion of the 'coloured' element, leadership should have been in the hands of a yellow or a very light man. There is more bitterness among us Negroes because of the caste of colour than there is between any other peoples, not excluding the peoples of India.[20]

GARVEY IN AMERICA

Marcus Garvey arrived in New York on 23 March 1916, on a fund-raising lecture tour for an industrial school to be built in Jamaica, and intended to stay for five months. He visited Tuskegee 'and paid my respects to the dead hero, Booker T. Washington', toured thirty-eight states and, at the end of the year, returned to New York city and set up base in Harlem. Scornful of existing Afro-American leadership, with its dependence on white support and neglect of the masses, Garvey decided to set up a division of the UNIA in America, and turned to the West Indian element in Harlem for assistance. Initially, Garvey planned to return to Jamaica after setting up an American branch of the UNIA, but faced with the opposition of Harlem's established black leadership, he resigned as president of the Jamaican chapter, decided to remain in Harlem, and began a campaign to recruit members. Within three weeks, Garvey claimed to have recruited 2,000 members in Harlem; by 1921 he estimated that the UNIA had six million members throughout the world. Neither contemporary observers nor later historians of the Garvey movement have agreed on its due-paying membership. In 1923 Du Bois stated that the UNIA had fewer than 20,000 members; by that date, Garvey could have reasonably claimed that within the United States the UNIA had twenty times the membership and support of all the other Negro organizations combined.

In 1919 Garvey began publication of a weekly newspaper, *The Negro World*, the official organ of the UNIA. As its masthead proclaimed, it was 'A Newspaper Devoted Solely to the Interests of the Negro Race'. With a weekly circulation of about 200,000, *The Negro World* was Garvey's greatest propaganda device, and his most successful publishing venture. It appeared in English, French and Spanish editions, and lasted until 1933. Every issue carried a front-page polemic by Garvey, and articles on black history and culture, racial news, and UNIA activities. The programme of the UNIA was stated in an eight-point platform in one issue of *The Negro World*:

1. To champion Negro nationhood by redemption of Africa.
2. To make the Negro race conscious.
3. To breathe ideals of manhood and womanhood into every Negro.
4. To advocate self-determination.
5. To make the Negro world-conscious.
6. To print all the news that will be interesting and instructive to the Negro.
7. To instill racial self-help.
8. To inspire Racial love and self-respect.[21]

(To underline the last point, *The Negro World* refused to print advertising copy for skin-whitening and hair-straightening compounds – staple revenue sources for much of the black press in America.)

Garvey's ideological statements in *The Negro World* spread the UNIA gospel not only throughout the United States, but also in Latin America, the Caribbean and Africa – much to the consternation of the colonial powers. The late C. L. R. James described a conversation with the Kenyan nationalist Jomo Kenyatta in 1921, in which he was informed that illiterate Kenyans 'would gather around a reader of Garvey's newspaper and listen to an article two or three times'. They would then run into surrounding areas 'carefully to repeat the whole, which they had memorized, to Africans, hungry for some doctrine which lifted them from the servile consciousness in which Africans lived'.[22] With his repeated calls for international black solidarity, denunciations of lynchings, and support for the Irish, Indian, and Egyptian independence movements, Garvey, initially seen as a charlatan, was quickly perceived as a threat to the established international order. His activities were carefully monitored by the British and American intelligence agencies, whose agents accused Garvey of fomenting racial strife. In America, the young J. Edgar

Hoover, then assistant to the attorney general (and who was later to mount a dirty tricks campaign against Martin Luther King), showed a marked interest in deporting Garvey as an undesirable alien. Addressing audiences in New York City, Detroit, Chicago, Pittsburgh, Cleveland Baltimore and Toronto, Garvey's message was essentially the same.

> The white man of the world has been accustomed to deal with the Uncle Tom cringing negro. Up to 1919 he knew no other negro than the negro represented through Booker Washington. Today he will find a new negro is on the stage. Every American negro and every West Indian negro must understand that there is but one fatherland for the negro, and that is Africa. And as the Germans fought and struggled for the fatherland of Germany; as the Irish man is fighting for the fatherhood of Ireland, so must the new negro of the world fight for the fatherland of Africa.

(Anticipating the rhetoric of Malcolm X and the Black Power advocates of the 1960s, Garvey informed a UNIA meeting at Carnegie Hall in 1919: 'The first dying that is to be done by the black man in the future will be done to make himself free'.)[23]

In July 1919 Garvey purchased a large auditorium in Harlem – 'Liberty Hall' – for UNIA meetings, and Liberty Halls were also opened by other UNIA branches. (By 1926 there were sixteen divisions and chapters of the UNIA in California.) Amy-Jacques Garvey described the multiple functions of these halls, designed to serve 'the needs of the people':

> Sunday morning worship, afternoon Sunday schools, Public meetings at nights, concerts and dances were held. Notice boards were put up where one could look for a room, a job or a lost article. In localities where there were many people out of work during the winter, Black Cross Nurses would organize soup kitchens and give them a warm meal daily....In the freezing winter days stoves had to be kept going to accommodate the cold and homeless until they 'got on their feet again'.[24]

The Negro Factories Corporation was established in 1919, and, according to *The Negro World*, was designed 'to build and operate factories in the big industrial centres of the United States, Central America, the West Indies and Africa to manufacture every marketable commodity'.[25] The corporation developed a chain of grocery stores, a restaurant, tailoring establishment, a hotel, printing presses, a (black) doll factory and a steam laundry in Harlem. (Garvey's advertising skills were revealed in the promise of the Negro Factories Corporation Laundry Service: 'We Return Everything But The Dirt'.) By 1920, the UNIA and its allied enterprises – putting into practice the Washington-derived precept of economic self-help – employed 300 people.

Garvey's most spectacular undertaking was the organization of an all-Negro steamship company that would link the coloured people of the world in commercial and industrial intercourse. The Black Star Steamship Line, incorporated in Delaware on 26 June 1919, was capitalized at $500,000, with 100,000 shares of stock at $5.00 a share. The Black Star Line also stemmed from Booker T. Washington's axiom that blacks must seek to become independent of white capital, and stock circulars for the projected company appealed directly to racial pride.

> The Black Star Line Corporation presents to every Black Man, Woman, and Child the opportunity to climb the great ladder of industrial and commercial progress. If you have ten dollars, one hundred dollars, or one or five thousand dollars to invest for profit, then take out shares in the Black Star Line, Inc. The Black Star Line will turn over profits and dividends to stockholders, and operate to their interest even whilst they will be asleep.[26]

Sale of BSL stock was limited to Negroes, with a maximum of 200 shares per person. In February 1920, the BSL was recapitalized at $10,000,000.

Garvey never intended that the line would be the agency for the mass transportation of Negroes back to Africa; rather it was conceived as a commercial operation, a source of justifiable racial pride, and a demonstration of black entrepreneurial (and nautical) skills. Amy-Jacques Garvey recalled that:

> The main purpose of the formation and promotion of the Black Star Line was to acquire ships to trade between the units of the Race – in Africa, the U.S.A., the West Indies, and Central America, thereby building up an independent economy of business, industry, and commerce, and to transport our people on business and pleasure, without being given inferior accommodation or refusal of any sort of accommodation.[27]

Unfortunately, the BSL's operations and administration were marked by financial failure, as well as by elements of farce and ineptitude.

In August 1920, Garvey and the Harlem branch of UNIA staged the First International Convention of the Negro Peoples of the World. Delegates representing twenty-five countries attended the proceedings in New York – although a Bureau of Investigation agent reported that many of the 'so-called foreign delegates' had, in fact, been 'living in the United States for years'. Consequently 'the majority of his followers and especially the general public are under the impression that *all* these delegates had just arrived here especially for Garvey's convention'.[28] Roi Ottley, a black journalist and social worker, remembered that as a child he had witnessed the 1920 Convention.

> During the whole month of August 1920, delegates from all the states, the West Indies, South America and Africa assembled in Liberty Hall, in a demonstration that proved to be a series of rousing 'bravos' and 'hallelujahs' to the black leader. People were fascinated by all the bustle, and animation in the streets. There were loud speeches, stock-selling from the curbstones, and indeed fisticuffs as men clashed. 'Is Garvey greater than Jesus Christ?' people asked. 'Give he a chance' shot back his devout West Indies followers in their quaint English dialect. 'He's a young mon yet!'[29]

The 1920 Convention was certainly a splendid and glamorous affair. Parades through Harlem of the various elements of the UNIA – the African Legion in blue and red uniforms, the Black Cross Nurses, dressed in dazzling white, the Black Flying Eagles, and the Universal African Motor Corps – attracted and delighted the Negro community. Garvey also took the opportunity to advertise the UNIA at the expense of his rivals. One of the slogans carried in the convention parade read: 'NAACP: Nothing Accomplished After Considerable Pretence/UNIA: United Nothing Can Impede Your Aspirations'.[30] The UNIA flag, red for Negro blood, green for Negro hopes and black for Negro skin, was prominently displayed, and the Convention speeches stressed the themes of African nationalism and the meaning of Garvey's movement. To the Reverend James David Brooks, UNIA secretary-general at the 1920 convention, Garveyism was:

> the spirit to help God work out the destiny of the black race. The spirit of Garveyism is the spirit to contend for that which belongs to you. Garveyism is the spirit of self-reliance. Garveyism is the freedom for Africa. You have got to get the spirit of Garvey and let it touch your heart until it becomes part of your life...until at night you dream Garveyism.[31]

(Two years later Brooks unsuccessfully sued Garvey for an unpaid loan of $1,000 and $7,000 in unpaid wages.) Garvey was elected Provisional President of the African Republic, and informed the delegates:

> We are here to celebrate the greatest event in the history of the Negro people for the last 500 years. We are in sympathy with the great Irish people who have been overrun for the last 700 years by the tyrants of Great Britain; we are in sympathy with the people of India...who are also dominated by Great Britain. We are in sympathy with the Chinese, with the Egyptians but one and all we are in sympathy with ourselves.[32]

Charles S. Johnson, writing in *Opportunity*, the magazine of the National Urban League, detected the possible inspiration for Garvey's exalted title:

Just prior to the first International Convention of the UNIA, De Valera
was elected Provisional President of Ireland. Garvey then became
Provisional President of Africa.[33]

The UNIA Convention also created a nobility – Knights of the Nile,
and honours – the Distinguished Service Order of Ethiopia. Delegates
drafted a 'Declaration of the Rights of the Negro Peoples of the
World', which included the demand that 'Negro' be spelled with a
capital N, condemnations of European imperialism in Africa and
lynchings in the United States.

But the UNIA rested on Garvey's charisma and energies rather than
on his administrative or organizational abilities. He undertook a series
of energetic promotional tours – including visits to Cuba, Jamaica,
Costa Rica, Panama and British Honduras – to sell Black Star Line
stock and memberships in the UNIA. But a series of misfortunes,
miscalculations and tactical blunders hastened his eventual American
downfall. In 1921 President Warren G. Harding, speaking in Alabama,
asserted his belief in the Washingtonian ideal of the separation of the
races. Garvey endorsed the speech, and was roundly condemned by
other black leaders. The following year Garvey went to Georgia for a
meeting with Edward Young Clarke, 'Imperial Kleagle' of the racist
and terroristic Ku Klux Klan, in an attempt to elicit Klan support for
the UNIA's African programme. From their opposing perspectives,
Clarke and Garvey shared a common belief in racial purity and racial
separation. As Garvey later announced: 'Whilst the Ku Klux Klan
desires to make America absolutely a white man's country, the UNIA
wants to make Africa absolutely a black man's country'.[34] Garvey's
black critics were astounded and outraged by the episode. William
Pickens of the NAACP, who had earlier shown interest in the UNIA,
broke with Garvey over the Klan meeting, and informed him bitterly:

> I gather you are now endorsing the Ku Klux Klan, or at least conceding
> the justice of its aim to crush and repress coloured Americans and
> incidently other racial and religious groups in the United States. You
> compare the aim of the Ku Klux in America with your aims in Africa –
> and if that be true, no civilized man can endorse either one of you....What
> is the earthly commonsense of bargaining what we have in the United
> States for what the Klan, and nothing like the Klan, can give us in Africa?
> If it is ever to be possible for you to negotiate a worse transaction than
> the Black Star Line, this must be IT....I would rather be a plain black
> American fighting in the ranks AGAINST the Klan and all its brood than
> to be the Imperial Wizard of the Ku Klux or the allied Imperial Blizzard
> of the UNIA.[35]

An editorial by Chandler Owen in *The Messenger*, the black
socialist paper, was headlined: 'Marcus Garvey! The Black Imperial

Wizard Becomes Messenger Boy Of The White Ku Klux Kleagle', and concluded:

> The issue is joined, and we shall spare no pains to inform the American, West Indian, African, South American and Canal Zone Negroes of the emptiness of all this Garvey flapdoodle, bombast and lying about impossible and conscienceless schemes calculated not to redeem Africa but to enslave Africa and the Negro everywhere...the *Messenger* is firing the opening gun in a campaign to drive Garvey and Garveyism from the American soil.

Robert W. Bagnall, an organizer for the NAACP, was reported in the *New York Times* as having told a 'Marcus Garvey Must Go' rally that:

> Garvey tells you to accept the Ku Klux Klan at its face value. He tells you not to oppose the Klan which has lynched and robbed you again and again. That's Garvey a leader who shows himself a cowardly, whining adventurer, an individual of doubtful honesty and a demagogic charlatan.[36]

In turn, Garvey stigmatized his black critics as proponents of 'racial equality' as distinct from his own philosophy of 'racial purity'. His continuing support for white segregationists, and his contacts with Theodore G. Bilbo, the Mississippi senator actively opposed to racial intermixing, who also espoused the repatriation of black Americans to West Africa, indicated that in his quest and zeal for black separatism, Garvey disregarded the sensibilities of most American Negroes.

After 1920 also, Garvey was repeatedly in financial and legal difficulties. The Black Star Line was economically unsound, and its operations were less than seaworthy. For example, the BSL's first ship, a small freighter, the 'S. S. Yarmouth', cost $165,000, and was in constant operational and legal trouble. Other ships purchased by the line, the aptly-named 'Shadyside', an old Hudson River excursion boat, and the steam yacht 'Kanawha', never realized a fraction of their purchase prices. The 'Yarmouth' (later named 'S. S. Frederick Douglass'), sailed for Cuba with a cargo of whiskey, narrowly escaped sinking, and arrived at its destination with a good part of the cargo having been disposed of by the crew.The Pan Union Company, the importers of the whiskey, were awarded $6,000 by a court for their losses. In less than five months' active service, the 'Shadyside' cost the BSL $11,000 in operating losses.

At the 1922 convention of the UNIA, Garvey repudiated his critics within the movement, and removed them from office after a series of acrimonious show trials. At the same time, he began to modify his demands for the expulsion of the European powers from Africa, disavowed his connection with radicalism, but continued to denounce his enemies (real and imagined) within the NAACP. Women were featured more prominently at the 1922 convention, after female delegates challenged male dominance of the proceedings and the UNIA as a male-run organization but featured mainly in fashion shows and pageants as 'Modistes and Milliners' and 'Manikins'. Bessie Coleman, the first black American to obtain a pilot's licence, was presented to the delegates (she was killed four years later after falling from her plane at a flying display at Jacksonville, Florida). A motion was debated that the women in UNIA should be given greater prominence in the organization.

> We, the women of UNIA and ACL know that no race can rise higher than its women. We need women in the important places of the organization to help refine and mould public sentiment, realizing the colossal programme of this great organization and...we are determined to reclaim our own land, Africa.[37]

In 1922 Garvey and three of his associates were arrested and charged with using the United States Mails to defraud – on the basis of information (unwittingly) supplied to the Bureau of Investigation by Cyril V. Briggs, leader of the African Blood Brotherhood, a radical group, which advocated human rights, an end to colonialism and a federation of 'all Negro organizations'. Garvey had attacked Briggs, who was of light complexion, as a 'white man' trying to pass as black. Briggs was also an ardent supporter of the Russian Revolution, leading Garvey to condemn him as a 'dangerous Bolshevik'.[38]

At his trial the prosecution declared that Garvey had promoted the sale of BSL stock, although he knew that the company was in serious financial trouble. Garvey conducted his own defence in a melodramatic fashion, and blamed his colleagues, white competitors, the NAACP and other enemies for the Line's collapse. He was fined $1,000, and sentenced to five years in prison. Released on bond, he returned to UNIA activity, and in particular attempted to obtain permission from the Liberian government to establish a UNIA base in that country. The Liberians, also engaged in financial transactions with the Firestone Rubber Company, informed the American government that they were 'irrevocably opposed, both in principle and fact to the incendiary policy of the Universal Negro Improvement Association headed by Marcus Garvey'.[39] In addition, Garvey faced the opposition of the European imperialist powers (and of Du Bois and J. Edgar Hoover) to his Liberian scheme. In 1925 Garvey's appeal against his mails fraud conviction was rejected by the United States Circuit Court of Appeals, and he was sent to the Atlanta penitentiary.

After two years President Calvin Coolidge (who had gained Garvey's declaration of support in the 1924 elections) commuted his sentence, and as an alien convicted of a felony, he was deported to Jamaica.

From 1927 to 1940 Garvey worked to rebuild the UNIA, and branches were opened in Paris and London – where he set up an office in West Kensington. In 1929 the Sixth International Convention of Negro Peoples of the World met in Jamaica, but Garvey disputed with the American delegates, whom he accused of financial malpractices. He also refused to accept their demand that the headquarters of the organization remain in New York, and with the defection of his remaining American followers, Garvey's influence in the United States declined even further – although offshoots of the UNIA were to reappear from time to time in the 1930s and 1940s. Garvey himself remained active. He denounced Italy's attack on Ethiopia in 1935, castigated the Harlem religious leader Father Divine for permitting his followers to refer to him as God, and continued to envision a world-wide organization of black people dedicated to African liberation. But none of his causes aroused the mass support which he had commanded in America. Garvey died in London in 1940 (after reading premature reports of his death in the press), impoverished and without ever having set foot in Africa.

GARVEYISM

The ideology of Marcus Garvey and the UNIA combined the various elements of black nationalism – religious, cultural, economic and territorial – into a distinctive philosophy. Basic to this world view was the emotive power of *blackness*. Garvey was essentially a racial Zionist who offered an eschatology of colour, in which black was good and white was evil. Garveyism advocated black economic self-determination and African redemption. It preached the revitalization of coloured people throughout the world and the power of the black race. Garvey was also well aware of the importance of religion in black culture and consciousness. The religious component of Garveyism was the African Orthodox Church, established in 1921, with the West Indian George Alexander McGuire as the UNIA's chaplain general. Garvey believed that as God was made in the image of man, black people ought to visualize and worship a black God and a black Christ. As he expressed it:

> Since the white people have seen their own God through white spectacles,
> we have now started out to see our God through our own spectacles. We
> Negroes believe in the God of Ethiopia, the everlasting God...but we shall
> worship Him through the spectacles of Ethiopia.[40]

To many of its followers, the UNIA was a surrogate or civil
religion, with Garvey a 'Black Moses', blacks the Chosen People, and
Africa the Promised Land. At the same time, the rituals, symbols and
beliefs of the UNIA's civil religion were sufficiently generalized to
permit members to continue to participate in their particular religious
denominations. Benjamin E. Mays, the Negro theologian and teacher
(and intellectual mentor of Martin Luther King, Jr) observed that
Garvey used the idea of a black God 'to arouse the Negro to a sense of
deep appreciation for his race...to stimulate [him] to work to improve
his social and economic conditions'.[41] Culturally, Garveyism extolled
and intensified the race consciousness which had already existed
among black Americans, only too painfully aware of their ethnic
identity in a racist society. It was Garvey's considerable achievement
to give this awareness a more positive (and international) focus. As a
statement of economic nationalism, Garveyism (deriving many of its
principal tenets from Booker T. Washington) espoused black
economic independence and self-sufficiency, but avoided endorsing
either capitalism or socialism. The Black Star Line and the Negro
Factories Corporation were, in fact, more cooperative than corporate
forms of business enterprise. The UNIA's proposed Liberian colony
would have comprised family units together with larger cooperative
farms administered by the Association.

The most important element in Garveyism, however, was its
emphasis on a return to Africa (whether in a physical or a spiritual
sense), the expulsion of European powers from the African continent,
and belief that once a strong and independent 'African nation' was
established, Negroes would gain automatically in power and prestige.
Although Garvey did not realistically expect all black Americans to
'return' to Africa, he viewed the UNIA as representing the vanguard
in the struggle for African liberation. As he informed an audience in
Madison Square Garden in 1924:

> The thoughtful and industrious of our race want to go back to Africa,
> because we realize it will be our only hope of permanent existence. We do
> not want all the Negroes in Africa. Some are no good here, and naturally
> will be no good there. The no-good Negro will naturally die in fifty years.
> The Negro who is wrangling about and fighting for social equality will
> naturally pass away in fifty years, and yield his place to the progressive
> Negro who wants a society and country of his own.[42]

Failing the peaceful resettlement of a black élite in colonized Africa, Garvey advocated the use of force, and the UNIA included such paramilitary units as the African Legion, The Black Eagle Flying Corps and the Universal African Motor Corps. Garvey informed delegates to the 1920 Convention (and the European colonialist powers in Africa):

We are striking homeward toward Africa to make her the big black republic...and we say to the white man who dominates Africa that it is to his interest to clear out now, because we are coming, not as in the time of Father Abraham, 2,000,000 strong but we are coming 400,000,000 strong and we mean to retake every square inch of the 12,000,000 square miles of African territory belonging to us by right Divine.[43]

At the Second International Convention in 1921 Garvey delivered an address at Liberty Hall which concluded with the ringing declaration:

It falls to our lot to tear off the shackles that bind Mother Africa. Can you do it? You did it in the Revolutionary War. You did it in the Civil War. You did it at the Battles of the Marne and Verdun. You can do it marching up the battle heights of Africa. Let the world know that 400,000,000 Negroes are prepared to live or die as free men. Climb ye the heights of liberty and cease not in well doing until you have planted the banner of the Red, the Black and the Green on the hilltops of Africa.[44]

The liberation of Africa from European colonial rule, and the repatriation there of the 'best' Afro-Americans (mulattos, by definition, were excluded), appear as constant – although not always clearly expressed – themes in Garvey's writings and speeches. But the mass appeal asserted by Garveyism transcended the impracticality and fantasy of its 'Back-to-Africa' ideology. For most Garveyites, the *idea* of an African homeland was more appealing than any actual desire (or ability) to leave the United States. Richard Wright, recalling his encounters with Garveyites in Chicago in the 1920s, felt that they

had embraced a totally racialistic outlook which endowed them with a dignity I have never seen before in Negroes. Those Garveyites I knew could never understand why I liked them but would never follow them, and I pitied them too much to tell them that they would never achieve their goal, that Africa was owned by the imperial powers of Europe, that their lives were alien to the mores of the natives of Africa, that they were people of the West....It was when the Garveyites spoke fervently of building their own country, of someday living within the boundaries of a culture of their own making, that I sensed the passionate hunger of their lives.[45]

Alain Locke, editor of and contributor to *The New Negro*, an anthology of the work of artists and writers of the Harlem

Renaissance, published in 1925, observed in his essay 'The New Negro' that:

> When the racial leaders twenty years ago spoke of developing race pride and stimulating race consciousness, and of the desirability of race solidarity, they could not in accurate degree have anticipated the abrupt feeling that has surged up and now pervades the awakened centres....With the American Negro, his new internationalism is primarily an effort to recapture contact with the scattered peoples of African derivation.

He viewed Garveyism as constituting perhaps 'a transient' but certainly a 'spectacular phenomenon' animated by 'the sense of a mission of rehabilitating the race in world esteem from the loss of prestige for which the fate and conditions of slavery have so largely been responsible'.[46]

GARVEY AND HIS BLACK CRITICS

Even more than Booker T. Washington, Garvey aroused critical responses from his black American contemporaries, but all were agreed on (as they deplored) his mass appeal. From the time of his arrival in Harlem until his deportation, Garvey faced the often bitter opposition of established and aspiring black leaders of differing ideological persuasions. To the middle-class, integrationist members of the NAACP and the Urban League, as well as to black socialists and radicals, Garvey was viewed as a visionary, a charlatan, a demagogue and a madman. He was accused of advocating racial segregation and of pandering to the prejudice of Southern whites, of injecting a divisive consciousness of colour among Afro-Americans and of duping his gullible followers.

Despite his expressed admiration for Booker T. Washington, members of the National Urban League, with its vested interest in economic opportunity for blacks within the American capitalist system (and its support for racial integration) were less than enthusiastic about Garvey's aims. Charles S. Johnson, writing for the NUL's journal *Opportunity* in 1923, characterized Garvey as a 'dynamic, blundering, temerarious visionary' and a trickster. Not only were his ideas unrealistic, his 'financial exploits were ridiculously unsound, his plans for the redemption of Africa absurdly visionary, and the grand result, the fleecing of hundreds of thousands of poor and ignorant Negroes'. By the standards of the NUL, Garveyism was 'a gigantic swindle', providing a 'dream-world escape for the "illiterati" from the eternal curse of their racial status in this country'. All that Garvey offered the urban poor was 'an opiate for their hopeless helplessness – a fantastic world beyond the grasp of logic and reason in which they might slake cravings never in this social order to be realised'.[47] Urban Leaguers (like most of Garvey's black opponents) saw him as an outsider, undereducated and bombastic. Board members of the NUL were also light-skinned, and this fact alone ensured animosity between the League and the UNIA. On all counts, then, Garvey and the NUL were antithetical. But Leaguers were not insensible to Garvey's mass appeal, based on the twin pillars of racial pride and the right of self-determination. Charles S. Johnson conceded that Garvey's personal characteristics, deplored by his critics, were precisely those which made him a charismatic figure.

> His extravagant self-esteem could be taken for dignity, his hard-headedness as self-reliance, his ignorance of law as transcendency, his blunders as persecution, his stupidity as silent deliberation, his churlishness and irascibility as the eccentricity of genius.[48]

On the left wing of the black protest movement, Garvey was to earn the enmity of the socialists A. Philip Randolph and Chandler Owen, joint editors of the *Messenger*. Randolph, the most notable black labour organizer of the 1920s, had helped to form the Brotherhood of Sleeping Car Porters in 1925. In later years he claimed to have given Garvey his first opportunity of addressing a Harlem street audience. (W. A. Domingo, who was the first editor of the *Negro World* , reported that Garvey's first public speech in New York was greeted with catcalls and jeers, while the speaker himself, visibly nervous, fell off the platform.) For a time, Randolph and Garvey, despite profound differences in their racial and political attitudes, enjoyed cordial relations. In 1919 Randolph addressed a UNIA meeting which considered sending a Negro delegate to the Paris Peace Conference. Earlier, Garvey had attended a conference organized by Randolph that led to the formation of the short-lived International League of Darker Peoples, which aimed to secure African liberation by an interracial alliance of radical, liberal, and labour movements.

As the UNIA grew, however, relations between Randolph and Garvey became increasingly strained. Garvey's glorification of black capitalism ran counter to the Randolph–Owen belief in democratic socialism, and other aspects of Garveyism earned their disapproval. In a series of articles in the *Messenger*, they attacked Garvey's African schemes as being based on simplistic reasoning, since the oppression of the masses, worldwide, was colour-blind. Garvey was also accused of stirring white prejudice against blacks and of fostering tensions between West Indians and Afro-Americans. In fact, the *Messenger's* critiques of Garvey had a pronounced anti-West Indian tone. Robert W. Bagnall, writing in the magazine in 1923, depicted Garvey as:

> A Jamaican Negro of unmixed stock, squat, fat and sleek,with protruding jaws and heavy jowls, small bright pig-like eyes and bull-dog-like face. Boastful, egotistical, tyrannical, intolerant, cunning, shifty smooth and suave, avaricious...gifted at self-advertisement, without shame in self-laudation, promising ever, but never fulfilling...a lover of pomp and tawdry finery and garish display,a bully with his own folk but servile in the presence of the Klan, a sheer opportunist. If he is not insane, he is a demagogic charlatan, but the probability is that the man is insane. Certainly the movement is insane, whether Garvey is or not.[49]

Following Garvey's overtures to the Ku Klux Klan, Chandler and Randolph served notice that they were going to campaign for his expulsion from America. The *Messenger* now adopted the slogan 'Garvey Must Go'. The Friends of Negro Freedom, a civil rights propaganda organization, founded by Randolph and Owen in May 1920, and which included several NAACP officials, also promoted anti-Garvey meetings. Randolph wrote sarcastically in the *Messenger*: 'I think we are justified in asking the question, that if Mr Garvey is seriously interested in establishing a Negro nation, why doesn't he begin with Jamaica, West Indies?'[50] (A *Messenger* editorial typified Garvey as 'A Supreme Jamaican Jackass').

In 1923 eight leaders of the 'Garvey Must Go' campaign, with Chandler Owen as secretary, wrote to the US Attorney General, urging the government to speed up its prosecution case against Garvey for mail fraud. (Garvey charged the committee with offences against race solidarity.) The signatories included Harry H. Pace of the NUL, William Pickens, field secretary of the NAACP, and Chandler Owen. A. Philip Randolph, despite his major role in the campaign, did not sign the letter. During Garvey's imprisonment, the *Messenger* advocated the total destruction of the UNIA, and commended Du Bois' critique (see p.99-100) of Garvey: 'Lunatic or Traitor', published in 1924. Randolph and Owen, like other commentators, rejected Garvey's intense black nationalism, and certainly resented his achievement in leading a movement composed almost entirely of the black working class. Above all, they resented his challenge to the Talented (Afro-American) Tenth's monopoly of race leadership. (Garvey himself observed with some accuracy that 'my success as an organizer was more than rival Negro leaders could tolerate'.)[51] Nowhere was this jealousy and resentment more apparent than in the responses of W.E.B. Du Bois to the rise (and fall) of Garvey in America.

DU BOIS AND GARVEY

In his first autobiography, Du Bois recalled that he had first heard of Garvey in 1915, on a visit to Jamaica, where he had been warmly-received 'by coloured people and white....Garvey and his associates, The United [sic] Improvement and Conservation Association, joined in the welcome'.[52] Du Bois reported Garvey's arrival in America in the *Crisis*, noting that he was on a visit to raise funds for the establishment of an industrial school for blacks in Jamaica. Four years later, Du Bois conceded that Garvey had 'with singular success capitalized and made vocal the great and long suffering grievances and spirit of protest among the West Indian peasantry', and commended his eloquence as an orator. And, Du Bois noted, 'he has become to thousands of people a sort of religion'.[53] But Du Bois' subsequent references to Garvey, open or veiled, became increasingly bitter and occasionally shrill. In a cryptic *Crisis* editorial in 1922, Du Bois was obviously referring to Garvey when he predicted that 'We must expect the Demagogue among Negroes more and more. He will come to lead, inflame, lie and steal. He will gather large followings and then disappear.'[54] Garvey did not let such oblique references pass unchallenged, and regularly blamed Du Bois and the NAACP for most of his problems, including the thwarting of his Liberian plans, the collapse of the Black Star Line, and his trial and imprisonment. Du Bois, in turn, was angered because Garvey's African schemes were competing – and often confused – with his own Pan-African philosophy and activities.

From 1920 onwards Du Bois began to aim *Crisis* editorials directly at Garvey and the UNIA. Among other misdemeanours, Garvey was charged with having attempted to introduce the black/mulatto schism in America where, Du Bois claimed unconvincingly, 'it has never had any substantial footing and where today it is absolutely repudiated by every thinking Negro'. In accentuating this division, Garvey had 'aroused more bitter colour enmity inside the race than has ever before existed'.[55] Two weeks before the UNIA's 1920 Convention, Garvey wrote to Du Bois, inviting him to stand for election as 'the accredited spokesman for the Negro people'. Du Bois icily refused the provocative invitation, and sent several requests to Garvey for information on UNIA membership, finances and activities, for a 'critical estimate' to be published in the *Crisis*. At the convention, Du Bois was reported as having said to an interviewer:

> I do not believe that Marcus Garvey is sincere. I think he is a demagogue, and that his movement will collapse in a short time....His followers are

the lowest type of negroes, mostly from the Indies. It cannot be considered an American movement....Most of his following are in Jamaica and other islands of the West and East Indies. They are allied with the Bolsheviks and the Sinn Feiners in their world revolution.[56]

Garvey, in retaliation, castigated Du Bois as 'the associate of an alien race', and accused him of being 'more of a white man than a Negro [and] only a professional Negro at that'. Warming to this theme, Garvey ridiculed Du Bois' 'aristocratic pretensions' and his professed Negro, French and Dutch ancestry.

I have but the ancient glories of Ethiopia to imitate. Anyone you hear always talking about the kind of blood he has in him other than the blood you can see, is dissatisfied with something and I feel sure that many of the Negroes of the United States know that if there is a man who is most dissatisfied with himself, it is Dr. Du Bois.[57]

With relations between the two men worsening rapidly, Du Bois denied that he was envious of Garvey's success, rather was he fearful of his failure.

He can have all the money and power he can efficiently and honestly use. If in addition he wants to prance down Broadway in a green shirt – let him – but do not let him foolishly overwhelm with bankruptcy and disaster one of the most interesting spiritual movements in the modern Negro world.[58]

Du Bois intensified his campaign against Garvey and again attempted (unsuccessfully) to secure details of BSL finances. In a long article published in *Century* magazine in 1923 Du Bois linked Booker T. Washington with Garvey, and deplored the influence of both the master and his declared disciple.

The present generation of Negroes has survived two grave temptations, the greater one fathered by Booker T. Washington, which said, 'Let politics alone, keep your place, work hard, and do not complain', and which meant perpetual caste status for the coloured folk by their own cooperation and consent, and the consequent inevitable debauchery of the white world; and the lesser, fathered by Marcus Garvey, which said, 'Give up, Surrender! The struggle is useless; back to Africa and fight the white world'.

In the same article, Du Bois also described having seen Garvey at a UNIA meeting:

A little fat black man, ugly but with intelligent eyes and a big head... seated on a plank platform beside a 'throne', dressed in a military uniform of the gayest mid-Victorian type.[59]

Garvey's response was immediate and savage. The *Negro World* carried the banner headline: 'W. E. B. Du Bois As A Hater Of Dark

People', subtitled 'Calls His Own Race "Black and Ugly", Judging From The White Man's Standard Of Beauty'. On the sensitive issue of physical and personal appearance, Garvey claimed that to Du Bois, anything black was repellent, and that was why 'in 1917 he had but the lightest of coloured people in his [NAACP] office, when one could hardly tell whether it was a white show or a coloured vaudeville he was running at 5th Avenue'. Du Bois, Garvey alleged, actually believed blacks to be ugly, sought out the company of whites, danced and even slept with them. Comparing their respective backgrounds to his own advantage in terms of self-reliance and achievements, Garvey conceded that Du Bois was highly educated, but if that education 'fits him for no better service than being a lackey for white people, then it were better that Negroes were not educated'. Du Bois, Garvey claimed, was the avowed enemy and known saboteur of the UNIA – an all-black organization grounded in the common people. But for the support of such white patrons as Mary White Ovington and Oswald Garrison Villard, the fastidious and mannered Du Bois 'would be eating his pork chops from the counter of the cheapest restaurant in Harlem like so many other Negro graduates of Harvard and Fisk'. Garvey concluded his indictment by pointing up the fundamental ideological differences which separated him from Du Bois and the NAACP:

> Du Bois cares not for an Empire of Negroes but contents himself with being a secondary part of white civilization. We of the UNIA feel that the greatest service that the Negro can render to the world and himself...is to make his independent contribution to civilization. It is only a question of time before coloured men and women everywhere will harken to the voice in the wilderness, even though Du Bois impugns the idea of Negro liberation.[60]

(Garvey chose to ignore Du Bois' charge that he was a Jamaican agitator uninterested in the struggle of Afro-Americans for civil rights.)

Following Garvey's trial and conviction, Du Bois published his most bitter attack on Garvey in a *Crisis* editorial headed 'A Lunatic or A Traitor'. It revealed that to Du Bois, the basic principles in conflict were those of racial integration as opposed to separation, and the interracial antagonisms fostered by Garvey's racial chauvinism. The 'half-concealed' planks in the UNIA platform were seen as meaning:

> That no person of African descent can ever hope to become an American citizen.
> That forcible separation of the races and the banishment of Negroes to Africa is the only solution to the race problem. That race war is sure to follow any attempt to realize the programme of the NAACP.

Garvey, Du Bois insisted, far from attacking white prejudice, was attacking fellow Negroes, for whom he only had contempt. He refused to accept that Garvey was now the victim of white prejudice since 'no Negro in America ever had a fairer and more patient trial'. Garvey had 'convicted himself by his own admissions and monkey-shines in court'.

> American Negroes have endured this wretch too long and with fine restraint and every effort at cooperation and understanding. But the end has come. Every man who apologises for and defends Marcus Garvey from this day forth writes himself down as unworthy of the countenance of decent Americans. As for Garvey himself, this open ally of the Ku Klux Klan should be locked up or sent home.

In a dramatic climax to his piece, Du Bois claimed that he had been advised not to publish it 'lest I be assassinated', and concluded with a heroic flourish: 'I have been exposing white traitors for a quarter of a century. If the day has come when I cannot tell the truth about black traitors it is high time that I died.'[61]

At the end of the 1924 UNIA Convention, a resolution was passed which declared:

> In view of the fact that W. E. B. Du Bois has continually attempted to obstruct the progress of the UNIA to the loss and detriment of the Negro race and that he has...gone out of his way to try to defeat the cause of Africa's redemption, that he be proclaimed as ostracized from the Negro race as far as the UNIA is concerned, and from henceforward be regarded as an enemy of the black people of the world.[62]

From his prison cell in Atlanta, Garvey continued to lambast Du Bois and the NAACP as deadly adversaries. After Garvey's release and deportation, Du Bois − with his *bête noir* removed from the American scene − denied that the NAACP had opposed the UNIA, and claimed that *the Crisis* had published only five articles on Garvey (ignoring those which had attacked him only indirectly). In later years, Du Bois was more magnanimous toward Garvey, and in *The World And Africa* (1947) characterized Garveyism as 'a poorly conceived but intensely earnest determination to unite the Negroes of the world, especially in commercial enterprise'. The strength of the UNIA 'lay in its backing by the masses of West Indians' and by substantial numbers of Afro-Americans. Its weakness and shortcomings 'lay in... demagogic leadership, poor finance, intemperate propaganda, and the natural apprehension it aroused among the colonial powers'.[63] In his second autobiography, Du Bois was concerned to disclaim any 'enmity or jealousy' in his feud with Garvey, and cited that part of his *Crisis* editorial (published after Garvey's deportation) which stated that Garvey had 'a great and worthy dream. We wish him well. He is free; he has a following; he still has a chance to carry on his work in his own home and among his own people and to accomplish some of his ideas. We will be the first to applaud any success he might have.'[64] The message was clear; with Garvey's spectacular American career at an end, Du Bois could consign him thankfully to the West Indies, and oblivion.

For his part, Garvey refused to come to even partial peace terms with his most influential black American protagonist. In the 1930s, when Du Bois began to espouse the idea of a nonprofit, cooperative racial economy, Garvey roundly accused him of stealing the UNIA's clothes and preaching latter-day Garveyism. The *Negro World* carried the headline: 'Dr. Du Bois agrees with UNIA leader – Takes Programme Over Finally – But Does Not Openly Confess It'. In a short essay, published in 1934, Garvey repeated his contention that Du Bois was 'exceptional' only in his admiration for and imitation of white culture.

> To us he was never a leader...just a vain opportunist who held on to the glory and honour showered on him because he was one of the first experiments of Negro higher education. He was never a born leader. He is too selfish to be anything but Du Bois.[65]

Writing from England in the following year, Garvey delivered a final verdict on Du Bois, a man with 'no racial self-respect, no independent ideas, nothing of self-reliance', and was prepared to compose (thirty years before it was required) Du Bois' obituary notice:

> When Du Bois dies he will be remembered as the man who sabotaged the Liberian colonization scheme of the Negro, the man who opposed the American Negro launching steamships on the seas, the man who did everything to handicap the industrial, educational system of Tuskegee, the man who never had a good word to say for any other Negro leaders, but who tried to down every one of them.[66]

ASSESSMENT

Where Du Bois and the NAACP failed to reach a mass black constituency, Marcus Garvey, through the UNIA, succeeded in building a popular movement and following for his programme of racial uplift and the 'redemption' of Africa. Garvey's greatest achievement was to arouse in poor and lower-class blacks, unaffected by or unaware of the Harlem Renaissance and the 'New Negro', a fierce pride in their colour and racial identity. Like all leaders, Garvey was a visionary. That his vision of the expulsion of the European colonial powers from Africa was, in the period between the two World Wars, impossible of realization, never appears to have occurred to him. In effect, he wanted to make Zionists of black Americans and of coloured people throughout the world. Garveyism struck a responsive chord among the Afro-American underclass of the 1920s partly because it exalted all things black and inverted white standards, while retaining, in large measure, the practices of the surrounding white society. For every white institution and belief, Garveyism offered a black counterpart: The Black Star Line, Black Cross Nurses, The *Negro World*, The Black Legion and The Black Flying Corps, a black God and a black Christ. Both a religious and circular impulse, Garveyism linked its constituent elements in the concept of blackness. (Marcus Garvey, rather than the Black Power theorists of the 1960s, deserves credit for the slogan 'Black is Beautiful'.) Again, the programme of the UNIA, with its stress on economic nationalism and African liberation, permitted (and encouraged) Afro-Americans to identify with 'primitive' Africans from a position of technological and material superiority. But the bulk of Garvey's followers, in common with most Afro-Americans during the 1920s, were never seriously attracted by the prospect of going 'Back-To-Africa'. The nation-wide interest the UNIA and its flamboyant leader aroused reflected the disillusionment of blacks for whom the promised land of the American city had turned into the harsh reality of the squalid ghetto. And, with the anti-Negro climate of the post World War I era, Garvey's rhetoric, together with UNIA pomp and ceremony, attracted a following. But, as in the nineteenth century, few black Americans were prepared to leave the United States and undertake the uncertain and thankless task of 'redeeming' Africa. Garvey's larger significance as a leader lies in the fact that he articulated the grievances of those blacks for whom the civil rights goals of desegregation and political rights were largely meaningless. Again, he made the established Afro-American leadership class (and its white allies) painfully aware of their distance from the rank-and-file of the urban underclass. After Garvey's deportation, and particularly during the Depression and New Deal, the established black protest organizations tried more strenuously than before to close the gap between the élitist concerns of the Talented Tenth and the day-to-day problems of the majority of American Negroes.

The less attractive face of Garveyism was its authoritarianism, paramilitarism, and racial chauvinism. Garvey himself has been portrayed as a charismatic leader and a shameless demagogue, a revolutionary and a reactionary, the father of the heightened black consciousness of the 1960s, and the purveyor of a falsified and incomplete version of the African past and the Afro-American experience. From his published *Papers*, he sometimes emerges as an artful dodger, hypersensitive to real or imagined criticism, and constantly (but not always convincingly) protesting his financial honesty. There is no doubt that Garvey, more than any previous leader, stimulated racial pride and confidence among black Americans. As the black sociologist E. Franklin Frazier observed perceptively in the 1920s, part of Garvey's success as the leader of a mass movement was due to the regalia, pomp and circumstances which the UNIA offered to its adherents.

> A uniformed member of a Negro lodge paled in significance beside a soldier of the Army of Africa. A Negro might be a porter during the day, taking his orders from white men, but he was an officer in the black army when it assembled at night at Liberty Hall.[67]

To the Reverend Adam Clayton Powell, Sr, pastor of Harlem's Abyssinian Baptist Church, Garvey's arrival in 1916:

> was more significant to the Negro than the World War, the Southern exodus and the fluctuation of property values....During the reign of Garvey there were two places in America – the federation of 48 states, and Harlem, and two million Negroes thought that Harlem was both of them....it is recording the truth to say that [Garvey] is the only man that ever made Negroes who are not black ashamed of their colour.[68]

Claude McKay, applauded Garvey's propagandistic skills, and the sheer audacity of the Black Star Line, which 'had an electrifying effect upon all the Negro peoples of the world'. Unfortunately, Garvey's revolutionary fervour had not been accompanied by a true revolutionary's consciousness. His ignorance of Africa was profound, taking no account of its tribal, geographic, linguistic and geographical divisions. His schemes of black capitalism had foundered with the collapse of the Black Star Line. But, McKay conceded, Garvey's 'five years of stupendous vaudeville' had made him 'the biggest popularizer of the Negro problem, especially among Negroes, since *Uncle Tom's Cabin*'.[69] James Weldon Johnson found little to praise in Garvey or the movement he led. A 'supreme egotist' who had surrounded himself with 'cringing sychophants' and 'cunning knaves', Garvey, in advocating the repatriation of black Americans, was simply plagiarizing ideas retailed by the American Colonization Society a century earlier, and rejected by the majority of Afro-

Americans then and in the 1920s:

> The central idea of Garvey's scheme was absolute abdication and the recognition as facts of the assertions that this is a white man's country in which the Negro has no right, no future, no chance. To that idea the overwhelming majority of thoughtful Negroes will not subscribe.[70]

Garvey's feuds with his American detractors drained the energies of all the participants, inhibited the development of both the unified black community he claimed to want, and polarized the black protest movement during a period of 'white backlash'. Garvey's movement (and its adherents) aroused only scorn and derision from the emerging black middle class. An affluent black physician in Chicago informed E. Franklin Frazier that the letters UNIA really stood for 'Ugliest Negroes in America'.[71] Verdicts on Garvey's leadership inevitably reflect attitudes toward the subsequent trends in American race relations. Certainly Marcus Garvey relished conflict and competition, and this was both a source of his appeal, and a factor in his defeat. As Myrdal observed, this Jamaican 'outsider':

> denounced practically the whole Negro leadership. They were bent upon cultural assimilation; they were all looking for support and they were making a compromise between accommodation and protest. Within a short time he succeeded in making enemies of practically all Negro intellectuals. Against him were mobilized most leaders in the Negro schools, the Negro organizations and the Negro press. He heartily responded by naming them opportunists, liars, thieves, traitors and bastards.[72]

On a visit to Jamaica in 1965, a notable black American placed a wreath on Garvey's memorial, and informed his audience:

> Marcus Garvey was the first man of colour in the history of the United States to lead and develop a mass movement. He was the first man on a mass scale and level to give millions of Negroes a sense of dignity and destiny, and make the Negro feel he is somebody. You gave Marcus Garvey to the United States of America, and gave to millions of Negroes... a sense of personhood, a sense of manhood, and a sense of somebodiness.[73]

The speaker on that occasion was Dr Martin Luther King, Jr.

REFERENCES

1. Isaacs, H. R., *The New World of Negro Americans* (London, 1964), p.19.
2. Jacques-Garvey, A., *Garvey and Garveyism* (Kingston, Jamaica, 1963), p.27.

3. Johnson, J. W., *Black Manhattan*, op. cit., p.147.
4. McKay, C., *Harlem: Negro Metropolis* (New York, 1940), p.143.
5. Jacques-Garvey, A. (ed.), *Philosophy and Opinions of Marcus Garvey* (New York, 1969), p.124.
6. Ibid., p.125.
7. Hill, R. A. (ed.), *The Marcus Garvey and Universal Negro Improvement Association Papers*, Vol. I, 1826-August 1919 (University of California Press, 1983), p.5. (Cited hereafter as *Papers*.)
8. Jacques-Garvey, *Garvey and Garveyism*, op. cit., p.8.
9. Jacques-Garvey, *Philosophy and Opinions of Marcus Garvey*, op. cit., p.126.
10. Jacques-Garvey, *Garvey and Garveyism*, op. cit., p.11.
11. *Papers, Vol I*, (1983), p.54.
12. Ibid., pp.55, 61.
13. Ibid., p.116.
14. Harlan, L. R., *Booker T. Washington: Wizard of Tuskegee*, op. cit., p.281.
15. *Papers, Vol. I*, (1983), p.166.
16. Martin, T., *Race First: The Ideological and Organizational Struggles of Marcus Garvey and the UNIA* (Westport, Connecticut, 1976), pp.281–3.
17. Jacques-Garvey, *Philosophy and Opinions of Marcus Garvey*, op. cit., p.56.
18. Vincent, T., *Black Power and the Garvey Movement* (San Francisco, California, 1972), p.26.
19. *Papers, Vol. I*, (1983), p.146.
20. Jacques-Garvey, *Philosophy and Opinions of Marcus Garvey*, op. cit., pp.127–8.
21. Jacques-Garvey, *Garvey and Garveyism*, op. cit., p.31.
22. James, C. L. R., *Black Jacobins* (London, 1980), p.396.
23. *Papers, Vol. I*, (1983), pp.503, 505.
24. Jacques-Garvey, *Garvey and Garveyism*, op. cit., p.91.
25. Cronon, E. D., *Black Moses: The Story of Marcus Garvey and the Universal Negro Improvement Association* (University of Wisconsin Press, 1962), p.60.
26. Ibid., p.52.
27. Jacques-Garvey, *Garvey and Garveyism*, op. cit., p.86.
28. *Papers, Vol. II* (1983), p.566.
29. Ottley, R., *New World A-Coming* (New York, 1969), p.75.
30. *Papers, Vol. II* (1983), p.647.
31. Ibid., pp.442-43.
32. Ibid., p.482.
33. *Opportunity*, I (August, 1923), p.21.
34. *Papers, Vol. IV* (1985), p.709.

35. Ibid., pp.748–9.
36. Ibid., pp.758, 933.
37. Ibid., p.1037.
38. Moore, R. B., 'Critics and Opponents of Marcus Garvey' in Clarke, J. H. (ed.), *Marcus Garvey and the Vision of Africa* (New York, 1974), p.224.
39. Cronon, *Black Moses*, op. cit., p.129.
40. Jacques-Garvey, *Philosophy and Opinions Of Marcus Garvey*, op. cit., p.44.
41. Mays, B. E., *The Negro's God as Reflected in His Literature* (New York, 1938), pp.184–5.
42. Jacques-Garvey, *Philosophy and Opinions of Marcus Garvey*, op. cit., p.122.
43. Johnson, *Black Manhattan*, op. cit., p.97.
44. Jacques-Garvey, *Philosophy and Opinions of Marcus Garvey*, op. cit., p.97.
45. Wright, R., *American Hunger* (New York, 1977), pp.28–9.
46. Locke, A. (ed.), *The New Negro* (New York, 1980), pp.7–15.
47. Weiss, N. J., *The National Urban League 1910–1940* (New York, OUP, 1974), pp.148–9.
48. *Opportunity*, I (August, 1923), p.232.
49. *Messenger* (March, 1923), p.368.
50. Kornweibel, *No Crystal Stair: Black Life and the Messenger, 1917–1928* (Westport, Connecticut, 1975), p.148.
51. *Papers, Vol. I*, (1983), p.11.
52. Du Bois, *Dusk of Dawn*, op. cit., p.277.
53. Lester, J., (ed.), *The Seventh Son*, op. cit., II, pp.175–6.
54. Rampersad, A., *The Art and Imagination of W. E. B. Du Bois* (London, 1976), p.149.
55. Lester, *The Seventh Son*, op. cit., p.183.
56. *Papers, Vol. II* (1983), p.620.
57. Rudwick, E. M., *W. E. B. Du Bois*, op. cit., p.219.
58. Lester, *The Seventh Son*, op. cit., p.183.
59. Martin, *Race First*, op. cit., pp.297–9.
60. Jacques-Garvey, *Philosophy and Opinions of Marcus Garvey*, op. cit., pp.310–20.
61. Lester, *The Seventh Son*, op. cit., pp.184–6.
62. Martin, *Race First*, op. cit., pp.306–7.
63. Du Bois, W. E. B., *The World and Africa* (New York, 1947), p.236.
64. Bu Bois, *The Autobiography of W. E. B. Du Bois*, op. cit., pp.273–4.
65. Essien-Udom, E. U. and A. Jacques-Garvey (eds), *More Philosophy and Opinions of Marcus Garvey* (London, 1977), p.124.

66 Martin, *Race First*, op. cit., p.311.
67. Frazier, E. F., 'Garvey as a Mass Leader', *Nation* (18 August 1926), pp.147–8.
68. Powell, A. C. Snr, *Against the Tide* (New York, 1938), pp.70–71.
69. McKay, C., 'Garvey as a Negro Moses' in W. Cooper (ed.), *The Passion of Claude McKay* (New York, 1973), pp.65–9.
70. Johnson, *Black Manhattan*, op. cit., pp.256–7.
71. Frazier, E. F., *Black Bourgeoisie: The Rise of a New Middle Class* (Toronto, 1965), p. 250.
72. Myrdal, *An American Dilemma*, op. cit., p.746.
73. Barrett, L. E., *Soul Force: African Heritage in Afro-American Religion* (New York, 1974), p.151.

CHAPTER FIVE

Martin Luther King, Jr: Apostle for Non-Violence

Redemptive suffering had always been the part of Martin's argument which I found difficult to accept. I had seen distress fester souls and bend peoples' bodies out of shape, but I had yet to see anyone redeemed from pain, by pain. [MAYA ANGELOU][1]

In 1960, my mother bought a television set...one day, there appeared the face of Dr Martin Luther King, Jr. What a funny name, I thought. At the moment I first saw him, he was being handcuffed and shoved into a police truck. He had dared to claim his rights as a native son, and had been arrested. He displayed no fear, but seemed calm, serene, unaware of his own extraordinary courage....At the moment I saw his resistance I knew I would never be able to live in this country without resisting everything that sought to disinherit me....He Was The One, The Hero, The One Fearless Person for whom we had waited

[ALICE WALKER][2]

PERSPECTIVES: A NEW DEAL FOR BLACKS? CIVIL RIGHTS AND NEGRO PROTEST, 1932–1954

For most black Americans, the collapse of the economy after 1929 simply aggravated an already desperate situation. Black unemployment figures were vastly out of proportion to their percentage of the population. In 1933, an Urban League report indicated that over 17 per cent of the entire Negro population was on relief (as contrasted with less than 10 per cent of the total white population). Conditions were equally bad in the North and the South, but in the Southern states, private charity organizations often refused to aid blacks. In the Southern farm belts, black tenant farmers and share croppers went increasingly into debt. Those organizations traditionally concerned with black welfare – the NAACP and the National Urban League – were unable to cope with the emergency crisis produced by the Depression. Beginning in the South Side of Chicago, 'Jobs-for Negroes' campaigns – utilizing boycotts against producers and retailers of goods and services who did not pursue fair policies with respect to the employment of blacks – soon spread across the country, but encountered difficulties as white merchants obtained court injunctions prohibiting Negro organizations from picketing their establishments. The National Urban League, primarily concerned with economic matters, offered its services to the Republican president, Herbert Hoover, successfully petitioned for the inclusion of a Negro on the President's Emergency Committee for Unemployment, and sought a fair share of jobs and relief measures for blacks. But with whites now willing to take even the most menial positions, the NUL's emphasis shifted from expanding opportunities to retaining those low-level jobs blacks already held. Increasingly, the NUL became more reliant than ever on the white philanthropic foundations, but could do little to improve either the employment status or the prospects of blacks during the Depression.

During the late 1920s and early 1930s, the American Communist Party publicized injustices against blacks and attacked the black bourgeoisie, and Negro protest organizations, but failed to attract a mass following. The National Negro Congress, with A. Philip Randolph as its first president, was formed in 1936. A Communist-inspired movement, critical of the conservatism of the NAACP and the NUL, it was to founder after the Soviet-Nazi non-aggression pact of 1939, when Randolph and other black leaders withdrew their support.

It was the election of the Democrat Franklin D. Roosevelt in 1932, with his promise of a 'New Deal', that raised black hopes and marked a turning point in American race relations. (Yet even the Depression had not immediately shaken the traditional Republican loyalties of Negroes. In the 1932 presidential election, blacks in Detroit, Cleveland, Philadelphia and other major cities voted for Herbert Hoover.) By 1934, the Negro vote began switching to the Democrats and in 1936, according to one estimate, 84.7 per cent of blacks favoured Roosevelt's re-election. Although New Deal reform policies and governmental agencies were not free of racial discrimination (and no major piece of civil rights legislation was adopted during Roosevelt's four terms of office), blacks shared in New Deal relief measures, and the administration eventually appointed black advisers in the major departments. Mary McLeod Bethune was made director of the

Division of Negro Affairs of the National Youth Administration, William H. Hastie served in various capacities, including that of civilian aide to the Secretary of War in the early years of World War II, and Robert C. Weaver was adviser to the Department of the Interior. If these appointments were largely symbolic, they were also the highest positions held by blacks in the federal government since the administration of William Howard Taft. But Roosevelt, although the most attractive president to black Americans since Abraham Lincoln, was a consummate politician, keenly aware that he must not offend Southern sensibilities on race issues because of his dependence on Southern Democratic votes in Congress for the passage of New Deal legislation. Yet precisely because blacks did benefit from New Deal measures, particularly in the areas of housing, education, health and labour, the established black protest organizations attempted to bring increased pressure on the government to make New Deal policies and programmes even more responsive to black needs.

In 1933, following an NAACP initiative, various race advancement organizations established the Joint Committee on National Recovery to fight discriminatory practices in federal relief agencies. The emergence of the Congress of Industrial Organizations (CIO) saw an attempt by the American Federation of Labour, under the leadership of John Lewis of the United Mine Workers, to organize black skilled and unskilled workers into industrial unions. The NAACP, in response, reversed its critical stance toward organized labour, and worked to build an alliance with the CIO. There was also a significant increase in the size of the black electorate in the North during the Roosevelt era, and the mobilization of organizations in the South to promote black voter registration. Again, Roosevelt's appointments to the Supreme Court of justices generally sympathetic to civil rights resulted in the gradual ending of such discriminatory practices as segregation in interstate transportation and inequalities in the pay of black and white school teachers. Eleanor Roosevelt also promoted civil rights causes. In 1938 at the opening session of the Southern Conference for Human Welfare in Birmingham, Alabama, Mrs Roosevelt defied a local segregation ordinance by taking a seat on the 'coloured' side of the auditorium. The following year, when the ultra-conservative Daughters of the American Revolution refused to let the black contralto, Marian Anderson, perform at Constitutional Hall in Washington, DC, Mrs Roosevelt resigned from the DAR, and arranged for Miss Anderson to give her concert from the steps of the Lincoln Memorial. In the election of 1940 black voters overwhelmingly supported Roosevelt for a third term.

However, the New Deal, although it raised black hopes, failed to satisfy them. A 1937 conference, sponsored by the National Youth Administration and organized by Mary McLeod Bethune, concluded that the majority of blacks still faced the problems of unemployment and lack of economic security, inadequate recreational and educational facilities, poor health and housing, and the continuing fear of mob violence. Two years later, another conference concluded that certain measures were imperative if there was to be any meaningful improvement in the status of blacks. These included federal legislation to outlaw lynching, the unrestricted use of the vote, the elimination of discrimination in the federal civil service, the expansion of low-rent housing, the extension of social security coverage to domestic and agricultural workers, additional black appointments to federal policy-making bodies and the expansion of federally-funded work-relief programmes. In 1940 the NAACP, in a *Crisis* editorial, commended Roosevelt for having included blacks in New Deal programmes, but condemned his failure to support a federal anti-lynching bill, and the persistence of racial discrimination in civilian life and in the United States armed forces.

On the eve of American involvement in World War II, black protest organizations were united in demanding full and equal participation in the military, and an end to discriminatory practices in the defence industries – which offered new employment opportunities for the blacks. Some sections of the black press came to adopt a more conciliatory tone, arguing (after the Japanese attack on Pearl Harbor) that the national crisis demanded that civil rights agitation should be suspended (or at least muted) for the duration of the war. More radical black leaders disagreed.

The March on Washington Movement (MOWM) was the most striking demonstration of more aggressive trends in black protest thought and action. In fact, the idea of exerting mass pressure on the government to end discrimination in the defence industries did not originate with A. Philip Randolph's call for a march on Washington, D.C. in early 1941. Agitation for mass pressure of some kind had grown since the failure of black leaders to gain any major concessions from Roosevelt in 1940, with protest meetings around the country sponsored by the NAACP and the Committee for the Participation of Negroes in National Defence. But in January 1941, Randolph suggested that 10,000 Negroes march on the nation's capital with the slogan: 'We loyal Americans demand the right to work and fight for our country'.

The MOWM – which was conceived as an all-black action on the part and on behalf of the black masses – anticipated the forms of black protest of the 1950s and 1960s. In the event, the March on Washington did not take place. Roosevelt issued Executive Order 8802 in June 1941, which stipulated that there should be no more discrimination in the defence industries 'because of race, creed, or national origin'. Yet the original MOWM agenda had also included the demand for an executive order forbidding the awarding of government contracts to firms practicing racial discrimination in their hiring practices, and a similar order ending segregation and discrimination in the armed forces and in all departments of the federal government, as well as a request for legislation forbidding the benefits of the National Labour Relations Act to unions denying Negro membership. In 1943 A. Philip Randolph began to plan a strategy of civil disobedience (based on the Gandhian example in India), to attack segregation and discrimination in the Northern states.

Gandhi's philosophy and techniques were also reflected in the formation of the Congress of Racial Equality (CORE) in 1942. Founded by James Farmer, a black Louisianan, and members of the Fellowship of Reconciliation (FOR), a Quaker pacifist social action organization, CORE was chiefly responsible for pioneering the use of non-violent protest as a civil rights strategy. CORE engaged in its first 'sit-in' in 1943, when Farmer and an interracial group of members employed the tactic against a Chicago restaurant which had refused to serve blacks. In 1947 CORE sponsored a 'Journey of Reconciliation' – a forerunner of the 1961 'Freedom Rides' – through the Upper South to test compliance with the Supreme Court decision, a year earlier, in *Morgan v. Virginia*, banning segregation in interstate transportation. CORE was to remain active in the direct-action protests of the 1950s and 1960s, concentrating its efforts on voter-registration drives in the Southern states. (In 1964 two CORE staff members, James Chaney and Michael Schwerner, together with Andrew Goodman, were abducted and murdered in Philadelphia, Mississippi – an episode recently portrayed in the movie 'Mississippi Burning'.)

World War II had created a climate in which blacks (and some whites) perceived possibilities for decisive changes in race relations. Black membership of labour unions and employment in white-collar and semi-skilled jobs increased, while returning black veterans, after 1945, spurred the increasing demands for civil rights. The heightened expectations of blacks, the growing importance of the Negro vote, and continuing migration out of the South combined to produce some improvements in several areas. In the South itself the number of blacks registered to vote increased from 2 to 12 per cent in the years 1940–47. Roosevelt's successor, Harry Truman, who appointed the President's Committee on Civil Rights in 1946, was the first president to address the NAACP, and urged a variety of civil rights measures on a Congress controlled by Southern Democrats and conservative Republicans. In response to the wartime complaints of black troops who had faced discriminatory and segregationist practices, Truman issued Executive Order 9981 in 1948, which called for 'equality of opportunity for all persons in the armed forces, without regard to race, colour, or national origin'. Although sections of the military were slow to implement the policy, by the time of the Korean War there was a substantial measure of racial integration in the armed forces.

In the presidential election of 1948 Truman's espousal of civil rights reforms provoked conservative Southern Democrats to bolt the party and form the 'Dixiecrat' party, which carried four Southern states for its candidate, Strom Thurmond. With the aid of a majority of black votes in the electorally crucial states of the North, Truman beat his Republican opponent, Thomas Dewey, but continued to face a Congress that was recalcitrant on racial matters. In fact, Truman's actual commitment to civil rights issues was very thin. In the 1948 presidential election he had tried to appease Southern Democrats on civil rights issues. During the Korean War, when he had the opportunity to create a wartime Fair Employment Practices Committee, Truman refused to do so. Again, more could have been done, through the use of Justice Department attorneys, to prosecute violators of civil rights in the South. But, during the same period, the Supreme Court of the United States was beginning to hand down decisions which were sympathetic to black aspirations.

In 1938 the Court had made an initial move against the doctrine of 'separate but equal' when it ruled that in failing to provide a law school for blacks, Missouri was in violation of the 14th Amendment, and in a 1950 ruling, the Court ordered the state of Texas to admit blacks to the university law school. NAACP attorneys, together with sympathetic black and white historians (including John Hope Franklin and C. Vann Woodward) and eminent sociologists, pushed the Court repeatedly on the 'separate but equal' principle. In 1954 Earl Warren – appointed as a Supreme Court justice by the racially conservative president Eisenhower – handed down the historic 'Brown' decision which held that separate educational facilities were 'inherently unequal' and, in the following year, ordered schools desegregation to proceed with 'all deliberate speed', provoking massive and well-organized opposition in the South. The Court's ruling in *'Brown versus Board of Education'* marked the triumphant conclusion of the NAACP's long campaign against segregated schools, and overturned the *'Plessy versus Ferguson'* decision of 1896. The Brown decision was immediately recognized – by its supporters and opponents – as a landmark step in American race relations, since it appeared to remove constitutional sanctions for the whole system of racial segregation and Jim Crow laws.

Eisenhower himself was largely indifferent (and frequently hostile) to black civil rights. In 1956 he campaigned throughout the South in an attempt to win segregationist votes. Ironically, he was compelled to use executive authority to implement the 1954 decision when Governor Orville Faubus of Arkansas, in September 1957, carried defiance of the ruling to the point of using state militia to halt token integration at Little Rock High School. Faubus removed the troops on court order, but when hysterical white mobs forced the removal of nine black children, Eisenhower ordered in federal troops to enforce the law. (Little Rock schools were closed in 1958–59, and blacks did not actually attend Little Rock High School until August 1959). Other Southern state governors employed less violent (but more effective) methods to circumvent the Brown decision – for example, providing state money to enable any white student 'threatened' with integration to attend a private school, or to allow any school district to close its schools if desegregation was against local community wishes.

In the face of executive disinterest and Southern white intransigence, Southern blacks became increasingly active. As a younger generation of black activists began to challenge racial discrimination and segregation in the South, they faced not only the opposition of a majority of whites, but also that of black 'conservatives' – the older-established leadership class which had practiced the politics of conciliation, caution and restraint in their dealings with the white power structure.

In Montgomery, Alabama, 'the cradle of the Confederacy', Jo Ann Gibson Robinson, an instructor in English at Alabama State College and an active member of Dexter Avenue Baptist Church, was president of the Women's Political Council (WPC), a local black women's organization founded in 1946 by one of her colleagues, Mrs Mary Fair Burks, when the local League of Women Voters had refused to integrate. In 1953 the WPC met with the City Commission to lodge complaints about the treatment of black passengers on the city's buses, a principal source of friction being the bus company's loosely defined seating policy which varied from route to route and driver to driver. Blacks were frequently required to shift their seats when peremptorily commanded to do so by white drivers. They were also compelled to get on at the front door of buses to pay their fare, and then get off and then reboard at the back door, instead of simply being allowed to walk down the aisle. Drivers sometimes moved off before black passengers had time to reboard. In 1954 Claudette Colvin, a 15 year-old black girl had refused to vacate her seat when ordered to do so by a driver and had been placed on probation. In May of that year Mrs Robinson, on behalf of the WPC, had written to Montgomery mayor W. A. 'Tacky' Gayle, insisting upon better conditions for black passengers on the city's buses, and threatened a boycott if significant improvements were not forthcoming.

On 1 December 1955, six days after the Interstate Commerce Commission banned segregation on all vehicles and in all facilities engaged in interstate travel, Mrs Rosa L. Parks, a 43-year old black seamstress in a downtown Montgomery store, refused a bus driver's orders to vacate her seat to a white man. A high school graduate and a former secretary of the local chapter of the NAACP, Mrs Parks had been ejected from Montgomery buses on several occasions for refusing to obey the Alabama segregation ordinance. This ordinance required blacks to give up their seats for whites, if ordered to do so by (white) bus drivers, acting under the provisions of a 1945 Alabama state statute which required the Alabama Public Service Commission to enforce racially-segregated seating by all bus companies under its jurisdiction. (Mrs Parks had also attended a workshop at the Highlander Folk School, founded by Myles Horton, a teacher and community activist, during the Great Depression. At Highlander, black and white labour and civil rights workers were trained in protest techniques, and, in 1955, Highlander instituted a programme in which black adults learned the rudiments of literacy – thereby qualifying them to vote.) On this occasion, however, she was arrested, charged with breaking a city segregation law, and fined $14.00. Following Mrs Parks' arrest, Jo Ann Gibson Robinson drafted, mimeographed and, with the help of her students, distributed a leaflet calling for a boycott of the bus company. As Mrs Robinson later recalled: 'We had planned the protest long before Mrs Parks was arrested. There had been so many things that happened, that black women had been embarrassed over, and they were ready to explode.' The leaflet read in part:

> Another Negro woman has been arrested and thrown in jail because she refused to get up out of her seat on the bus for a white person to sit down....If we do not do something to stop these arrests, they will continue. The next time it may be you, or your daughter, or mother....We are, therefore, asking every Negro to stay off the buses Monday in protest of the arrest and trial. Don't ride the buses to work, to town, to school or to anywhere on Monday....Please stay off all buses on Monday.

Mrs Robinson, recalling the episode, also remembered that before writing the leaflet, she had written some notes 'on the back of an envelope':

> The Women's Political Council will not wait for Mrs Parks' consent to call for a boycott of the city buses. On Friday, December 2, 1955, the women of Montgomery will call for a boycott to take place on Monday, December 5.[3]

Edgar D. Nixon, president of the local chapter of the International Brotherhood of Sleeping Car Porters, and a dominant figure in the Montgomery NAACP, remembered calling on Mrs Parks after her arrest and telling her: 'We can break this situation on the bus with your case'. After talking to her husband and mother, Mrs Parks replied: 'You know, Mr Nixon, if you say so, I'll go along with it'.[4] Following the initiative of Mrs Robinson and the WPC, and under the direction of E. D. Nixon, a group of black ministers formed the Montgomery Improvement Association (MIA) to direct and coordinate what became a 382-day boycott of the City Lines bus company, owned by the Chicago-based National City Lines. Nixon and Robinson shrewdly recognized that blacks could be more effectively organized for a mass protest through the indigenous black church, which bridged social classes and political factions – than through a secular movement. Again, the facilities of the black churches – in providing meeting-places and fund-raising machinery – were particularly important in a community which did not have a black-owned radio station or newspaper. The majority of bus passengers were blacks, and the company stood to lose $3,000 a day in revenues, the city of Montgomery part of its $20,000 a year in taxes on the bus line, and Montgomery department stores could anticipate over one million dollars in lost sales, if the proposed boycott proved effective.

The original demands of the MIA, however, were quite modest, and had been accepted by other Southern municipalities: two years earlier, blacks in Baton Rouge, Louisiana had boycotted the city's buses and forced an agreement that passengers would be given 'first come, first served' segregated seating. The MIA asked for greater courtesy from bus drivers; the hiring of black drivers on predominantly black routes, the seating of blacks from the back toward the front of buses and whites from the front to the back, without a section always to be kept clear for each race. Essentially, then, the initial thrust of the Montgomery bus boycott was for *modification* of segregationist practices. Montgomery whites, however, were not prepared to compromise on racial segregation, and the MIA, through a law suit, came to demand the elimination of segregation on the city's buses. By charging Mrs Parks with violating the segregated transportation statute, the Montgomery authorities inadvertently made possible an appeal to a federal court and, ultimately, to the Supreme Court, challenging the constitutionality of segregation in interstate transportation.

Martin Luther King, Jr, a twenty-six year old Negro minister, who had arrived in Montgomery from Atlanta only a year before, was unanimously elected to preside over the MIA. E. D. Nixon agreed to serve as treasurer, but refused to run for the presidency of the new organization because he would be away from Montgomery for long periods on railroad business. By all accounts, including his own, King was surprised to gain leadership of the MIA. During his first year in Montgomery, he had concentrated his energies on his pastorate of the Dexter Avenue Baptist Church, serving a black middle-class congregation (which included faculty members of Alabama State College), and on completing his doctoral dissertation. King later recalled that his election as MIA president 'caught me unawares. It happened so quickly I did not even have time to think it through. It is probable that if I had, I would have declined the nomination.'[5] In fact, a month before his nomination, King had refused the presidency of the city chapter of the NAACP, had not engaged in any organized civil rights protest, and had not met Mrs Parks. But on several counts, King was an ideal choice for the MIA presidency. As a relative newcomer, he was not involved in the factionalism of local black politics, and had not been compromised by his dealings with the white community. His selection also reflected hostility within the MIA to the Reverend L. Roy Bennett, a Methodist minister, and president of the Interdenominational Ministerial Alliance. In addition, as E. D. Nixon recognized, King possessed the personal and educational qualities necessary in a leader who would have to conduct negotiations at a high level. In other respects, however, Martin Luther King, Jr was an unknown quantity. The Montgomery bus boycott was to make him into a figure of national (and international) stature. In his first (hastily-prepared) speech as leader of the MIA, King issued a ringing call to action, coupled with a plea for an orderly protest:

> We are here this evening to say to those who have mistreated us for so long that we are tired – tired of being segregated and humiliated; tired of being kicked about by the brutal feet of oppression....For many years we have shown amazing patience. We have sometimes given our white brothers the feeling that we like the way we were being treated. But we come here tonight to be saved from that patience that makes us patient with anything less than freedom and justice...if you will protest courageously and yet with dignity and Christian love, when the history books are written in future generations the historians will pause and say: 'There lived a great people – a black people – who injected new meaning and dignity into the veins of civilization.' This is our challenge and our overwhelming responsibility.[6]

MARTIN LUTHER KING, JR: THE MAKING OF A LEADER

The son of a sharecropper who had attended Morehouse College and entered the Baptist ministry, Martin Luther King, Jr was born in Atlanta, Georgia. His maternal grandfather, the Reverend Alfred Daniel Williams, had founded the Ebenezer Baptist Church, and Martin Luther King, Sr, a forceful preacher, member of the NAACP, and an active Republican, was a strong personality. Martin Luther King, Jr, grew up in a close-knit, middle-class and deeply religious family, and seemed himself destined for the ministry. At the age of fifteen he entered Morehouse College in Atlanta, where he was influenced by its president, Benjamin E. Mays, a leading black theologian and church historian. Mays' attacks on racial injustice, and his beliefs in Christian social responsibility and political engagement greatly impressed King (who had considered law or medicine), and he elected to continue the family tradition and become a Baptist minister. At Morehouse, King read Henry David Thoreau's classic essay *Civil Disobedience*, and accepted its central assertion that the individual should refuse to cooperate with an evil system, and is entitled to disobey unjust laws.

In 1948 King graduated from Morehouse with a degree in sociology, and enrolled at Crozer Theological Seminary in Chester, Pennsylvania, to study for the ministry. At Crozer, he was introduced to the writings of the Social Gospel theologian Walter Rauschenbusch, and endorsed his contention that the church should concern itself with social conditions, as well as with the salvation of souls. In his first book, an account of the Montgomery bus boycott, King asserted:

> It has been my conviction ever since reading Rauschenbusch, that any religion which professes to be concerned about the souls of men and is not concerned about the social and economic conditions that scar that soul, is a spiritually moribund religion.

At Crozer, King also became interested in the teachings of Mohandas K. Gandhi, after he heard a lecture in Philadelphia, delivered by Mordecai W. Johnson, president of Howard University, who had recently returned from a trip to India. Already a declared pacifist, King added Gandhi's philosophy of non-violent resistance to injustice to his intellectual system, and later came to celebrate the redemptive power of love and suffering as forces for social change. King was to write that:

> Gandhi was probably the first person in history to lift the love ethic of Jesus above mere interaction between individuals to a powerful and effective force on a large scale. It was in this Gandhian emphasis on love and nonviolence that I discovered the method of social reform for which I had been seeking. I came to feel that this was the only morally and practically sound method open to oppressed people in their struggle for freedom. My study of Gandhi convinced me that true pacifism is not nonresistance to evil, but nonviolent resistance to evil.

As a student, King was introduced to the writings of the American Protestant theologian Reinhold Niebuhr's concept of 'collective evil' (but did not accept Niebuhr's break with pacifism), and rejected Marxism as atheistic and materialistic – although he endorsed its social concerns, and believed that 'Communism grew as a protest against the hardships of the underprivileged'.[7] After a distinguished career at Crozer, King entered the doctoral programme at Boston University in 1951. Here he met and married Coretta Scott, from Alabama, then a student at the New England Conservatory of Music. Before completing his PhD thesis on the opposing theological views of Paul Tillich and Henry Nelson Wieman, King was offered and accepted a pastorship at the Dexter Avenue Baptist Church in Montgomery. In addition to his intellectual abilities and credentials, King brought to his first appointment a love for the South, a supportive wife, and a social philosophy based on a belief in Christian activism. As leader of the MIA, he quickly came to display considerable powers as an orator and public performer – qualities which were to distinguish his subsequent career as the prophet and practitioner of non-violent resistance to denials of civil and human rights.

As president of the MIA, which included twenty black ministers in its membership, King, (who was aware that their initial demands did not meet the NAACP's minimum standard for racial integration) united and inspired the boycott movement. When Montgomery blacks followed the call not to ride on the city's buses, the MIA created and maintained a car pool, which gave more affluent Negroes an opportunity to participate in the protest by giving lifts to the walkers. After Montgomery whites put pressure on insurance companies to cancel the policies of these motorists offering their services to the MIA, the organization turned to Lloyd's of London for coverage. When an attempt to divide the black community into its traditional factions failed, the mayor and city fathers resorted to other tactics. King was arrested for an alleged speeding offence (and jailed for the first time in his life), and in January 1956 his house was bombed. On 21 February, a Montgomery Grand Jury indicted 115 blacks for allegedly breaking a 1921 anti-labour law which held that it was illegal to injure a legitimate business enterprise without 'just cause or legal excuse'. Faced by such provocations, King continued to preach a message of non-violent resistance, and the boycott began to attract national support and financial donations from various sources including the NAACP, the United Auto Workers and overseas.

During this period, King also developed a close working relationship with Ralph Abernathy, Negro pastor of the First Baptist Church, and an activist preacher. Following the attack on his home, King was visited by Bayard Rustin, and Glenn E. Smiley, members of the Fellowship of Reconciliation, admirers of Gandhi and followers of the American pacifist, A. J. Muste. But, according to his own account, it was a white woman, Miss Juliette Morgan, in a letter to the *Montgomery Advertizer*, who first alerted King to the parallels between the bus boycott and Gandhi's strategy in India:

> The Negroes of Montgomery seem to have taken a lesson from Gandhi – and our own Thoreau, who influenced Gandhi. Their task is greater than Gandhi's, however, for they have greater prejudice to overcome. One feels that history is being made in Montgomery these days. It is hard to imagine a soul so dead, a heart so hard, a vision so blinded and provincial as not to be moved with admiration at the quiet dignity, discipline and dedication with which the Negroes have conducted their boycott.

King remembered that Miss Morgan 'sensitive and frail, did not long survive the rejection and condemnation of the white community', but that before her death in 1957:

> ...the name of Mahatma Gandhi was well-known in Montgomery. Non-violent resistance had emerged as the technique of the movement, while love stood as the regulating ideal. Christ furnished the spirit and motivation, while Gandhi furnished the method. This philosophy was disseminated mainly through the regular mass meetings which were held in the various Negro churches of the city.[8]

Despite a Supreme Court ruling against segregation on interstate buses in South Carolina, the Montgomery city government obtained a local court injunction ordering it to continue the practice. On 4 June 1956 a Federal District Court ruled that the city ordinance violated the United States Constitution, but the city appealed, and the boycott continued. However, as King and his associates were awaiting a court decision regarding the continuing operation of the car pool, news came of the United States' Supreme Court decision declaring Alabama's state and local laws upholding segregation on the buses to be unconstitutional. King and the MIA now worked to prepare the black community for the arrival of the desegregation order, and urged blacks to behave courteously when they went back on the buses. They were instructed to 'read, study and memorize' a list of 'Integrated Bus Suggestions' which included the following:

> Pray for guidance and commit yourself to complete non-violence as you enter the bus. Be quiet but friendly; proud but not arrogant; joyous, but not boisterous. If cursed, do not curse back. If pushed, do not push back. If struck, do not strike back, but evidence love and goodwill at all times.[9]

Montgomery's buses were desegregated, but there was retaliatory violence against blacks, and Negro churches in the city were firebombed. But for King, the boycott provided a demonstration and vindication of the efficiency of non-violent direct action. While the boycott was still in progress, he declared:

We now know that the Southern Negro has become of age, politically and morally. Montgomery has demonstrated that we will not run from the struggle, and will support the battle for equality. This is a protest – a *non-violent* protest against injustice. We are depending on moral and spiritual forces...this is a movement of passive resistance, and the great instrument is the instrument of love...no matter what sacrifices we have to make, we will not let anybody drag us down so low as to hate them.[10]

Rufus A. Lewis, former football coach at Alabama State College, a successful businessman, and chairman of the Citizens' Steering Committee formed in 1953 to press for better treatment of Montgomery's blacks, believed that King's 'greatest contribution' to the boycott 'was interpreting the situation to the mass of the people. He could speak better than any man I've ever heard in expressing to the people their problem and making them see clearly what the situation was and inspiring them to work at it.'[11] Yet there is also evidence to suggest that the mass of Montgomery blacks, although supporting the boycott, were confused by or indifferent to the Gandhian gloss which King (with the advice of Rustin and Smiley) attempted to put on the movement. In retrospect, it is clear that the Montgomery boycott was a seminal event, yet it did not touch off a national Negro revolt. Refusing to ride the buses, although a form of direct action, was also an essentially conservative protest – the withdrawal of patronage, an act of omission rather than one of commission. It involved participants in considerable hardship and inconvenience, but little actual physical danger. Again, the boycott had been initiated by the Women's Political Council and Mrs Robinson, and not by the black ministers of Montgomery. In effect, they were presented with a *fait accompli*, and as Mrs Robinson wryly observes after her circular was made public:

It was then that the ministers decided that it was time for them, the leaders, to catch up with the masses....Had they not done so, they might have alienated themselves from their congregations.[12]

THE SOUTHERN CHRISTIAN LEADERSHIP CONFERENCE

In 1957 King and other black clergymen, with the advice of Bayard Rustin and Stanley Levison, a white New York attorney, formed the Southern Christian Leadership Conference (SCLC), to spread and coordinate the strategy of non-violent civil rights protest across the South. Its statement of purpose declared that:

> SCLC believes that the American dilemma in race relations can best and most quickly be resolved through the actions of thousands of people, committed to the philosophy of nonviolence, who will physically identify themselves in a just and moral struggle. SCLC is firmly opposed to segregation in any form...and pledges itself to work unrelentingly to rid every vestige of its scars from our nation through nonviolent means. Our ultimate goal is genuine intergroup and interpersonal living – *integration*.[13]

An unstructured and unorthodox organization, SCLC did not offer individual memberships – wishing to avoid direct competition with the NAACP. (Many of SCLC's founders were members of the NAACP.) Baptist ministers were heavily represented in SCLC affiliates, and provided the leadership of the organization, but were atypical of a group which, drawing its salaries and support from the black community, was traditionally conservative, possessing a vested interest in the racial *status quo*. For the remainder of his life, King was to be identified with the SCLC, while the organization itself deliberately capitalized on King's growing fame and prestige.

Bayard Rustin and Stanley Levison also urged King to remain non-partisan, since there was little fundamental difference between the Republicans and Democrats on civil rights issues. SCLC, they believed, in stressing non-violence and Christian principles, would appeal to a wide liberal constituency. In May 1957 King (as part of SCLC strategy to present him as a national figure) attended a 'Prayer Pilgrimage' to Washington, D.C., in the company of Roy Wilkins, executive secretary of the NAACP, and A. Philip Randolph. The event attracted little media attention, but King received the greatest ovation after an address in which he demanded that blacks now be given the ballot to enforce their constitutional rights.

The SCLC's original aim of spreading the Montgomery example by supporting similar boycotts in other cities had met with little success, and in Montgomery the MIA did little to challenge directly other forms of segregation. Believing that Southern whites were less opposed to black voting rights than desegregation, the SCLC, during its first three years, engaged in an (unsuccessful) effort to double the number of black voters in the South. Ella Baker, the SCLC's temporary executive director (and the only woman on its board), initiated this 'Crusade for Citizenship', but with inadequate financial resources and lack of effective organization at the local levels, little was achieved. Baker (who believed that mass protest movements should be organized from the grass-roots level) became increasingly critical of King's leadership abilities, and regarded him as pompous and condescending toward women. Certainly before 1960 SCLC was inadequately staffed and, without a clearly-defined purpose, undecided as to whether to instigate its own protests or simply to assist in local actions.

In 1959 after surviving a stabbing by a deranged black woman as he was signing copies of *Stride Toward Freedom* in a New York bookstore, King (who had earlier visited Ghana, Nigeria and several European capitals, including London) made a spiritual pilgrimage to India, and went to Gandhi's shrine. The Indian visit was a significant event in King's intellectual and political growth. In particular, he was impressed by prime minister Nehru's explanation that under the Indian constitution, caste discrimination was punishable by imprisonment, and concluded that India had made greater progress against the iniquitous caste system than had the United States against racial discrimination. He returned to America with the renewed conviction that non-violent resistance 'is the most potent weapon available to the oppressed people in their struggle for freedom'.[14]

In November 1959 King resigned as Pastor of Dexter Avenue Church, and moved to Atlanta to concentrate his energies on the SCLC. Its strategy for the election year 1960 was to continue with the voter registration drive, together with direct-action protests against segregation. With many of Atlanta's established black leaders hostile to civil rights agitation (and with his father resident in the city as well), King diplomatically agreed that the SCLC would not undertake any protests there.

It was the 'sit-in' movement, pioneered at Greensboro, North Carolina, in February 1960, when four black students from the North Carolina Agricultural and Technical College sat down at a Woolworth's lunch counter and demanded service, that had already inaugurated a new – and more aggressive – phase of the civil rights struggle. Various forms of non-violent direct action protests, utilizing the Greensboro strategy, quickly followed – 'wade-ins' at municipal swimming pools and segregated beaches, 'stand-ins' at theatres refusing to sell tickets to blacks, and 'pray-ins' at segregated churches. Many of the student activists had been inspired by the Montgomery boycott and had read King's account, *Stride Toward Freedom*. In turn, King was aware that a new element had been injected into the black protest movement, and was concerned to retain the influence of the SCLC in the face of growing competition (and rivalry) among civil rights organizations.

When Ella Baker arranged a meeting of student leaders at Shaw University in Raleigh, North Carolina in April 1960, out of which emerged the Student Nonviolent Coordinating Committee (SNCC), King attempted to mould the movement in the image of the SCLC, which initially accepted (and adopted) his non-violent philosophy. King advised the student leaders to collect volunteers willing to go to jail rather than pay fines for alleged infractions of the law, to adhere to the doctrine of non-violence, and, by direct action protests, to compel the federal government to intervene in the civil rights struggle. Although it was soon to move beyond what it came to regard as King's cautious, conciliatory and unrealistic approach, SNCC, at its inception, embraced SCLC principles:

> We affirm the philosophical or religious ideal of non-violence as the foundation of our purpose, the presupposition of our faith, and the manner of our action. Non-violence as it grows from the Judaic-Christian tradition seeks a social order of justice permeated by love....Love is the central motif of non-violence. It matches the capacity of evil to inflict suffering with an even more enduring capacity to absorb evil, all the while persisting in love.[15]

Yet Ella Baker, aware of the growing dissatisfaction among the student generation with the established civil rights leadership, urged SNCC to maintain a separate identity. Diane Nash, a student at Fisk University in Nashville, and a leader in the student sit-in movement, recalled that Ella Baker 'was very important in giving direction to the student movement... in terms of seeing how important it was that the students should set the goals and directions and maintain control of the student movement'. After the founding of SNCC, Ella Baker noted that the conference had made it very apparent 'that the current sit-in and other demonstrations are concerned with something bigger than a hamburger. The Negro and white students, North and South, are seeking to rid America of the scourge of racial segregation and discrimination – not only at lunch counters but in every aspect of life.'[16]

MLK AND JFK

Whereas King had been unhappy with the record of the Eisenhower administration on civil rights – apart from the president's reluctant stand during the Little Rock crisis – he entertained greater hopes for the Democratic challenger in the 1960 election, John F. Kennedy. When King was given a four month prison sentence for an alleged driving offence in Georgia, he was released following Senator Kennedy's intervention. Although King himself did not officially come out for Kennedy, 'Daddy' King, in gratitude, reversed his traditional Republican loyalties and declared that he would be urging blacks to vote for the Democratic candidate, despite his Catholic faith. Certainly black support was crucial in Kennedy's narrow victory over Richard Nixon in 1960; a post-election Gallup poll indicated that Kennedy had received 68 per cent of the black vote.

But despite his declared commitment to civil rights, Kennedy did not keep his campaign promise to prohibit housing discrimination in federally-funded housing projects by executive order, and awarded three 'strict constructionists' to federal judgeships in the South. A month before Kennedy's inauguration civil rights activists gained a victory in the Supreme Court when it ruled that bus terminals serving interstate travellers must be integrated. In 1961 CORE sponsored a series of 'Freedom Rides' into the South to test compliance with the decision. When the Freedom Riders were met by white violence in Alabama and Mississippi, the Kennedy administration was forced to intervene to protect the riders, but, concerned not to alienate Southern Democrats, began to stress voter registration projects as a less provocative form of civil rights activity. King did not participate directly in the Freedom Rides, but quickly realized that the intensive press coverage of Southern attacks on the Freedom Riders should be utilized by SCLC and its allies, and he became involved in several forms of direct-action protest, with varying degrees of success and failure. SCLC, under Wyatt Walker, a Baptist minister, who replaced Ella Baker as executive director, determined to capitalize on King's image, and regain leadership of the civil rights coalition.

ALBANY AND BIRMINGHAM

From December 1961 to the summer of 1962, King and the SCLC led a mass direct-action campaign in Albany, Georgia, demanding not only integrated facilities, but employment for blacks in the city's police force and other municipal jobs. The Albany campaign failed because of divided energies and loyalties between the SCLC, SNCC and local blacks. James Forman of SNCC, suspicious of 'charismatic' leadership, did not want King in Albany, believing that blacks should rely on grass-roots organization. Although King was arrested and jailed, along with his supporters, police chief Laurie Pritchett did not employ violence against the demonstrators, thus denying them media exposure, and possible federal intervention. Again, attorneys for the city were able to secure a federal injunction that halted demonstrations for ten days, effectively sapping their momentum. Although King and Abernathy were given jail sentences (when they refused to pay $78 fines) for marching without permits, they were quickly released after Chief Pritchett arranged for payment of their fines. The city closed its parks rather than integrate them, and the town's library was 'integrated' only after all its chairs had been removed. As King later conceded, SCLC had gone into Albany inadequately briefed on the local situation.

But the lessons of Albany were well-learned, and SCLC's next campaign (already planned) was carefully executed. Within SCLC itself, new staff members, with direct experience of voter registration campaigns and Freedom Rides, made the organization more efficient and effective. New SCLC members included James Lawson, C. T. Vivian, James Bevel, Hosea Williams and Andrew Young. King himself had also come to realize that, in Bayard Rustin's words, 'protest becomes an effective tactic to the degree that it elicits brutality and oppression from the power structure', and privately conceded that the success of the 'non-violent' resistance depended on the existence (or fostering) of 'creative tension' – attacks by whites on demonstrators, coverage by the media, consequent national outrage and subsequent federal intervention. All of these ingredients were to be present in the Birmingham, Alabama campaign of 1962–3.

The South's major industrial city, Birmingham was also a stronghold of racial oppression, fully-fledged segregation and an administration pledged to resist even minimal change. Eugene 'Bull' Connor, Birmingham's police commissioner, exercised total power, and had earlier closed the city's parks to blacks in order to avoid integration. From 1957 to 1963 there were seventeen 'unsolved' bombings of Negro churches and the homes of local civil rights leaders. Inspired by the Montgomery boycott, the Reverend Fred Shuttlesworth, pastor of Baptist Bethel Church, had formed the Alabama Christian Movement for Human Rights (later an affiliate of the SCLC). With the support of local black college students, Shuttlesworth had led a boycott of Birmingham stores, in an effort to desegregate lunch counters and open up jobs for Negroes. Shuttlesworth invited King and the SCLC to come to Birmingham to focus and direct a campaign against the business community. King accepted, and decided to concentrate on three demands: the integration of lunch counters, fitting and restrooms and drinking fountains in department stores; the upgrading and hiring of blacks in business and industry, and the creation of a bi-racial committee to work out a time-table for desegregation in other areas of municipal life. Boycotts and sit-ins of down-town stores were to be combined with disruptive street demonstrations, and Wyatt Walker collected the names and addresses of 300 Birmingham residents prepared to go to jail. A. G. Gaston, a local black millionaire entrepreneur, provided the campaign with rent-free head quarters at his hotel, while outside support was organized by the black actor Harry Belafonte.

Demonstrations were twice postponed – once to allow for (abortive) negotiations with business leaders, and, a second time, to await the (disputed) outcome of a mayoralty election between commissioner 'Bull'

Connor, and a racial moderate, Albert Boutwell. When Connor obtained a court order enjoining all demonstrations pending a court decision, King (prepared to defy an injunction of a state rather than a federal court), marched on city hall, wearing the denim overalls that had become the field uniform of the SCLC. King was arrested and held for two days without being allowed to contact his wife or SCLC lawyers but, following the intervention of President Kennedy and his brother, Robert, the attorney general (neither of whom sympathized with the SCLC campaign), was allowed to communicate with Coretta and his attorneys.

When King's activities in Birmingham were criticized by eight white clergymen in the city, who described him as an extremist and outside agitator, and urged blacks to end their demonstrations, his response was to produce a classic statement on civil rights and non-violence. In 'Letter from Birmingham Jail', King asserted that he had been invited to the city by the Alabama Christian Movement for Human Rights, and claimed that no one could be an 'outsider' to injustice. He observed that direct action must always precede negotiation, and reiterated his belief in resistance to unjust laws. King expressed disappointment that his fellow (black and white) clergymen confused non-violence with extremism, and warned that black disaffection had already produced the Black Muslim sect 'made up of people who have lost faith in America, who have absolutely repudiated Christianity, and who have concluded that the white man is an incurable "devil"'. In contrast, King presented himself as a responsible moderate, as having 'tried to stand between these two forces saying that we need not follow the "do-nothingism" of the complacent or the hatred and despair of the black nationalist'.[17]

Released on bail after eight days in prison, King left Birmingham, and, in his absence, James Bevel put hundreds of black schoolchildren into direct confrontation with the white authorities. Bull Connor met the marchers with fire hoses, police dogs and clubs, and 2,500 were arrested and jailed. No serious injuries were inflicted on the marchers, but television and press coverage of the episode shocked the nation, with Bull Connor as the villain of the piece. The federal government was forced to act, and with the arrival of Burke Marshall, head of the Civil Rights Division of the Justice Department, negotiations were opened between the SCLC and the city government. The agreement finally reached fell short of the original SCLC demands. Stores agreed to desegregate their facilities, but only within ninety days, and accepted the 'gradual' hiring of black employees. It was the white business community, anxious to restore some measure of racial harmony (and prosperity) which pushed for the limited settlement. Again, the Birmingham agreement left untouched the issue of school desegregation, and some black leaders (including Fred

Shuttlesworth) accused King of accepting only token gains, when total victory could have been achieved by further protests. (Yet it was probable, as King believed, that continuing demonstrations would have been counter-productive.)

Whatever its limitations, the Birmingham campaign provoked the Kennedy administration into introducing civil rights legislation. In a television address, Kennedy acknowledged as much when he stated that: 'the events in Birmingham and elsewhere have so increased the cries for equality that no city or state or legislative body can prudently choose to ignore them'. Kennedy's successor, Lyndon Johnson, was finally to secure congressional cooperation resulting in the landmark Civil Rights Act of 1964, which not only included Kennedy's proposals but also gave the executive powers to withdraw federal funds from state and local governments practising discrimination. The Birmingham protest also atoned for the miscalculations of SCLC's Albany campaign, and propelled King into leadership of the civil rights coalition. A *Newsweek* opinion poll of blacks indicated that 95 per cent regarded King as their most successful spokesman.

In the March on Washington of August 1963, when a quarter of a million people (about 20 per cent of them white) converged on the capital in an effort to obtain passage of the Civil Rights bill, King delivered his 'I have a dream' oration – one of the great speeches of the twentieth century – from the steps of the Lincoln Memorial. Some of the impact of the speech (the 'dream' imagery of which King had already used in a speech in Detroit two months earlier) derived essentially from its context rather than from its contents. But the cadences of King's oratory, and the repetition of his central theme (not unlike that of a skilled jazz improviser), had a cathartic effect on his audience:

> I have a dream that one day on the red hills of Georgia the sons of former slaves and the sons of former slave holders will be able to sit down together at the table of brotherhood. I have a dream that one day even the state of Mississippi, a desert state sweltering with the heat of injustice and oppression, will be transformed into an oasis of freedom and justice....I have a dream that one day the state of Alabama, whose governor's lips are presently dripping with the words of interposition and nullification, will be transformed into a situation where little black boys and black girls will be able to join hands with little white boys and white girls and walk together as sisters and brothers.[18]

But not all of the marchers assembled at the Lincoln Memorial shared King's integrationist vision. John Lewis of SNCC had to be persuaded to modify his speech because SCLC leaders considered it too critical of the Kennedy administration. The young black civil rights activist Anne Moody remembered:

I sat on the grass and listened to the speakers, to discover we had 'dreamers' instead of leaders leading us. Martin Luther King went on and on talking about his dream. I sat there thinking that in Canton [Mississippi] we never had time to sleep, much less dream.[19]

In 1964 King appeared on the cover of *Time* magazine, in which he was credited with 'an indescribable capacity for empathy that is the touchstone of 'of leadership'. In the same year, King was awarded the Nobel Peace Prize. Significantly, in his acceptance speech, he linked the civil rights movement with the larger cause of world peace and human rights. Ironically, King was already under investigation by the FBI which, under J. Edgar Hoover's directive had begun to keep the SCLC under close surveillance because of alleged Communist infiltration of the organization (and also because of King's alleged philandering). Robert Kennedy, convinced that King's close associate and advisor, Stanley Levison, was an active member of the American Communist Party, had authorized FBI wiretaps on King.

ST AUGUSTINE, FREEDOM SUMMER AND SELMA

In 1964 the SCLC, anxious to induce Kennedy's successor, Lyndon Johnson, to secure passage of the Civil Rights bill, undertook a protest campaign in St Augustine, Florida. Wyatt Walker believed that the SCLC could exploit the city's dependence on tourism (and its expectation of federal funding for its 400th anniversary celebrations) by launching an attack against the discrimination faced by St Augustine's blacks, who constituted about 25 per cent of the city's population of 15,000. As in Birmingham, SCLC strategy was to apply economic pressure on the business community that would compel the city, faced with federal intervention, to negotiate concessions. But Lyndon Johnson, aware that the civil rights would be a major issue in the forthcoming election, and afraid that the conservative Republican, Barry Goldwater, would appeal to Democrats in the Deep South, was reluctant to act. SCLC protestors in St Augustine were attacked by whites, including Klansmen, and Florida governor Farris Bryant defied a federal court injunction protecting the right of peaceful protest in St Augustine by reinstating a ban on night marches, and refused to use the National Guard to protect demonstrators. Although the St Augustine campaign ended in stalemate, with some of the city's hotels, motels, restaurants (anticipating passage of the pending Civil Rights Bill) agreeing to desegregate their facilities, but with no agreement reached on other issues, SCLC believed that it had induced Johnson to secure the passage by Congress of the historic 1964 Civil Rights Act, and thus vindicated direct action protest.

During the summer of 1964 King and the SCLC went to Mississippi to assist SNCC and CORE in a 'Freedom Project' – a voter registration drive resulting from a mock election organized by Robert Moses of the SCLC, who was also director of the Council of Federated Organizations (COFO), a coalition of SNCC, CORE, the SCLC and the NAACP. It led to the founding of a new political party, the Mississippi Freedom Democrats (MFDP) in the spring of 1964, that was to challenge the all-white Mississippi delegation at the Democratic National Convention.

Fannie Lou Hamer, born in 1917, the last of 20 children of a black sharecropping family in Montgomery County, Mississippi, was a major force in the MFDP. Because she was literate Mrs Hamer had been promoted to the post of timekeeper on the W. D. Marlon plantation near Ruleville, Mississippi, having previously worked there as a field hand. In 1962 she lost her job after attempting to register as a voter, and became a civil rights activist in the SNCC, organizing voter registration projects and attempting to obtain welfare benefits for poor black families. On one occasion she was arrested and severely beaten for attempting to use the 'rest room' in a Mississippi bus station. At the Democratic National Convention, Mrs Hamer told the credentials committee how she (and other blacks) had been brutally treated when they attempted to vote in Mississippi. Despite her dramatic (and nationally televised) testimony - during which she declared 'Is this America? The land of the free and the home of the brave? Where we have to sleep with our telephones off the hook, because our lives be threatened daily?'-Lyndon Johnson refused to allow the 'Freedom Democrats' voting rights in the convention. Instead it was proposed that at future conventions, no delegations would be allowed from states discriminating against black voters, and that two Freedom Democrats – Aaron Henry, president of the Mississippi NAACP, and Edward King, the white chaplain of Tougaloo College – be allowed to sit in the convention as delegates-at-large with full voting rights. King, along with Roy Wilkins of the NAACP, James Farmer of CORE and Bayard Rustin, was in favour in accepting the proposals, believing that blacks could not afford to alienate the Democratic party, but SNCC, angered by the treatment of the MDFP, drew increasingly away from the 'conservatism' of King and the SCLC. After her appearance at the Democratic Convention, Mrs Hamer attempted (unsuccessfully) to run for the United States House of Representatives as the MFDP candidate from Mississippi's Second Congressional District. In 1965 she was the plaintiff in a legal action which resulted in the overturning of local election results in two Mississippi counties because blacks had not been allowed to vote.

In great demand as a public speaker and an (accomplished) performer of civil rights songs, Mrs Hamer later served on the Democratic National Committee and the board of directors of the Fannie Lou Hamer Day Care Centre, founded in Ruleville in 1970 by the National Council of Negro Women. The recipient of many honorary degrees and awards, Mrs Hamer died in 1977 in the historic black township of Mound Bayou, Mississippi – a year after the mayor of Ruleville announced the observance of a Fannie Lou Hamer Day. Shortly after her death, the Mississippi state legislature unanimously passed a resolution praising her services to the state. In her autobiography *To Praise Our Bridges*, Fannie Lou Hamer recalled:

> I married in 1944 and stayed on the plantation until 1962, when I went down to the courthouse in Indianola to register to vote. That happened because I went to a mass meeting one night. Until then I'd never heard of no mass meeting and I didn't know that a Negro could register and vote. Bob Moses, Reggie Johnson, Jim Bevel, and James Forman were some of the SNCC workers who ran that meeting. When they asked for those to raise their hands who'd go down to the courthouse the next day, I raised mine...The only thing they could do to me was to kill me and it seemed like they'd been trying to do that a little bit at a time ever since I could remember...I've worked on voter registration here [in Mississippi] ever since I went to that first mass meeting...I went to Africa in 1964 and I learned that I sure didn't have anything to be ashamed of from being black. Being from the South we never was taught much about our African heritage. The way everybody talked to us, everybody in Africa was savages and really stupid people. But I've seen more savage white folks here in America than I've seen in Africa...I was treated much better in Africa than I was treated in America.[20]

Since its 'Crusade for Citizenship' in 1960 black suffrage had been a major goal of King and the SCLC. Although the 1964 Civil Rights Act had dealt a heavy blow to segregation, it had not guaranteed the constitutional right to vote. In 1965 SCLC decided to join with SNCC and CORE in a voter-registration drive in Selma, Alabama, to dramatize the need for additional legislation, by again provoking crisis and confrontation with the white authorities. It was Mrs Amelia Platts Boynton, a civil rights activist in Selma, instrumental in bringing SNCC workers into town, who persuaded King and the SCLC to make Selma the target for their voting rights project. SNCC field workers (who had been active in Selma since 1963) were ambivalent about cooperating with King and the SCLC.

Although King's presence would bring valuable publicity to the campaign, the SNCC disliked his excessive religiosity, tendency to compromise at critical junctures, and SCLC's penchant for provoking crisis and then leaving the scene for other engagements. When King, leading a march from Selma to Montgomery, refused to break through a police barricade, led the marchers in prayer, and then turned back to Selma (with many of his followers singing 'Ain't Gonna Let Nobody Turn Me 'Round') SNCC workers were openly contemptuous. (King had, in fact, decided against a confrontation with the Alabama police after discussions with the Attorney General, but had not informed SNCC of his resolve.) But again, King's presence had dramatized an already violent situation. Dallas County sheriff James G. Clark, like Bull Connor in Birmingham, had been provoked into violence against the demonstrators, notably on 'Bloody Sunday' at the Edmund Pettus bridge on the road out of Selma, where marchers were tear-gassed and beaten by mounted police. C. T. Vivian of the SCLC had been publicly assaulted by Clark, and the murder of the white Unitarian minister James J. Reeb, by Selma whites, produced a highly-charged atmosphere which moved Lyndon Johnson to call Congress into special session to enact new voting rights legislation.

On 17 March 1965, a federal court approved the Selma-to-Montgomery march, Johnson mobilized Alabama state militia to protect the procession (which was also accompanied by Justice Department officials), and on 25 March King spoke to 25,000 people from the capitol steps in Montgomery, bringing the black protest movement back full circle to the scene of the bus boycott ten years earlier. The Selma campaign also marked the culmination of the civil rights movement in the South and, in retrospect, was King's finest hour. On 6 August Lyndon Johnson signed the Voting Rights Act, a direct consequence of the Selma campaign.

CHICAGO, BLACK POWER AND VIETNAM

The urban racial riots of the 1960s (euphemistically termed 'civil disorders') alerted King to the problems of poverty and social pathology, and the need for reaching the black underclass of the nation's inner city ghettos. Concurrently, he was also beginning to express concern over the cause and implications of the escalating American presence in Vietnam. These two issues – poverty and American imperialism – which King also believed were intimately related, were to dominate his thought and actions for the remaining three years of his life. Together, they offer convincing evidence to support the contention that King became increasingly radical (and less reformist) in his last years. Although King's position on Vietnam allied him with the younger elements of the civil rights coalition – SNCC and CORE – it alienated him from the established black leadership and earned him the enmity of Lyndon Johnson (as well as the renewed attentions of the FBI).

In 1966 despite the disapproval of Bayard Rustin, King decided to move to Chicago to lead a non-violent demonstration against segregated slum housing, *de facto* segregated schools, black unemployment and job discrimination. (In 1956 Edwin C. Berry of the Chicago Urban League had called his city the most segregated one in the United States.) James Bevel, the strategy organizer for SCLC in Chicago, asserted that the black unemployment rate was twice that of the whites, detailed the extent of black family breakdowns, and charged the Democratic party machine with allowing merchants to make minimal investments in black areas of the city, inflating prices and syphoning off profits to the affluent white suburbs. In going to Chicago, King was aware that he was taking on its formidable mayor, Richard J. Daley, a consummate politician and power broker in the national Democratic party. As the Reverend Arthur Brazier, leader of the South Side Woodlawn Association observed:

> King decided to come to Chicago because he thought Chicago was unique in that there was one man, one source of power, who you had to deal with. He knew this wasn't the case in New York or any other city. He thought if Daley could be persuaded on the rightness of open housing and integrated schools that things would be done.[21]

But although Daley treated King outwardly with respect, the considerable resources of the city government were used to frustrate the campaign. When King, in a move to highlight the housing crisis, moved into a rat-infested apartment, Daley sent in building inspectors with slum violation notices. When SCLC marched through Chicago's blue collar suburbs, they encountered bitter and violent opposition from working-class whites, and King himself was assaulted, but Daley argued that SCLC had encouraged rioting.

As events in Chicago were to prove, SCLC strategies did not transpose easily from the rural South to the urban North. Despite Jesse Jackson's attempts in 'Operation Breadbasket', consumer boycotts organized with the help of black ministers against white employers practicing hiring discrimination, SCLC discovered that urban preachers lacked the prestige they enjoyed in the South, while the black church was also less efficient as an organizing institution for protest movements. Again ill-prepared and inadequately briefed, SCLC workers did not even possess appropriate clothing for the severe Chicago winter. Moreover, the gathering protest against the Vietnam war was diverting funds and energies away from the civil rights movement. Although SCLC claimed some success in working with Chicago street gangs – members of which acted as King's bodyguards – they rejected the philosophy of non-violent protest. In Chicago, King who was increasingly attracted to democratic socialism of the kind he had witnessed in Sweden, was demanding drastic redistributions of wealth and political power, in favour of the poor and dispossessed. But The Chicago Freedom Movement succeeded only in persuading Daley to concede an open housing agreement with the city's banking and real estate interests which achieved little in practice. When Daley was re-elected to a fourth term of office in 1967, he disavowed the open housing policy. SCLC's first campaign outside the South had achieved little, while calling King's philosophy and strategies into question.

The growing rift between SCLC and SNCC deepened during the continuation of James Meredith's one-man 'March Against Fear' in 1966. Meredith had become the first black student to enroll at the University of Mississippi in 1962, but only after a confrontation between President Kennedy and the state's segregationist governor, Ross Barnett, the deployment of 600 United States marshals and 15,000 federalized National Guardsmen, and riots which resulted in the loss of two lives and the injury of 375 people. When Meredith was shot and wounded by a white sniper in Mississippi, King joined with Stokely Carmichael of SNCC and Floyd McKissick of CORE to complete Meredith's march. Carmichael's use of the emotive slogan 'Black Power' (see Chapter 7) became a source of tension, when King, opposed to the phrase because of its connotations of racial separatism and apparent acceptance of violence, threatened to withdraw from the march unless its leaders made a commitment to non-violence. King was to recall:

> I pleaded with the group to abandon the Black Power slogan. It was my contention that a leader has to be concerned about the problems of semantics. Each word, I said, has a denotative meaning – its explicit and recognized sense – and a connotative meaning – its suggestive sense. While the concept of Black Power might be denotatively sound, the slogan 'Black Power' carried the wrong connotations. I mentioned the implications of violence that the press had already attached to the phrase.[22]

While agreement was reached between King, Carmichael and McKissick not to use the competing slogans of 'Black Power' and 'Freedom Now' for the remainder of the march, the dispute was indicative of the approaching split of the civil rights coalition along racial as well as ideological and class lines.

Since 1965 King (although not a strict pacifist) had questioned the morality of the war in South-East Asia but, aware of Lyndon Johnson's support for civil rights, did not join the anti-war lobby until early in 1967, when he appeared in demonstrations with Dr Benjamin Spock. Coretta

King, an ardent pacifist, and a member of Women Strike for Peace, supported her husband's new stance. Increasingly convinced that the war was deflecting the administration's attention from civil rights, and aware that his opposition to it would damage the SCLC financially, King, after reading an article on 'The Children of Vietnam' in *Ramparts* magazine, which featured a photograph of a Vietnamese woman holding a dead baby killed by the American military, decided to join the peace movement.

In an address delivered at Riverside Church in New York City in April 1967, King expressed sympathy for the Vietcong and for the revolutionary movements in the Third World. The following month, King, in a talk to SCLC staffers, praised Ho Chi Minh as the dedicated leader of a popular movement against a corrupt dictatorship. As he continued to protest against the war, King aroused hostile press comment; *Newsweek* magazine accused him of displaying 'simplistic political judgement' and of being 'in over his head' in issues about which he was singularly ill-informed. *Life* magazine published an editorial on 'Dr King's Disservice to His Cause', in which it asserted that by linking the civil rights movement with the opposition to the American position in Vietnam, he had come 'close to betraying the cause for which he has worked so long'. It concluded:

> Dr King has claimed that the budgetary demands of the war in Vietnam are the key hindrance to progress in civil rights. Not so. If the drive for equal rights falters now, in the difficult time when life must be given to laws already on the books, Dr King and his tactics must share the blame.[23]

Carl Rowan, a black journalist who had met King during the Montgomery boycott, published an article in *Reader's Digest*, in which he argued that King's involvement in a conflict between the United States and Communists would raise further suspicions concerning his loyalties and might endanger impending civil rights legislation. King's response to such attacks, was to argue that there was an interrelationship between racism and poverty and American imperialism and militarism – a conviction that deepened after the racial riots in Newark and Detroit. King now asserted that it would be morally inconsistent for him to denounce the violence against blacks in the ghettos, and to condone American violence in Vietnam. Again, as winner of the Nobel Peace Prize, he felt an obligation to oppose war, particularly one which violated the right of self-determination by the Vietnamese. The FBI kept Lyndon Johnson informed of King's anti-war activities, and intensified its surveillance of the SCLC.

THE POOR PEOPLE'S CAMPAIGN AND THE MEMPHIS STRIKE

In an effort to bridge the divisions within the civil rights ranks (the NAACP and the Urban League were vehemently opposed to involvement in the anti-war movement) King, by the end of 1967, had conceived an interracial alliance that would both reassert the principle of non-violence and unite a coalition of the poor along class rather than racial lines. Stanley Levison, with memories of the 1942 'Bonus March' on Washington, D.C., suggested that a small 'army' of demonstrators should erect a shanty town or tent city on government property in the capital. Within the SCLC, Jesse Jackson and James Bevel opposed the idea, believing that priority should be given to ending American involvement in Vietnam. King, desperate to reignite the spirit of protest which had brought success to the South, and aware of his precarious position as a spokesman for non-violence, explained the rationale behind the Poor People's Campaign in an article published after his assassination.

> The time has come to return to mass non-violent protest....Our Washington demonstration will resemble Birmingham and Selma in duration. Just as we dealt with the social problem of segregation through massive demonstrations, and...with the political problem – the denial of the right to vote – through massive demonstrations, we are now trying to deal with economic problems – the right to live, to have a job and income – through massive protest. It will be a Selma-like movement on economic issues...no structural changes have taken place as a result of the riots. We plan to build a shantytown in Washington, patterned after the bonus marches of the thirties, to dramatize how many people have to live in slums.[24]

The planned march (which took place after his death) also revealed King's conviction that American society needed a fundamental redistribution of wealth and economic power. (The immediate purpose of the projected march was to pressure Congress into enacting King's proposed Bill of Rights for the Disadvantaged – a massive federally-funded anti-poverty programme.) He informed an interviewer:

> America is deeply racist and its democracy is flawed both economically and socially...the black revolution is much more than a struggle for the rights of Negroes. It is forcing America to face all its interrelated flaws – racism, poverty, militarism, and imperialism. It is exposing evils that are deeply rooted in the whole structure of our society.[25]

In February 1968 Negro sanitation workers in Memphis, Tennessee, went on strike to win union recognition, improved wages and working conditions. King, who saw the Memphis strike as the beginning of the projected Poor People's Campaign, accepted an invitation from James

Lawson, an old friend and Methodist minister, to lead a protest march in Memphis. The demonstration ended in disorder, when police shot a black youth during a pitched battle with protestors. King conceded that he had gone to Memphis inadequately briefed, and left abruptly. Sections of the press, taking their cues from FBI informants, predicted that the violence in Memphis would be repeated on a larger scale during the Washington march. The *Memphis Commercial Appeal* commented tartly: 'Dr King's pose as a leader of a non-violent movement has been shattered. He now has the entire nation doubting his word when he insists that his April project [the Poor People's Campaign] can be peaceful.'[26] King was deeply disturbed by events in Memphis, and media comment on his own culpability. But Lyndon Johnson's surprise announcement that he would not seek re-election in 1968, appeared to offer hope that the anti-war and anti-poverty movements might achieve a unified front under a new Democratic president. (In the event, the conservative Republican, Richard Nixon, won the election.)

King returned to Memphis in a more optimistic mood to lead a new march. On 3 April King addressed a small but enthusiastic audience at Mason Temple, and referred to the increasing number of threats on his life. In a startling peroration he declared that:

> ...it really doesn't matter with me now, because I've been to the mountaintop, and I don't mind. Like anybody, I would like to live a long life; longevity has its place. But I'm not concerned about that now. I just want to do God's will. And he's allowed me to go up to the mountain. And I've looked over. And I've seen the Promised Land. So I'm happy tonight. I'm not worried about anything. I'm not fearing any man. 'Mine eyes have seen the glory of the coming of the Lord.'[27]

The next day, Martin Luther King, Jr, was shot and killed by a white sniper as he stood on the balcony of the Lorraine Motel. James Earl Ray, a small-time criminal was convicted (and sentenced to a 99-year prison sentence) for King's murder, but there is strong evidence to suggest FBI and Central Intelligence Agency implication in his assassination. King's death touched off a wave of violence across America, in which more than twenty people died. *Newsweek* magazine, in a memorial issue, commented:

> King's martyrdom on a motel balcony did far more than rob Negroes of their most compelling spokesman, and whites of their most effective bridge to black America. His murder, for too many blacks, could only be read as a judgement upon his non-violent philosophy – and a license for retaliatory violence.

Floyd McKissick, in the same issue, announced simply: 'Dr Martin Luther King was the last prince of non-violence. Non-violence is a dead philosophy and it was not black people that killed it.'[28] Ironically, King's murder may have helped the Memphis strikers. Following his death, 300 ministers (black and white) marched to city hall to demand recognition of the union, and Memphis businessmen also began to press for a settlement of the dispute. Again, the passage of the 1968 Civil Rights Act, which incorporated fair housing proposals, absent from the 1966 Act, may have been facilitated by King's murder and the congressional sympathy it evoked.

ASSESSMENT

From the time of the Montgomery bus boycott in 1955, until the Memphis sanitation workers' strike thirteen years later, Martin Luther King, Jr, was the outstanding advocate of non-violence as both a method of protest and as a way of life. To his admirers (black and white) King was the outstanding black leader of the twentieth century, whose unique contributions to the civil rights cause derived from his intense religious faith, expressed in the idioms and symbols of Southern black Christianity. King's personal bravery, and engagement with the forces of Southern racism resembled (as they were intended) a medieval passion play in which the forces of good confronted those of evil. To his critics, King was the exponent of an unrealistic, if not pathological doctrine which enjoined its adherents to love their oppressors and to abdicate the right of self-defence. King, his critics also charged, had not initiated the black protests of the 1950s and the 1960s (which began as local campaigns), had failed to gain mass support for either his reformist or radical ideas, and among his personal failings was pompous, sexist, and overbearing to subordinates. The divergent views of King's admirers and detractors deserve consideration and amplification.

During and after the Montgomery boycott, King served as a catalyst of increasing symbolic and charismatic significance, able to direct attention on and support for protests started by others.It was King's ability to bring these local crises to the attention of the news media (and to the federal government) which made him a pivotal figure. Again, his expressed devotion to non-violence and religious terminology (as well as his openness to compromise) made King appear 'moderate', 'respectable' and 'reasonable' in the eyes of many Americans.

Until the emergence of the Black Power slogan, King, through his prestige and force of personality, was able to hold together an obviously fragmenting civil rights coalition. In this respect, he served as the vital centre of the movement, standing between the 'conservatism' of the NAACP and Urban League, and the 'radicalism' of SNCC and CORE. But King also recognized that 'non-violence' provoked violence, and the SCLC came to expect (and deliberately precipitate) assaults on black demonstrators in order to gain public sympathy for civil rights legislation. In this respect, also, King deserves credit for having inspired (through his oratory and personal example) Southern blacks – and their white supporters – to gain a sense of individual and collective worth through political action. It is often not fully appreciated that to engage in civil rights activities in the Southern states was to actively risk death or injury. As the acquittal by an (all-white) Mississippi jury in 1955 of two local white men accused of murdering Emmett Till, a Chicago teenager, who had allegedly made 'familiar' remarks to a white woman indicated, *any* infraction of the rigid standards of Southern racial etiquette could lead to violent death for black 'offenders', and the absolution of their murderers – should they even be brought to trial. Again, as Richard King has observed, in their willingness to go to prison for their beliefs, the student activists who were initially inspired by the Montgomery boycott 'undermined the traditional negative connotations of jail and turned it from a place of shame to one of political honour'.[29]

It was also Martin Luther King's achievement to invest civil rights protest with universal significance, his declared purpose being 'to redeem the soul of America' by appeals to its moral conscience and national values. By 1966, however, and despite tangible victories over segregation and discrimination, King felt some empathy for Black Power and Marxist critiques of American society, and had moved perceptibly to the left in his social attitudes and awareness. The Vietnam War, urban violence, and the realization that with legal victories achieved, protest movements needed to embrace economic rights, all contributed to King's latter-day radicalism. (That King even privately expressed admiration for Scandinavian-type democratic socialism is difficult for even his most ardent American admirers – black and white – to concede).

Recent disclosures of King's chequered private life and sexual appetite should in no way affect judgements of his stature as a race leader, but it remains unexplained why he and his SCLC colleagues (and other elements in the civil rights movement), aware of FBI surveillance and 'dirty tricks', did little, if anything to curb or conceal their more intimate activities. David Garrow suggests that King's sexual proclivities and practices were simply 'standard ministerial practice in a context where intimate pastor-parishioner relationships had long been winked at'. (Garrow quotes King as having said to a worried acquaintance: 'I'm away from home twenty-five to twenty-seven days a month. Fucking's a form of anxiety reduction'.)[30] But King's weaknesses as a leader need to be acknowledged.

Primarily a strategist, negotiator and charismatic speaker, King was not, in any sense, an organization man. But the SCLC, with which he was identified after the conclusion of the Montgomery boycott, also came to be identified solely with King himself. Ralph Abernathy, its vice-president, called SCLC simply 'a faith operation'.[31] (Yet many Southern black clergymen did not share the SCLC's Social Gospel orientation. Wyatt Walker estimated that probably 90 per cent of black ministers in Birmingham remained aloof from the campaign there.) Poorly organized, SCLC was frequently inefficient and always male dominated. Septima Clark, active in the Highlander Folk School, was also a member of the SCLC's executive staff. Like Ella Baker, she discovered that King (and his male associates) 'didn't think too much of the way women could contribute' to the movement. Frequently patronized by King, Mrs Clark, in retrospect, remembered that:

> ...in those days I didn't criticize Dr King, other than asking him not to lead all the marches. I adored him. I supported him in every way I could because I greatly respected his courage, his service to others, and his non-violence. The way I think about him now comes from my experience in the women's movement. But in those days...in the black church men were always in charge. It was just the way things were.[32]

SCLC was also flexible, informal, and because of its ministerial base, able to mobilize effectively Southern blacks. Andrew Young (who joined SCLC in 1961, became its principal negotiator and played a decisive role in the negotiations that ended the Birmingham campaign) observed that although King was in nominal charge of SCLC, it was more like 'a jazz combo', in which each staff member had 'a chance to solo'.[33] With King's death, SCLC lost an accomplished orchestrator/arranger, and was to engage in a leadership struggle between his appointed successor, Ralph Abernathy and Jesse Jackson, until Jackson's resignation in 1971 (see Chapter 7). If, as is now generally acknowledged, King's fame was created by the civil rights movement (rather than vice versa) it is also true that through his leadership and example, black protest in the Southern states achieved its most significant victories. Judged only by his contribution to the 'classic' phase of black protest, his influence in shaming Congress into enacting the Civil Rights, Voting Rights and Housing Acts, King will be remembered as the greatest black visionary leader of the twentieth century. That the majority of Americans, black and white, were unable to endorse King's later critiques of capitalist society, suggests that he was also, at the end of his life, a leader in advance of most of his followers. Yet King never abandoned his fundamental belief in the aspirations of African-Americans for integration into the American way of life. In a eulogy to King, delivered at his funeral service at Atlanta on 9 April 1968, Benjamin E. Mays, President Emeritus of Morehouse College, declared that::

> No reasonable person would deny that the activities and personality of Martin Luther King, Jr., contributed largely to the success of the student sit-in movements in abolishing segregation in downtown establishments; and that his activities contributed mightily to the passage of the Civil Rights legislation of 1964 and 1965....He had faith in his country. He died striving to desegregate and integrate America....nonviolence to King was total commitment not only in solving the problems of the race in the United States but in solving the problems of the world.[34]

Ironically, the integrationist movement of the 1950s and 1960s, of which King was the symbolic leader, also gave rise to a revived sense of black nationalism, with demands for racial separatism and violent resistance against the forces of white oppression. As King himself became painfully aware, no one voiced these views more articulately than the son of another black minister – Malcolm X.

REFERENCES

1. Angelou, M., *The Heart of a Woman* (London, 1986), p.93.
2. Walker, A., *In Search of Our Mother's Gardens: Womanist Prose* (New York, 1984), pp.143–4.
3. Garrow, D. J., *Bearing the Cross: Martin Luther King, Jr., and the Southern Christian Leadership Conference* (New York, 1986), p.16; Garrow, D. L. (ed.), *The Montgomery Bus Boycott and the Women Who Started It: The Memoir of Jo Ann Gibson Robinson* (University of Tennessee Press, 1987), pp.45–6.
4. Raines, H., *My Soul Is Rested: Movement Days in the Deep South Remembered* (Penguin Books, Harmondsworth, 1983), p.43.
5. King, M. L., Jr, *Stride Toward Freedom: The Montgomery Story* (London, 1958), p.54.
6. Williams, J., *Eyes on the Prize: America's Civil Rights Years 1954–1965* (Penguin Books, New York, 1988), p.76.
7. King, *Stride Toward Freedom*, op. cit., pp.91–3.
8. Ibid., p.79.
9. Ibid., p.158.
10. Meier, A., E. Rudwick and F. L. Broderick (eds), *Black Protest Thought in the Twentieth Century* (2nd edn, New York, 1971), pp.293–300.

11. Fairclough, A., *To Redeem the Soul of America: The Southern Christian Leadership Conference and Martin Luther King, Jr.* (University of Georgia Press, London, 1987), p.27.
12. Garrow, *The Montgomery Bus Boycott and the Women Who Started It*, op. cit., pp.53–4.
13. Meier, et al.,*Black Protest Thought in the Twentieth Century*, op. cit., pp.303–6.
14. Lewis, D. L., *King: A Critical Biography* (London, 1970), p.105.
15. Meier, *et al.*, *Black Protest Thought in the Twentieth Century*, op. cit., pp.307–8.
16. Williams, *Eyes on the Prize*, op. cit., p.137.
17. King, M. L. Jr., 'Letter From Birmingham Jail', in *Why We Can't Wait* (New York, 1964), pp. 86–7.
18. Meir, *et al.*, *Black Protest Thought in the Twentieth Century*, op. cit., pp.49–50.
19. Moody, A., *Coming of Age in Mississippi* (New York, 1968), p.307.
20. Hamer, Fannie Lou, *To Praise Our Bridges: An Autobiography* (1967), quoted in Juan Williams, *Eyes on the Prize: America's Civil Rights Years 1954-1965* (Penguin Books, New York, 1988), pp.245-247. Mrs Hamer also recounts her civil rights activities in Howell Raines, *My Soul Is Rested: Movement Days In The Deep South Remembered* (Penguin Books, New York, 1983), pp.249-255.
21. Royko, M., *Boss: Mayor Richard J. Daley of Chicago* (London, 1972), p.141.
22. King, M. L., Jr, *Where Do We Go From Here: Chaos or Community?* (New York, 1967), p.30.
23. Ansboro, J. J., *Martin Luther King, Jr,: The Making Of A Mind* (New York, 1983), p.256.
24. Meier, *et al.*, *Black Protest Thought in the Twentieth Century*, op. cit., pp.586–93.
25. Garrow, D. J., *The FBI and Martin Luther King, Jr., from 'Solo' to Memphis* (London, 1981), p.214.
26. Fairclough, *To Redeem The Soul Of America*, op. cit., p.377.
27. Ibid., pp.380–1.
28. *Newsweek*, 15 April 1958.
29. King, R. H., 'Citizenship and Self-Respect: The Experience of Politics in the Civil Rights Movement', *Journal of American Studies*, 22 (1988), p.12.
30. Garrow, *Bearing the Cross*, op. cit., p.375.
31. Fairclough, *To Redeem The Soul Of America*, op. cit., p.1.
32. Clark, S., *Ready From Within: Septima Clark and the Civil Rights Movement*, ed. with an introduction by Cynthia Stokes Brown (Navarro, California, 1986), pp.78–9.

33. Colaiaco, J. A., *Martin Luther King, Jr.: Apostle of Militant Nonviolence* (New York, 1988), p.53.

34. Mays, B. E., 'Eulogy of Dr Martin Luther King, Jr.', in *The Morehouse College Bulletin*, 36 (summer, 1968), pp.8–12.

CHAPTER SIX

Malcolm X: Sinner and Convert

If Malcolm X were not a Negro, his autobiography would be little more than a journal of abnormal psychology, the story of a burglar, dope pusher, addict and jailbird – with a family history of insanity – who acquires messianic delusions and sets forth to preach an upside down religion of 'brotherly' hatred.

[*The Saturday Evening Post*][1]

It does not promote the cause of responsible leadership to deny the importance of Malcolm X to the particular segment of people whose political and/or ideological leader he was, or sought to be....Malcolm X made an impact on the minds of the black masses irrespective of his criminal past or his strong pro-black ideology.

[C. ERIC LINCOLN][2]

PERSPECTIVES: BLACK NATIONALISM AFTER GARVEY, THE SEPARATIST IMPULSE, 1930–1950

Marcus Garvey's deportation in 1927, and the onset of the Great Depression effectively ended black American support for the separatist Universal Negro Improvement Association. Negro organizations and leaders, concerned with ensuring the sheer survival of blacks, stressed interracial cooperation, and the political and economic advancement of blacks within the United States. From the advent of the New Deal in 1932, to the climax of the civil rights movement in the mid-1960s, integration remained the dominant black ideology. The goals of integration and equal rights coincided with the aspirations of a growing black middle class. During the period of World War II, NAACP branches increased from 335 in 1940 to 1,073 in 1946, and its total membership rose from 50,000 to 450,000. The publication in 1944 of Gunnar Myrdal's monumental *An American Dilemma*, with its optimism, deprecation of separatist movements, and acceptance of racial integration as the proper goal of protest activity, also helped to set the ideological tone accepted by most civil rights activists and theoreticians. Not until the mid-1960s, with the emergence of the Black Power slogan, growing disillusionment on the part of many younger blacks with the 'tokenism' of civil rights legislation, and their rejection of non-violence as a strategy and a philosophy, did black nationalist theories and organizations enjoy the currency (and publicity) which had attended Garvey and the UNIA. But even in the 1930s and 1940s, not all black leaders subscribed to the integrationist ethic. W. E. B. Du Bois, as has been seen, clashed with the NAACP over his advocacy of a separate black economy.

The American Communist Party, founded in 1919, made some converts among black intellectuals with its Stalinist-derived call for 'self-determination' for African-Americans, including a proposal to create an all-black '49th State' out of the heart of the Southern 'black belt'. But the Communist appeal to the mass of blacks was minimal and by 1935, operating on the (mistaken) assumption that the proletarian revolution was at hand, American Communists reversed their nationalistic stance in favour of a policy of equal rights for blacks in the United States.

But the mass unemployment of the Depression saw the flowering of various mystic, black nationalist sectarian cults in the black urban ghettos. Noble Drew Ali's Moorish-American Science Temple, founded in Newark, New Jersey, in 1913, gained in strength with the influx of a large number of former Garveyites in the late 1920s. Drew insisted that black Americans would find salvation only when they realized that they were Moorish Americans or Asiatics, whose true African homeland was Morocco.

More significant was Father Divine's Peace Mission Movement, established on Long Island in 1919, which instituted a collectivist economy among its followers (who also included ex-Garveyites), and functioned as much as a social as a religious black nationalist movement. From 1931-36, Father Divine's Peace Mission grew from a handful to over a million followers or 'angels'. Wages and benefits acquired by converts (who were required to surrender any insurance policies and to withdraw from fraternal organizations) were used to purchase missions and houses ('Heavens'), which were turned into sexually segregated living quarters. Members were employed in Father Divine's laundries, restaurants and communal farms in New York and New Jersey. During their heyday, the Peace Missions provided wholesome meals at minimal prices to the unemployed. Father Divine (born George Baker) became the most successful black evangelist of the 1930s and 1940s, and was the most arresting black nationalist since Marcus Garvey. Through the collective efforts of his followers, Divine (who was opposed to trade unions and social welfare legislation) was able to provide food, accommodation and employment for large numbers of blacks untouched by New Deal programmes. But Father Divine had little interest in the civil rights protests of the period. Although he took part in street demonstrations against department stores in Harlem which practiced discrimination, Divine had little impact as a reform leader. He died in 1965 in his mansion on a 75 acre estate outside Philadelphia. His obituary in the *New York Times* related that:

> Father Divine's height was 5 feet 2 inches, and his customary dress was a carefully tailored $500 silk suit. He was bald and paunchy....His rhetoric was replete with malapropisms, and many of his sentences were virtually unintelligible. However, to the thousands who looked upon him and heard him speak, Father Divine was God Almighty, who had arrived full grown on earth...to divulge a creed of peace, communal living, celibacy, honesty, and racial equality....In practice, Father Divine fostered a mass cooperative primitive communism, based on the Last Supper.[3]

Emigrationist and repatriation ideas were confined during the 1930s to such organizations as the Ethiopian Pacific Movement, established in Chicago in 1932, by Mittie Gordon, a former president of the city's division of the UNIA. In 1939, 300 members of the movement set out for Washington, D. C., to lobby the federal government in support of Senator Theodore Bilbo's proposal to allocate federal funds to blacks who wished to emigrate to Africa. Most never arrived in the capital, as their transportation began breaking down even before they had left the Chicago city limits. (In 1941 Miss Gordon was charged with inciting blacks to avoid conscription.)

In 1930 the most influential black nationalist/separatist religion, the Nation of Islam (the Black Muslims) was founded by Wallace D. Fard in Detroit, Michigan. Presenting himself as a Muslim prophet, Fard preached a message of black redemption within Islam. Whites were castigated as 'devils' and mankind itself was said to have begun with the black race which had brought civilization to the world. The white race – a degenerate mutation of the original inhabitants of the earth – the 'Asiatic Black Man' – had been given 6,000 years of domination by God to test the capacity and strength of the Black Nation. But the day of judgement was at hand, when the 'Caucasians' and their religion, white Christianity, would be destroyed. Fard attracted a following, founded the Temple of Islam and a University of Islam (actually a combined elementary and secondary school), and taught young Muslim women the rudiments of domestic science. The fruit of Islam – a paramilitary organization – drilled its male members in the use of firearms.

In 1933, following Fard's disappearance, leadership of the Nation (which had gained about 33,000 adherents) passed to Elijah Poole, the son of Georgia tenant farmers and former slaves, and a Garveyite. Poole changed his name to Elijah Muhammad, and declared that he was 'Allah's Prophet'. During the 1930s and 1940s, the Nation of Islam grew slowly, drawing support mainly from the black lower class. Muhammad organized Temples in Chicago, Milwaukee, and Washington, DC, and amplified the precepts of the faith. According to Elijah Muhammad, the black race originally inhabited the moon, and at one time the moon and the earth were one planet. But following an explosion – produced by a mad black scientist called Yakub – the two were separated. 'Original Man' – the first people to inhabit the earth – were black, members of the tribe of Shabazz.

Under Elijah Muhammad, the Black Muslims advocated racial separatism, self-determination and the setting up of an independent black republic within the borders of the United States – or a 'return' to Africa. Black Muslims published their own history books which stressed the glories of the African past. They rejected the term 'Negro' as derogatory and favoured the term 'Afro-American', and discarded black surnames as marks of the slave past, substituting the suffix 'X'. Converts were enjoined to follow a strict code of personal conduct which included a prohibition on the eating of pork, extra-marital sexual relations, and the use of tobacco, alcohol or narcotics. Muslims were not allowed to engage in any kind of political activity or to serve in the armed forces.

In 1942 Muhammad and sixty-two of his followers were convicted of draft evasion and jailed for three years. It was in prison that Muhammad realized that the existing civil rights organizations had made no attempt to reach or recruit criminals, delinquents or the black underclass; in the post-war era, the Nation of Islam concentrated on just these elements, and with often remarkable results. Drug addicts were rehabilitated and prostitutes 'reformed' after they joined the Nation. Discipline within the organization was strict; indolence and laziness were sternly reproved, and habits of thrift, personal cleanliness and economic self-help were extolled as positive virtues. Until the government granted them a separate state, Muslims elected to avoid any social, religious or political contacts with whites. During the Depression and New Deal, they refused to accept relief checks, Social Security numbers, or any form of federally-sponsored employment.

In addition to being allowed to set up an independent state, Muslim demands, as formulated by Muhammad, included the following:

> We want the government of the United States to exempt our people from ALL taxation as long as we are deprived of equal justice under the laws of the land.
> We believe that intermarriage or race mixing should be prohibited.
> We believe that the offer of integration is hypocritical and is made by those who are trying to deceive black peoples into believing that their 400-year-old enemies of freedom, justice and equality are, all of a sudden, their 'friends'. We believe that such deception is intended to prevent black people from realizing that the time in history has arrived for the separation from the whites of this nation.
> We believe that Allah (God) appeared in the Person of Master W. Fard Muhammad, July, 1930; the long-awaited 'Messiah' of the Christians and the 'Mahdi' of the Muslims.[4]

In several respects, the Black Muslims represented a latter-day version of Garveyism. The separatism of the Nation of Islam was motivated by similar forces to those which had prompted Garveyites to discover their individual and group identity in racial separation. The group economy practiced by the Muslims – dry cleaners, grocery stores, restaurants, dairy farms and bakeries – duplicated those of the UNIA (and of Father Divine). Again, in its commitment to racial uplift and redemption, the Nation of Islam retained fundamental tenets of Garveyism, which had itself drawn selectively on Booker T. Washington's economic nationalism. But where Washington, in the racial climate of the early 1900s, was a 'conservative' separatist, Elijah Muhammad, in the predominantly integrationist atmosphere of black thought during and after World War II, preached a more militant, assertive separatism, based on his version of the Muslim faith. The Nation of Islam, although it attracted increasing attention, might have remained a relatively obscure sect during the integrationist phase of the black protest movement, had it not attracted the attentions of its most notable convert, later to become its most famous apostate.

MALCOLM LITTLE AND MALCOLM X

Malcolm Little was born in Omaha, Nebraska, in 1925 (the fourth of eight children), the son of a West Indian mother and a black American Baptist preacher, who was a follower of Marcus Garvey. In his *Autobiography*, Malcolm remembered:

> My father the Reverend Earl Little, was...a dedicated organizer for Marcus Garvey's UNIA. With the help of such disciples as my father, Garvey, from his headquarters in Harlem, was raising the banner of black-race purity and exhorting the Negro masses to return to their ancestral African homeland – a cause which made Garvey the most controversial man on earth.[5]

When Malcolm was very young , his family, following warnings by the Ku Klux Klan that the Reverend Little's UNIA activities were unsettling local blacks, moved to Lansing, Michigan. Malcolm accompanied his father on UNIA missions around Lansing. At meetings held in private houses, Malcolm remembered seeing 'big shiny photographs of Marcus Garvey', which his father always carried, being passed around.

> The pictures showed that what seemed to me millions of Negroes thronged in parade behind Garvey riding in a fine car, a big black man dressed in a dazzling uniform with gold braid on it...wearing a thrilling hat with tall plumes. I remember hearing that he had black followers not only in the United States but all around the world, and...the meetings always closed with my father saying, several times, and the people chanting after him, 'Up, you mighty race, you can accomplish what you will!'[6]

When Malcolm was six, his father was beaten and thrown to death under a tramcar by members of a local white supremacist group – the Black Legion – who had earlier burned the Little family home. An intelligent and promising high school student, Malcolm hoped to become a lawyer, an ambition that was summarily dismissed by his teacher as being unrealistic for a Negro (she suggested that he become a carpenter). The episode, together with his father's death, his mother's commitment to a mental hospital and the subsequent fragmentation of the family, increased Malcolm's early sense of alienation from an unremittingly hostile white society. In 1941 he left school and went to live with his older half-sister in Roxbury, Massachusetts, the black ghetto of Boston. Employed as a shoeshine boy at the Roseland Ballroom (where he met such famous jazzmen as Lionel Hampton and Johnny Hodges), and as a dining-car porter on the Boston-New York route, Malcolm became a petty criminal, with the nickname 'Detroit Red' and operated for a time in Harlem during much of World War II. Returning to Boston in 1945, he was soon arrested for burglary and sentenced to seven years in prison, a severe penalty probably reflecting the fact that one of his accomplices was his white mistress. He was not yet twenty-one years old.

During his first year in prison, in Charleston, Malcolm continued to behave as a delinquent, baiting the guards, sniffing nutmeg and other substances, and, by his own account, raging against God and the Bible to such an extent that he was called 'Satan' by the other inmates. But he met and came to respect a fellow prisoner, Bimbi, who was studious and articulate. With his encouragement, Malcolm began correspondence classes in English and Latin, copied out an entire dictionary, and read so voraciously in his cell after lights out that he permanently impaired his vision. In 1948, after his transfer to Concord prison, Malcolm received a letter from his brother, Philbert, stating that he had discovered the 'natural religion for the black man', and had joined the Nation of Islam. It also instructed him, 'don't eat any more pork, and don't smoke any more cigarettes. I'll show you how to get out of prison'.[7] Malcolm's natural curiosity was aroused. Further letters from his family, including his brothers Reginald and Philbert, and his sister, Hilda, all of whom were Black Muslims, and correspondence with Elijah Muhammad himself, together with his own reading, introduced Malcolm to the Black Muslim faith. He embraced the new creed with all the enthusiasm of the convert. In addition to Black Muslim literature, he also read Du Bois' *The Souls of Black Folk*, H. G. Wells' *Outline of History* and Will Durant's *Story of Civilization*.

Released from prison in 1952, Malcolm went directly to Detroit to meet Elijah Muhammad, was made a formal member of the Nation, and took the surname X. He advanced rapidly within the Muslim hierarchy to become assistant minister to Temple No. 1 in Detroit. He also became the movement's most effective preacher and proselytizer. In 1954 he was given the ministry of Temple No. 7 at Lennox Avenue and 116th Street in Harlem, and quickly built a following in New York. As a trusted minister and disciple of Elijah Muhammad, Malcolm preached orthodox black Muslim doctrine. At the Harlem rally 1960, he declared:

> The Western World is filled with drunkenness, dope, addiction, lying, stealing, gambling, adultery, fornication, prostitution and hosts of other evils. The God of Peace and Righteousness is about to set up His Kingdom...here on this earth. Mr Muhammad is trying to clean up our morals and qualify us to enter into this new Righteous Nation of God...stop carrying guns and knives...drinking whiskey, taking dope, reefers and even cigarettes. No more gambling! Elevate the black woman....Your thirst for integrating makes the white man think you want only to marry his daughter. We [Muslims] who follow Mr Muhammad don't think God ever intended for Black men to marry white women....WE MUST HAVE SOME LAND OF OUR OWN. How else can 20 million black people who now constitute a nation within our own right, a NATION WITHIN A NATION, expect to survive...in a land where we are the last ones hired and the first ones fired....WE MUST HAVE SOME LAND. We will then set up our own farms, factories, business and schools...to become self-sustaining, economically and otherwise.[8]

Yet despite Malcolm's dedication and considerable oratical skills, the Black Muslim appeal was limited, and members had few rights. Muslim theology was bizarre (and bogus), while the call for 'separation', however appealing emotionally, was vague, and to the black majority, unrealistic. Malcolm began to attract increasing attention and support from lower-class ghetto blacks, less from his exegesis of Black Muslim tenets than for his blistering condemnations of white racism and critiques of the civil rights movement's stress on non-violence and integration. Some of his most stinging comments were reserved for Martin Luther King's doctrine of redemptive black suffering. Drawing an analogy with slavery, Malcolm asserted that the two classes of slaves were the 'House Negro', loyal to the master, and the 'Field Negro', who hated both the master and servitude. Their modern counterparts were the 'Uncle Toms' – accommodating, peaceable and self-serving, and the 'New Negro' who had a pride in his colour and culture, and who demanded racial separation. Martin Luther King belonged firmly in the first category, an 'Uncle Tom' whose

> primary concern is in defending the white man, and if he can elevate the black man's condition at the same time, then the black man will be elevated. But if it takes the condemnation of a white man in order to elevate the black man, you'll find that Martin Luther King will get out of the struggle. Martin Luther King isn't preaching love – he's preaching love the white man.[9]

Asked by the noted black psychologist Kenneth B. Clark if his strictures against Negroes 'talking about "love everybody" [when] they don't have any love whatsoever for their own kind' was an oblique reference to King, Malcolm replied tartly:

You don't have to criticize Reverend Martin Luther King. His actions criticize him. Any Negro who teaches other Negroes to turn the other cheek is disarming that Negro...of his God-given right...his moral right...his natural right to defend himself. Everything in nature can defend itself except the American Negro. And men like King – their job is to go among Negroes and teach Negroes 'Don't fight back'. He doesn't tell them, 'Don't fight each other'. 'Don't fight the white man' is what he is saying....*White* people follow King....*White* people subsidize King. *White* people support King...the masses of black people don't support King [who is] the best weapon that the white man, who wants to brutalize Negroes, has ever gotten in this country, because he is setting up a situation where, when the white man wants to attack Negroes, they can't defend themselves, because King has put this foolish philosophy out – you're not supposed to fight, or...to defend yourself.[10]

Malcolm gave a similar assessment of King to the black journalist Louis Lomax, adding on this occasion that:

The goal of Dr Martin Luther King is to give Negroes a chance to sit in a segregated restaurant beside the same white man who has brutalized them for years...to get Negroes to forgive the people who have brutalized them for 500 years...but the masses of black people today don't go for what Martin Luther King is putting down.[11]

When King was honoured at a ceremony in Harlem after his receipt of the Nobel Peace Prize, Malcolm commented sarcastically:

He got the peace prize, we got the problem. I don't want the white man giving me medals. If I'm following a general and he's leading me into battle, and the enemy tends to give him rewards, or awards, I get suspicious of him. Especially if he gets a peace award before the war is over.[12]

That Malcolm was prepared to act directly against white provocation was dramatically illustrated in 1957, when he led a group of followers, and surrounded a Harlem police station, following the beating of a Black Muslim by the police. Malcolm demanded the victim's release and hospitalization, and filed a $70,000 claim for damages against the New York City police department. The widely publicized action caught the attention of the media and of blacks throughout the country, and membership of the Nation increased rapidly. According to one estimate, by 1959 the annual income of the Nation was $3,000,000; by 1961 the eight Temples founded by Malcolm in the Eastern states had completed payment of nearly $39,000 to the Nation's headquarters in Chicago. (Malcolm's own

New York Temple No. 7 contributed over $23,000.)

A frequent guest on TV and radio shows, Malcolm, by 1964, was also the second most requested speaker on college campuses – the first being the ultra conservative Republican (and presidential contender), Barry Goldwater. In his numerous public addresses and in the Nation's newspaper (which he founded), *Muhammad Speaks*, Malcolm, gaining in confidence and awareness, pointed out the major issues confronting blacks: inadequate housing and high rents, inferior welfare and educational facilities, and political powerlessness. He was also increasingly uneasy with the conservatism of Elijah Muhammad, and in particular, his refusal to allow Black Muslims to participate in civil rights protests. Recalling this period, Malcolm reflected:

> If I harboured any personal disappointment...it was that privately I was convinced that our Nation of Islam could be an even greater force in the American black man's overall struggle – if we engaged in more action.... I felt privately that we could have amended or relaxed our general non-engagement policy. I felt that, wherever black people committed themselves, in the Little Rocks and Birminghams... militantly disciplined Muslims should be there....It could be heard increasingly in the Negro communities: 'Those Muslims talk tough, but they never do anything, unless somebody bothers Muslims.'[13]

It is also clear, in retrospect, that the insularity and exclusiveness of the Muslims, as well as their theological mysticism, no longer satisfied the intellectually mature Malcolm. The occasion of the break with the Nation was provided by the assassination of John F. Kennedy in November 1963. Disregarding Muhammad's directive that Muslim spokesmen should refuse to comment on the event, Malcolm, when asked for his thoughts (at the end of an address prepared a week before Kennedy's murder in Dallas, and entitled 'God's Judgement of White America'), remarked that it was simply a matter of 'chickens coming home to roost'. In his *Autobiography*, Malcolm remembered:

> I said that the hate in white men had not stopped with the killing of defenseless black people, but that hate, allowed to spread unchecked, finally had struck down his country's Chief of State I said it was the same thing as had happened with Medgar Evers, with Patrice Lumumba, with Madame Nhu's husband.[14]

Malcolm's impromptu comments were widely reported, and Elijah Muhammad suspended him from the Nation for a 90-day period, during which he was forbidden to speak as a Muslim minister. Malcolm correctly suspected that his suspension (he was not to be reinstated) was an attempt to curb his influence within the movement, as it also reflected the growing divergence between his ideas and those of Muhammad. (Malcolm's well-founded suspicion that Muhammad had not adhered to the Nation's strict code of sexual conduct had also weakened his respect for the man and his movement.)

MALCOLM X: MUSLIM

In March 1964, Malcolm resigned from the Nation and announced that he was going to organize a new mosque in New York City – to be known as the Muslim Mosque, Inc. – which would provide both a spiritual and an activist base for Muslims and non-Muslims and adopt a black nationalist, direct-action approach to the racial problem. Although he publicly still endorsed Muhammad's policies of racial separatism and an ultimate return to Africa, Malcolm was aware that the theology and political inactivism of the Nation did not appeal to the Black youth of the ghettos. His splinter group would, therefore:

> ...be organized in such a manner as to provide for the active participation of all Negroes in our political, economic, and social programmes....Our accent must be upon youth....We are completely disenchanted with the old, adult, established politicians.

Malcolm also reiterated his contention that blacks should (and would) retaliate in self-defence when provoked:

> Concerning non-violence: it is criminal to teach a man not to defend himself when he is the constant victim of brutal attacks. It is legal...to own a shotgun or rifle. When our people are being bitten by dogs, they are within their rights to kill those dogs. We should be peaceful...but the time has come for the American Negro to fight back in self-defence whenever and wherever he is being unjustly and unlawfully attacked.[15]

From its inception, the Muslim Mosque, Inc., was weak, poorly organized, and without sufficient funding. The radical wing of the civil rights coalition – SNCC and CORE – rejected Malcolm's overtures to form a working alliance. Despite his breach with the Black Muslims, Malcolm was initially regarded by younger black militants as a lone agitator and self-publicist, and a potential (if not actual) rival for leadership of the urban black proletariat. For his part, Elijah Muhammad never forgave Malcolm's apostasy, and the Nation's newspaper published weekly diatribes, comparing him with such notable traitors as Judas, Brutus and Benedict Arnold. The established black leaders, already embarrassed and angered by Malcolm's attacks, were in no mood to form alliances with him. In fact, Malcolm was now in an ambivalent position: a confirmed Black Muslim and an aspiring civil rights leader, a religious and secular black nationalist. Moreover, he was now beginning to review the plight of black Americans in a world-wide context and perspective.

In 1964 Malcolm made a tour of the Middle East and African states, where he was well-received by heads of state, politicians and students. The turning point of this tour was his pilgrimage to Mecca, where his exposure to the true Islamic faith broke his remaining ties with the bowdlerized version preached by Elijah Muhammad. Malcolm was particularly impressed by the fraternal relations between pilgrims of all colours and nationalities at Mecca, and the interest expressed in the American racial situation by Arab and African leaders. He returned to the United States as a Sunni Muslim: El-Hajj-Malik El-Shabazz – although he continued to be known as Malcolm X – convinced that if they must remain in America physically, Afro-Americans should 'return' to Africa culturally and metaphysically within the framework of Pan-Africanism. On his return from Africa, Malcolm informed a reporter:

> Every time you see another nation on the African continent become independent, you know that Marcus Garvey is alive. All the freedom movement that is taking place right here in America today was initiated by the philosophy and teachings of Garvey. The entire Black Nationalist philosophy here in America is fed upon the seeds that were planted by Marcus Garvey.[16]

In June 1964 Malcolm announced the formation of the Organization of Afro-American Unity (OAAU) which with distinct overtones of Garvey's Universal Negro Improvement Association, declared itself:

> *Dedicated* to the unification of all people of African descent in this hemisphere and to the utilization of that unity to bring into being the organizational structure that will project the black people's contribution to the world.

Among its objectives, the OAAU asserted the 'Afro-American's right of self-defence' against all oppressors, complete independence for all black people, 'a voter-registration drive to make every unregistered voter in the Afro-American community an independent voter', 'the establishment of a cultural centre in Harlem' to offer courses and workshops in the arts and in Afro-American history, and Afro-American principals for black schools. It also called for the formulation of a petition to be presented to the United Nations Human Rights Commission, calling for the prosecution of the United States government, on the grounds that the deteriorating condition of Afro-Americans constituted a threat to world peace.[17] As Peter Goldman observes, the OAAU prospectus 'read like a Black Power manifesto two years ahead of its time'.[18]

An organization of never more than 900 members, the OAAU, despite its impressive title, was more the institutional embodiment of Malcolm's changing and developing views on the racial situation at home and abroad, rather than an activist movement. OAAU rallies were not membership meetings but public relations and educational events during which Malcolm explained his thinking and strategies on a variety of issues. He criticized blacks for supporting Lyndon Johnson's candidacy in 1964, and castigated the black bourgeoisie for its commitment to private enterprise. He urged supporters to organize 'rifle clubs' to defend the Afro-American community against white vigilante violence and police brutality. But Malcolm's most attractive theme for black audiences was his exposition of the history of racial discrimination in America, generally with references to 'the legacy of slavery'. Like Booker T. Washington and Marcus Garvey, Malcolm made frequent allusions to the debilitating effects of enslavement on the black psyche. However, after his break with the Nation of Islam, Malcolm did not preach the divine deliverance of blacks from racial oppression, but the need for blacks to deliver themselves. Following his second visit to African capitals in 1964, during which he attended the meeting of the Organization of African Unity in Cairo, and urged it to support his moves to indict the American government before the United Nations, Malcolm began to appeal to non-racist whites for their support in the civil rights struggle. He declared:

> We will work with anyone, with any group, no matter what their colour is, as long as they are genuinely interested in taking the type of steps necessary to bring an end to the injustices that black people in this country are afflicted by. No matter what their colour is, no matter what their political, economic or social philosophy is, as long as their aims and objectives are in the direction of destroying the vulturous system that has been sucking the blood of the black people in this country, they're all right with me.[19]

In his last speeches, Malcolm also made passing references to socialism. At an OAAU meeting in Harlem in December 1964, he observed that:

> Almost every one of the countries that has gotten independence has
> devised some kind of socialistic system, and this is no accident....You
> can't operate a capitalistic system unless you are vulturistic; you have
> to have someone's blood to suck to be a capitalist. You show me a
> capitalist, and I'll show you a bloodsucker.[20]

But despite such assertions, Malcolm never moved beyond a
vague critique of capitalism, and never endorsed Marxism. As one
confidant remarked: 'he had no use for Marxism. He considered
Marxism as another political ideology invented by white men for
white men, to shift the seat of power from one group of white
men to another group of white men. He thought it had no relevance
to the black man.'[21] Essentially an inspired agitator, public moralist
and revivalist (he once called himself a 'black Billy Graham'),
Malcolm (unlike Martin Luther King) addressed a dispossessed
and almost entirely black constituency, and never envisioned a
coalition of the underprivileged across racial lines. He informed
one interviewer:

> The history of America is that working class whites have been just as
> much against not only working Negroes, but all Negroes, because all
> Negroes are working class within the caste system. The richest Negro
> is treated like a working class Negro. There never has been any good
> relationship between the working class Negro and working class
> whites...there can be no worker solidarity until there is first some
> black solidarity....I think one of the mistakes Negroes make is this
> worker solidarity thing. There's no such thing – it didn't even work in
> Russia.[22]

From his conversion to the Nation of Islam to the end of his
life, Malcolm remained a black nationalist, committed to the
spiritual and material elevation of Afro-Americans through the
affirmation of his own faith in the redemption of the individual.
Like Booker T. Washington, Malcolm produced an authorized and
inspirational account of his own life, completed shortly after his
assassination by three members of the Nation of Islam in Harlem,
on 21 February 1965. Published after his death, it became a cardinal
text for the emerging Black Power movement. Malcolm's posthumous
Autobiography presented his search for identity (as well as his
claim to leadership) to an audience that had been largely indifferent
or actively opposed to him during his comparatively short public
career. It is possible to regard it as his greatest achievement.

THE AUTOBIOGRAPHY OF MALCOLM X

Like *Up From Slavery*, Malcolm's Autobiography (dictated in instalments to the then struggling black writer, Alex Haley) is a black success story, but one profoundly different in content and tone. It contains graphic descriptions of Malcolm's youth in Omaha, Nebraska, and Lansing, Michigan, his subsequent criminal activities, prison experiences, conversion to the Nation of Islam, changing relationships with Elijah Muhammad, and the discovery of 'true' Islam on his journey to Mecca. In many respects, it belongs to the genre of spiritual conversion autobiography, and is, in effect, a black *Pilgrim's Progress*, in which Malcolm describes the episodes of his life in the form of parables; an incident is described, and then the appropriate moral dawn. Thus, in a notable passage, Malcolm describes how, as a ghetto youth, he allowed his friend Shorty to 'straighten' his hair at home, with a near-lethal mixture of lye, eggs and other ingredients. In every respect, the experience was hair-raising:

> The congolene just felt warm when Shorty started combing it in. But then my head caught fire. I gritted my teeth and tried to pull the sides of the kitchen table together. The comb felt as if it was raking my skin off. My eyes watered, my nose was running. I couldn't stand it any longer; I bolted to the washbasin. I was cursing Shorty with every name I could think of when he got the spray going and started soap-lathering my head.

When the painful operation was completed, Malcolm looked in the mirror and the sight 'blotted out the hurting...on top of my head was this thick, smooth sheen of shiny red hair – real red – as straight as any white man's'. In retrospect, to the intellectually mature Malcolm, the episode was revealing and cautionary:

> This was my really big step toward self-degradation: when I endured all that pain, literally burning my flesh with lye, in order to cook my natural hair until it was limp, to have it look like a white man's hair. I had joined the multitude of Negro men and women in America who are [so] brainwashed into believing that black people are 'inferior' – and white people 'superior' – that they will even mutilate their God-created bodies to try to look 'pretty'.[23]

Throughout his book, Malcolm shrewdly adjusts his language to parallel and evoke the particular stages of his life. Recounting his career as a street-wise hustler, running narcotics, working the 'numbers' racket, and providing black prostitutes for white customers, Malcolm (also showing his sense of humour) says:

> Shorty would take me to the groovy, frantic scenes in different chick's
> and cat's pads, where with the lights and the juke down mellow,
> everybody blew gage and juiced back and jumped. I met chicks who
> were as fine as May wine, and cats who were hip to all happenings.

And then adds laconically:

> That paragraph is a bit deliberate of course; its just to display a bit
> more of the slang that was used by everyone I respected as 'hip' in
> those days.[24]

As in his public speeches and addresses, so too in the
Autobiography, Malcolm could employ parody and satire. In a
devastating passage, he both conveys and mocks the world of un-
reality inhabited by the aspiring black bourgeoisie of the Roxbury
section of Boston, who imitated white middle-class life-styles.

> I'd guess that eight out of ten of the Hill Negroes of Roxbury, despite
> the impressive-sounding job titles they affected, actually worked as
> menials and servants. 'He's in banking', or 'He's in securities'. It
> sounded as if they were discussing a Rockefeller or a Mellon – and
> not some grey-headed, dignity-posturing bank janitor or bond-house
> messenger. 'I'm with an old family', was the euphemism used to
> dignify the professions of white folks' cooks and maids who talked so
> affectedly among their own kind in Roxbury that you couldn't even
> understand them. I don't know how many forty or fifty-year old errand
> boys went down the Hill dressed like ambassadors in black suits, to
> down-town jobs in 'government', 'in financing', or 'in law'. It has
> never ceased to amaze me how so many Negroes, now and then, could
> stand the indignity of that kind of self-delusion.[25]

But, he was also prepared to admit, as a teenager, Malcolm had
himself slavishly conformed to sartorial trends and fashions, as in
the hilarious account of his purchase of a 'zoot' suit:

> I was measured, and the young salesman picked off a rack a suit that
> was just wild; sky-blue pants thirty inches in the knees and angle-
> narrowed down to twelve inches at the bottom, and a long coat that
> pinched my waist and flared out below my knees. As a gift, the
> salesman said, the store would give me a narrow belt with my initial
> 'L' on it. Then he said I ought to buy a hat, and I did – blue, with a
> feather in the four-inch brim. Then the store gave me another present:
> a long, thick, gold-plated chain that swung down lower than my coat
> hem.

Again a moral is drawn: 'I was', Malcolm recalls ironically,
'sold forever on credit'.[26] Following his (false) conversion to the
Nation of Islam, Malcolm's dictated life-story adopts a more formal,
sober and suitably dignified form.

Never in prison have I studied and absorbed so intensely as I did now under Mr Muhammad's guidance....I went to bed every night ever more awed. If not Allah, who else could have put such wisdom into the little humble lamb of a man from the Georgia fourth grade and saw mills and cotton patches. The 'lamb of a man' analogy I drew for myself from the prophecy in the Book of Revelations of a symbolic lamb with a two-edged sword in its mouth. Mr Muhammad's two-edged sword was his teachings, which cut back and forth to free the black man's mind from the white man. My adoration of Mr. Muhammad grew, in the sense of the Latin root and word *adorare*.[27]

After his break with the Nation, Malcolm, converted to the true Islamic faith during his visit to Mecca, reflects on his earlier ingenuousness in having followed his acknowledged mentor without question.

I guess it would be impossible for anyone ever to realize fully how complete was my belief in Elijah Muhammad. I believed in him not only as a leader in the ordinary human sense, but I also believed in him as a divine leader. I believed he had no human weaknesses or faults.... There on a Holy World hilltop, I realized how very dangerous it is for people to hold any human being in such esteem, especially to consider anyone some sort of a 'divinely guided' or 'protected' person.[28]

In recounting the story of his life – whether as schoolboy, petty criminal, autodidact, Muslim minister or putative black leader – Malcolm (like Booker T. Washington) presents himself as eminently successful. He relates his receptions in Saudi Arabia with ostensible modesty and a certain disingenuousness, in a letter written at the time:

Never have I been so highly honoured....Who would believe the blessings that have been heaped upon an *American Negro*? A few nights ago, a man who would be called in America a 'white' man, a United Nations diplomat, an ambassador, a companion of kings, gave me *his* hotel suite, *his* bed....His Holiness Sheikh Muhammad Harkon himself okayed my visit to Mecca...he told me he hoped I would be a successful preacher of Islam in America. A car, a driver, and a guide have been placed at my disposal. Never would I have thought of dreaming that I would ever be a recipient of such honours – honours that in America would be bestowed upon a King – not a Negro.[29]

Embracing his new faith with enthusiasm and obvious sincerity, Malcolm, in the chapter of his *Autobiography* entitled 'El-Hajj Malik El-Shabazz', reveals that he also retained and displayed the self-confidence and boosterism of the American entrepreneur abroad:

> Behind my nods and smiles...I was doing some American-type
> thinking and reflection. I saw that Islam's conversions around the
> world could double and triple if the colourfulness and the true
> spiritualness of the Hajj pilgrimage were properly advertized and
> communicated to the outside world....The Arabs said 'insha Allah'
> ('God willing') – then they waited for converts. Even by this means,
> Islam was on the march, but I knew that with improved public
> relations the number of new converts turning to Allah could be turned
> to millions.[30]

As the late I. F. Stone, a journalist sympathetic to Malcolm,
wryly observed, El-Hajj Malik El-Shabazz 'had become a Hajj but
remained in some ways a Babbit, the salesman archetype of American
society. A creed was something to sell. Allah, the Merciful, needed
better merchandising.'[31] In a real sense, in his *Autobiography*,
Malcolm was 'merchandizing' himself, attempting to assure and
reassure his readers that as a consequence of the experiences
described, he was no longer a threat to society, but rather a figure
of integrity and stature. He was, however, prepared to admit to
Alex Haley that certain incidents had been exaggerated in the
telling to increase their dramatic impact. For example, as a young
gang leader, concerned to establish his credentials, he had not
actually played Russian roulette with a pistol, but had palmed the
bullet. When Haley offered to amend the passage, Malcolm replied
that it should stand since he did not want to be regarded as a
bluffer. Throughout the book, Malcolm presents himself as a man
constantly in motion and the process of change, who only came to
rest – physically and metaphysically – at the Holy City of Mecca.
His sense of spiritual kinship with fellow pilgrims is conveyed in
the following passage:

> ...the Muslim world's customs no longer seem strange to me. My
> hands readily plucked up food from a common dish shared with
> brother Muslims; I was drinking without hesitation from the same
> glass as others; I was washing from the same little pitcher of water;
> and sleeping with eight or ten others on a mat in the open. I remember
> one night...I lay awake among sleeping Muslim brothers and I learned
> that pilgrims from every land – every colour, and class, and rank;
> officials and beggars alike – all snored in the same language.[32]

Malcolm's autobiography does not end with his spiritual and
political illumination at Mecca, but rather in passages expressing
anxiety and uncertainty. Like Martin Luther King, Malcolm was
aware that he might, at any moment, be killed by either his black
or white enemies. He predicted with grim accuracy that 'I do not
expect to live long enough to read this book in its finished form',

and wondered only who 'would meet a fatal catastrophe first – "non-violent" Dr King, or so-called "violent" me'.[33] In the event, Malcolm was murdered three years before his great rival. Although King had deplored Malcolm's apparent preoccupation with violence and advocacy of racial separatism, he deplored Malcolm's untimely death. When a young white student informed him that his grandmother had just read *The Autobiography of Malcolm X* and thought 'it was a marvelous book of love', King reportedly replied:

> It was tragic that Malcolm was killed, he was really coming around, moving away from racism. He had such a sweet spirit...right before he was killed he came down to Selma and said some pretty passionate things against me, and that surprised me because after all it was my own territory down there. But afterwards he took my wife aside, and said he thought he could help me more by attacking me than praising me. He thought it would make it easier for me in the long run.[34]

During his lifetime, however, Malcolm elicited less generous responses from leaders of the civil rights coalition.

MALCOLM X AND HIS BLACK CRITICS

As an impassioned agitator, moralist and cynic, Malcolm found the integrationism, gradualism and non-violence espoused by the established civil rights leadership to be misguided and not a little ridiculous. In 1963, in a 'Message to the Grassroots', Malcolm informed his audience that the contemporary civil rights movement did not qualify as a social revolution. The American, French, Russian and Chinese revolutions had been marked by violence and bloodshed and had effected radical change. With heavy irony and emphasis, he suggested that the:

> only kind of revolution that is nonviolent is the *Negro* revolution. The only revolution based on loving your enemy is the *Negro* revolution. The only revolution in which the goal is a desegregated lunch counter, a desegregated theatre, a desegregated park, and a desegregated toilet. You can sit down next to white folks – on the *toilet*.

At a Harlem rally late in 1964, Malcolm declared 'I don't believe we're going to overcome [by] singing. If you're going to get yourself a .45 and start singing "We Shall Overcome", I'm with you.'[35] Asked about his view of the activities of Martin Luther King and the SCLC in Birmingham, Alabama, Malcolm replied harshly: 'Martin Luther King is a chump not a champ. Any man who puts his women and children on the front lines is a chump, not a champ.'[36] Nationally-recognized black leaders, Malcolm maintained, had betrayed their constituents. He informed a Detroit conference in 1963 that:

> When Martin Luther King failed to desegregate Albany, Georgia, the civil rights struggle in America reached its lowpoint. King became bankrupt almost, as a leader. The Southern Christian Leadership Conference was in financial trouble; and it was in trouble, period, with the people when they failed to desegregate Albany, Georgia. Other Negro civil rights leaders of so-called national stature became fallen idols...began to lose their prestige and influence [but] local leaders began to stir up the masses...at the grass roots level. This was never done by these Negroes of national stature....They control you, they contain you, they have kept you on the plantation.[37]

Asked in an interview in March 1964 about his attitude toward 'Christian-Gandhian groups', Malcolm retorted:

> Christian? Gandhian? I don't go for anything that's nonviolent and turn-the-other-cheekish....I've never heard of a nonviolent revolution or a revolution that was brought about by turning the other cheek, and so I believe that it is a crime for anyone to teach a person who is being brutalized to continue to accept the brutality without doing something to defend himself. If this is what the Christian-Gandhian philosophy teaches, then it is criminal – a criminal philosophy.[38]

Again, Malcolm's insistence on separatism and identification with Africa, was at odds with the integrationism and 'Americanism' of the civil rights movement. In a conversation with the Southern white writer, Robert Penn Warren, Malcolm derided the possibility of 'the political and economic system of this country' producing 'freedom, justice...equality and human dignity for twenty-two million Afro-Americans' and declared that:

> I believe that a psychological, cultural, and philosophical migration back to Africa will solve our problems. Not a physical migration, but a cultural, psychological [and] philosophical migration back to Africa – which means restoring our common bond – will give us the spiritual strength and the incentive to strengthen our political and social position right here in America...And at the same time this will give incentive to many of our people to also visit and even migrate physically back to Africa, and those who stay here can help those who go back and those who go back can help those who stay here, in the same way as the Jews who go to Israel.[39]

Such statements by Malcolm, whether as a Black Muslim or independent minister, earned him the condemnation of most black leaders and spokesmen. The substance of much of their criticism echoed that of earlier Afro-American indictments of Marcus Garvey. Malcolm, it was generally conceded, had touched the sensitivities of urban blacks by exhorting them to reassert racial pride and to resist white oppression and denigration. Martin Luther King reportedly once remarked to a friend: 'I just saw Malcolm X on television. I can't deny it. When he starts talking about all that's been done to us, I get a twinge of hate, of identification with him'.[40] But King also deplored Malcolm's apparent obsession with violence and asserted that:

> ...violence is not going to solve our problem...in his litany of articulating the despair of the Negro without offering any positive, creative alternative, I feel that Malcolm has done himself and our people a great disservice. Fiery, demagogic oratory in the black ghettos, urging Negroes to arm themselves and prepare to engage in violence, as he has done, can reap nothing but grief.[41]

In the last months of his life, Malcolm was also seen by his black critics (and with some justification) as confused and uncertain. Bayard Rustin informed Robert Penn Warren in October 1964 that Malcolm (then returning from the Near East) was only a marginal figure.

> He has very little in the way of an organization – practically nothing. They're a few frustrated youngsters and a few confused writers...but even before he left here, these Sunday meetings which he was always having got smaller and smaller, because he doesn't have any real answers to the immediate problems which Negroes want an answer to.

Whitney M. Young of the National Urban League believed that despite frequent appearances in headlines and on television:

> ...there aren't ten Negroes who would follow Malcolm X to a separate state. The only appeal he has is to give a Negro who's been beaten down all day a chance to get a vicarious pleasure out of hearing someone cuss out the white people.

James Farmer, of the Congress of Racial Equality, felt that 'Malcolm has done nothing but verbalize – his militancy is a matter of posture, there has been no action'.[42] To Roy Wilkins of the NAACP, Malcolm's greatest limitation was that 'the only way you could judge things was whether you did the thing that was manly, no matter if it was suicidal or not. A prosecutor like Malcolm has to be able to put himself in the shoes of people who did the best they could under the circumstances', and this, Wilkins believed, Malcolm was congenitally unprepared or unwilling to do.[43] Only after his death and canonization as the patron saint of Black Power by the younger elements in the black protest movement were established black leaders prepared to offer more favourable estimates of Malcolm X.

ASSESSMENT

As a black Muslim minister and independent spokesman after his break with Elijah Muhammad, Malcolm X was consistently dedicated to the spiritual regeneration of Afro-Americans. He employed the rhetoric of racial separatism to affirm the resolve of blacks to exist on their own terms within (but culturally and mentally apart from) the surrounding white society. An accomplished , polished and artful public speaker, Malcolm portrayed and analysed the plight and dilemma of black Americans with remarkable vividness and clarity. His speeches were filled with visual images, metaphors, slogans and allusions to black history, music and folk lore, all of which struck an immediate chord with his audiences. In the following exchange with Richard Penn Warren, Malcolm responds to a question about 'nonselective reprisal' against whites with a parable:

> Well, I'll tell you, if I go home and my child has blood running down her leg and someone tells me a snake bit her, I'm going out and kill snakes, and when I find a snake I'm not going to look and see if he has blood on his jaws.
> WARREN: You mean you'd kill any snake you could find?
> MALCOLM X: I grew up in the country, on a farm. And whenever a snake was bothering the chickens, we'd kill the snakes. We never knew which was the snake did it.
> WARREN: To read your parable, then, you would advocate nonselective reprisals?
> MALCOLM X: I'm just telling you about the snakes.[44]

In Malcolm's imagery, society was a jungle, infested with snakes, foxes, wolves and vultures, yet black 'leaders' themselves, were often no more than 'parrots', repeating 'what the [white] man says.'[45]

The most remarkable feature of Malcolm's remarkable life was his capacity for intellectual growth. From the parochial and simplistic outlook of his Black Muslim phase, he came to embrace a more sophisticated and informed spiritual and political world-view by the time of his death. But he never abandoned his role as an evangelist for a form of black nationalism which owed much to

Marcus Garvey's example. As a Black Muslim minister, Malcolm energized and greatly increased the membership and vitality of what had been a relatively obscure and largely elderly sect. By 1963 he had become increasingly impatient with the political disengagement forced on the Nation of Islam by Elijah Muhammad. Simultaneously, he pointed out the weaknesses in the objectives and achievements of a civil rights coalition which, after some successes in the South, had come to regard racial integration as a panacea. Again, as an independent minister, Malcolm voiced the feelings of a younger black generation either hostile or indifferent to Martin Luther King's philosophy of non-violence and the power of redemptive suffering. And, before King's own move to the left, Malcolm highlighted the socio-economic condition (and needs) of blacks, and the failure of the civil rights movement to effect meaningful change in the lives of the ghetto proletariat. Malcolm espoused (and personified) black leadership from the grass roots of local organizations, free from the domination of the middle classes. Bayard Rustin, in conversation with Peter Goldman, conceded that Malcolm had brought a kind of psychic satisfaction and compensation to the dispossessed:

> King had to be measured by his victories. But what King did, what the NAACP did, what Roy Wilkins did, all that was for the benefit of the Southern Negro. There were no obtainable, immediate results for the Northern ghettoized black, whose housing is getting worse; who is unable to find work; whose schools are deteriorating ....He...must find victory somewhere, and he finds victory within. He needed Malcolm, who brought him an internal victory, precisely because the external victory is beyond his reach. What can bring satisfaction is the feeling that he is black, he is a man, he is internally free. King had to win victories in the real world. Malcolm's were the kind you can create yourself.[46]

The sociologist C. Eric Lincoln expressed a similar view of Malcolm's appeal and achievement:

> He was always challenging the white man, always debunking the white man. I don't think he was ever under any illusion that a powerless black minority could mount a physical challenge to a powerful white majority and survive. But they could mount a psychological challenge, and if they were persistent, they might at least produce some erosion in the attitudes and the strategies by which the white man has always protected himself and his interests. His challenge was to prove that you are as great as you say you are...as moral as you say you are...as kind as you say you are...as loving as you say you are...as altruistic as you say you are...as *superior* as you say you are.[47]

Like Marcus Garvey, Malcolm X has been claimed as a revolutionary and a reactionary, a black nationalist and a black racist, a prophet and a demagogue. Like Garvey also, Malcolm had more followers than those who belonged to the Organization of Afro-American Unity. Where Garvey spoke to the despairing mood of the 1920s, Malcolm was receptive to the hopelessness of the enduring black ghettos of the 1960s, which he sought to transform into centres of black consciousness, enterprise and spiritual liberation. Two differing estimates of Malcolm, both delivered after his assassination, illustrate his essentially *psychological* appeal as perceived by admirers and critics. Asked why he 'eulogized' Malcolm X, Ossie Davis, the black actor, director and playwright, replied:

> We used to think that protocol and common sense required that Negroes stand back and let the white man speak up for us, defend us, and lead us from behind the scenes in our fight. This was the essence of Negro politics. But Malcolm said to hell with that! Get up off your knees and fight your own battles....That's the way to make the white man respect you. Malcolm...was refreshing excitement....He could make you angry as hell, but he could also make you proud. It was impossible to remain defensive and apologetic about being a Negro in his presence....I never doubted that Malcolm X, even when he was wrong, was always the rarest thing in the world among us Negroes: a true man.[48]

James Baldwin, writing seven years after Malcolm's death, observed correctly that Malcolm had never been a 'racist':

> His intelligence was more complex than that.... What made him unfamiliar and dangerous was not his hatred for white people but his love for blacks, his apprehension of the horror of the black condition, and the reasons for it, and his determination so to work on their hearts and minds that they would be enabled to see their condition and change it for themselves.[49]

Although he rejected Malcolm's racial separatism and advocacy of retaliatory violence, Martin Luther King, his widow believed, occupied some common ground with him.

> he shared with Malcolm the fierce desire that the black American reclaim his racial pride, his joy in himself and his race – in a physical, a cultural, and a spiritual rebirth. He shared with the nationalists the sure knowledge that 'black is beautiful' and that, in so many respects, the quality of the black people's scale of values was far superior to that of the white culture which attempted to enslave us....Martin too believed that white Christianity had failed to act in accordance with its teachings. Martin also believed in nonviolent

Black Power. He believed that we must have our share of the economy, of education, of jobs of free choice.[50]

With the violent deaths of Martin Luther King, Jr, and of Malcolm X, the urban riots of the 1960s, and the fragmentation of the civil rights coalition on the rocks of Black Power and the polarization caused by the Vietnam War, American society appeared to be in turmoil. Legislation designed to improve the citizenship status of blacks – notably, the Civil Rights Act of 1964 and the Voting Rights Act of 1965 – served also to heighten their expectations. Yet in 1966 the unemployment rate for blacks was 7.8 per cent, or twice the national average, with 40 per cent of black families earning less than $3,000 a year. Again, ten years after the Supreme Court's historic decision on school desegregation, the United States Commissioner of Education could report that the majority of American children still attended racially segregated schools. Most disturbingly, perhaps, the nation's black ghettos, despite the efforts of Martin Luther King and Malcolm X, remained as appalling reminders of the persistence (if not the intensification) of white racism impervious to the appeals of either integrationists or black nationalists. The disillusioned mood of urban blacks was most frighteningly revealed in the wave of 'civil disorders' which engulfed the country's major cities in the 1960s: Harlem (1964), Watts, Los Angeles (1965), Newark, New Jersey; Detroit, Michigan, and Cleveland, Ohio (1967 – 68), suffered major racial disturbances which resulted in over 200 deaths (mostly of blacks), with at least 10,000 injured and 60,000 arrested, and the widespread destruction of property. Opinion polls indicated that while most blacks agreed that rioters and looters were guilty of criminal acts, many also regarded rioting as a justifiable form of political protest against police brutality, unremitting white racism, and the dreadful condition within the black ghettos. As President Lyndon Johnson's National Advisory Commission on Civil Disorders reported:

> What white Americans have never fully understood – but what the Negro can never forget – is that white society is deeply implicated in the ghetto. White institutions created it, white institutions maintain it, and white society condones it....Our nation is moving toward two societies, one black, one white – separate and unequal.[51]

REFERENCES

1. *The Saturday Evening Post*, 12 September 1964, quoted in *The Autobiography of Malcolm X* (Penguin, Harmondsworth, 1980 edn.), p.44.
2. Lincoln, C. E., 'The Meaning of Malcolm X', in J. H. Clarke (ed.), *Malcolm X: The Man and His Times* (Toronto, 1969), p.10.
3. Whitman, A., 'Father Divine', in *The Obituary Book* (New York, 1971), pp.64–5.
4. Muhammad, E., 'The Muslim Programme', in J. H. Bracey, A. Meier and E. Rudwick, *Black Nationalism in America* (New York, 1970), pp.404–7.
5. *The Autobiography of Malcolm X*, op. cit., p.79.
6. Ibid., p.85.
7. Ibid., pp.248–9.
8. Bracey *et al.*, *Black Nationalism in America*, op. cit., pp.410–20.
9. Goldman, P., *The Death and Life of Malcolm X* (London, 1974) p.75.
10. Clark, K. B., *The Negro Protest: James Baldwin, Malcolm X and Martin Luther King Talk With Kenneth B. Clark* (Boston, 1963), pp.26–7.
11. Lomax, L. E., *When the World is Given: A Report on Elijah Muhammad and the Black Muslim World* (New York, 1964), p.174.
12. Goldman, P., 'Malcolm X: Witness for the Prosecution', in J. H. Franklin and A. Meier (eds), *Black Leaders of the Twentieth Century* (University of Illinois Press, 1982), p.317.
13. *The Autobiography of Malcolm X*, op. cit., p.397.
14. Ibid., p.411.
15. Breitman, G., *Malcolm X Speaks* (New York, 1965), pp.18–22.
16. Weisbord, R. G., *Ebony Kinship: Africa, Africans and the Afro-Americans* (Westport, Connecticut, 1973), p.82.
17. Malcolm X, 'Statement of the Basic Aims and Objectives of the Organization of Afro-American Unity', in Bracey *et al.*, *Black Nationalism in America*, pp.421–7.
18. Goldman, *The Death and Life of Malcolm X*, op. cit., p.190.
19. Breitman, G., *The Last Year of Malcolm X* (New York, 1967), p.46.
20. Blair, T. L., *Retreat to the Ghetto: The End of a Dream* (London, 1977), p.46.
21. Goldman, *The Death and Life of Malcolm X*, op. cit., p.234.
22. Breitman, *The Last Year of Malcolm X*, op. cit., p.46.
23. *The Autobiography of Malcolm X*, op. cit., pp.137–8.
24. Ibid., p.140.
25. Ibid., p.123.

26. Ibid., p 135.
27. Ibid., pp.310–11.
28. Ibid., pp.482–3.
29. Ibid., pp.455–6.
30. Ibid., p.469.
31. Stone, I. F., *In a Time of Torment* (New York, 1967), p.117.
32. *The Autobiography of Malcolm X*, op. cit., pp.457–8.
33. Ibid., pp.496, 500.
34. Halberstam, D., 'When "Civil Rights" and "Peace" Join Forces', in C. E. Lincoln (ed.), *Martin Luther King Jr.: A Profile* (London, 1972), pp.66–7.
35. Goldman, 'Malcolm X: Witness for the Prosecution', op. cit., p.319.
36. Lomax, *When the World is Given*, op. cit., p.74.
37. Epps, A. (ed.), *The Speeches of Malcolm X at Harvard* (New York, 1969), p.70.
38. Breitman, G. (ed.), *By Any Means Necessary: Speeches, Interviews and a Letter by Malcolm X* (New York, 1970), pp.8–9.
39. Warren, R. P., *Who Speaks for the Negro?* (New York, 1965), p.259.
40. Ibid., p.266.
41. Oates, S. B., *Let the Trumpet Sound: The Life of Martin Luther King, Jr.* (London, 1982), p.253.
42. Warren, *Who Speaks for the Negro?* op. cit., pp.161, 197, 244.
43. Goldman, *The Death and Life of Malcolm X*, op. cit., p.385.
44. Warren, *Who Speaks for the Negro?* op. cit., p.261.
45. Epps, *The Speeches of Malcolm X at Harvard*, op. cit., p.49.
46. Goldman, 'Malcolm X: Witness for the Prosecution', op. cit., p.311.
47. Ibid., p.312.
48. Davis, O., 'Why I Eulogized Malcolm X', in J. H. Clarke, *Malcolm X: The Man and His Times*, op. cit., pp.128–31.
49. Baldwin, J., *No Name in the Street* (London, 1972), pp.66–7.
50. King, C. S., *My Life With Martin Luther King, Jr.* (New York, 1970), pp.256–7.
51. *Report of the National Advisory Commission on Civil Disorders* (New York, 1968), p.1.

CHAPTER SEVEN

Jesse Jackson: Populist Preacher

I've always developed a tension – a tension in my own mind about the place I'm assigned I deserve to be. That's why I resist the press calling me a black leader. I'm a moral leader who just happens to be black.   [JESSE JACKSON][1]

We can move from the slave ship to the championship! From the guttermost to the uppermost! From the outhouse to the courthouse! From the state house to the White house!
        [JESSE JACKSON: Los Angeles Rally, August 1982]

Jackson's rise to prominence in 1984 was fueled by a number of factors; central among them were his impressive knack for self-promotion and the dispirited and uncertain conditions prevailing within the Afro-American population. [ADOLPH L. REED, JR][2]

PERSPECTIVES: FROM BLACK POWER TO POLITICAL POWER, 1966–1984

By 1966 what Milton Viorst has called the 'reformist phase' of the black protest movement had achieved its notable victories.[3] The Civil Rights Act of 1964, and the Voting Rights Act of 1965, abolished the formal practices of segregation and eliminated 'literacy' and other tests which had been used to prevent blacks from registering as qualified voters. Yet there were, as has been seen, divisions within the civil rights coalition which came increasingly into the open. The older established organizations and their leaders resented the publicity given to younger elements, such as CORE and SNCC, while there were also tensions and jealousies between the older leaders themselves. Roy Wilkins of the NAACP, for example, resented Martin Luther King's preeminence as the primary symbol and spokesman of the civil rights struggle.

At the height of the SCLC's Birmingham campaign, Attorney General Robert Kennedy reminded the president that in responding to the crisis, the administration should keep in mind the fact that 'Roy Wilkins hates Martin Luther King'.[4] Young activists in the Student Nonviolent Coordinating Committee also believed that King's style of leadership discouraged grass roots organization, came to question (and then reject) integration as the proper goal of militant black protest, and began to define its purpose as the creation of autonomous political and economic institutions. By the mid-1960s, SNCC had disavowed non-violence and had also rejected alliances with white liberals. CORE advocated working within the Democratic party, but sanctioned the use of violence in self-defence, and called for black economic boycotts as well as all-black businesses and financial institutions based on and located within the ghettos. In 1968 whites were excluded from active membership of CORE. These 'radical' critics of the civil rights movement criticized it as a subterfuge for the maintenance of white supremacy, rejected the assumptions of integration, and stressed instead the virtues of black life-styles and black consciousness.

At the other end of the black ideological spectrum, the Nation of Islam continued to denigrate Malcolm X as an apostate. In a two-page editorial in *Muhammad Speaks*, published six years after his assassination, it warned that:

Some people want to build a backward nation by goading unstable youths to violence....Such people are attempting to use Malcolm to mislead his sincere admirers. His good qualities – the long hard study put in under the guidance of Mr Muhammad – are ignored...what youths are really being told is that by being a degenerate, hustler, and quick-to-kill, they are being 'revolutionary' like the 'real Malcolm', the pre-Muslim Malcolm. Other young blacks are being told that Malcolm discovered some great, abstract...'humanistic' 'Truth' in the last eleven months of his life. This nameless, mythical abstraction they would have impressionable Blacks substitute for a programme of real social progress...for dignity bestowed on hard work...which are consistently advanced by Messenger Muhammad year in year out.[5]

The Nation's expressed concern over the growing cult of Malcolm X was not misplaced. In many respects, he was the inspiration for and posthumous examplar of a revitalized nationalism that began as a slogan and gradually acquired a supporting rationale – the ideology of Black Power.

BLACK POWER: 'OLD WINE IN NEW BOTTLES'?

During the continuation of James Meredith's 'March Against Fear' in the summer of 1966, Stokely Carmichael of the SNCC, informed a crowd at Greenwood, Mississippi:

> The only way we gonna stop them white men from whuppin us is to take over....We been sayin' 'freedom ' for six years and we ain't got nothin'. What we gonna start sayin' now is....BLACK POWER[6]

Precisely what the new slogan meant was unclear. Julius Lester, a former field secretary of SNCC, offered a simplistic interpretation of the concept in his half-humorous but sharply bitter account: *Look Out Whitey! Black Power's Gon' Get Your Mama*, published in 1968. Black Power, Lester asserted, meant that 'Black People would control their own lives, destinies and communities', and he ridiculed the 1963 March on Washington as:

> ...a great inspiration to those who think that something is being accomplished by having black bodies next to white ones...nothing but a giant therapy session that allowed Dr. King to orate about his dreams of a nigger eating at the same table with some Georgia cracker, while most black folks just dreamed of eating.[7]

As a black nationalist ideology, Black Power came to acquire a variety of connotations. It was most obviously a reaction against persistent white racism and paternalism, which viewed integration as either 'tokenism' or 'assimilationism'. Stokely Carmichael and Charles V. Hamilton, in their elucidation of Black Power asserted that: 'The goal of black people must not be to assimilate into middle-class America, for that class, as a whole, is without a viable conscience as regards humanity'.[8] They also rejected the notion of an equal working partnership with whites in the black protest movement, and dismissed the efforts of 'many young, middle-class, white Americans, [who] like some sort of Pepsi-Cola generation, have wanted to "come alive" through the black community and black groups'.[9] Black Power also represented a disillusionment with the 'gradualism' and legislative achievements of the civil rights coalition – a recognition that its apparent victories had not produced any discernible changes in the lives of most Afro-

Americans. Most obviously, Black Power was an assertion (or rather, a reassertion) of racial pride, a rejection of white standards of physical and cosmetic beauty, evident in the slogan 'Black is Beautiful', and the vogue of 'natural' Afro-American hair styles (or wigs), adopted by such entertainers as James Brown and Nina Simone. In the 1960s the sound of black jazz grew harsher, evident in the work of Miles Davis, Sonny Rollins and John Coltrane. There was also a renewed interest in the African background and heritage (real or imagined) of black Americans, together with demands for Black Studies programmes in colleges and universities, with black instructors and separate facilities for black students.

In politics, Black Power was synonymous with independent black action and exercise of power in the urban ghettos, either through the creation of a black political party or control of the political machinery within the ghettos, without white involvement. Economically, Black Power called for the creation of independent, self-sufficient black business enterprises through the encouragement of black entrepreneurs and the formation of black cooperatives. In the area of education, Black Power theoreticians demanded local community control of public schools in predominantly black neighbourhoods. Essentially, Black Power stressed self-help, racial unity and voluntary segregation. Owing a great deal to Malcolm X's black nationalist statements, Black Power as Lyndon Johnson's Commission on Civil Disorders concluded, was in some respects also 'Old Wine in New Bottles':

> Black Power advocates feel that they are the most militant group in the Negro protest movement. Yet they have retreated from a direct confrontation with American society on the issue of integration and, by preaching separatism, unconsciously function as an accommodation to white racism. Much of their economic programme, as well as their interest in Negro history, self-help, racial solidarity and separation, is reminiscent of Booker T. Washington. The rhetoric is different, but the programmes are remarkably similar.[10]

From its inception, Black Power was never a coherent ideology, and failed to formulate demands that were supported by a majority of its proponents. (It also contained disturbing elements of anti-Semitism, which many American commentators chose to ignore.) Moreover, as Manning Marable has observed, Black Power was quickly appropriated by conservative interests, black and white. The Black Power conference held in Philadelphia in June 1968 was co-sponsored by Clairol, a white corporation, whose president endorsed the concept as meaning black 'ownership of apartments, ownership of homes, ownership of businesses, as well as equitable treatment for all people'. Again, the Republican Richard Nixon, running for the presidency in 1968, defined (and defused) Black Power as another form of 'free enterprise':

> What most of the militants are asking is not separation but to be included in – not as supplicants, but as owners, as entrepreneurs – to have a share of the wealth and a piece of the action. And this is precisely what the Federal central target of the new approach ought to be. It ought to be oriented toward more black ownership, for from this can flow the rest – black pride, black jobs, black opportunity and yes, black power.[11]

In these formulations, Black Power had been transmuted simply into Black Capitalism. Theodore Draper has suggested plausibly that:

> Both the strengths and weaknesses of the Black Power slogan may be traced to its ambiguity....It sprang from a nationalist urge without getting into any of the nationalist dilemmas. It avoided trouble by the simple expedient of leaving undefined what kind of 'power' it had in mind. Black capitalists as well as black separatist revolutionaries could adopt it for very different purposes.[12]

The Black Panther party, founded in Oakland, California by two black college students, Huey Newton and Bobby Seale in 1966, was perhaps the most extreme example of Black Power in action. Its original 'Ten Point Programme' stated the following demands:
1. We want freedom. We want power to determine the destiny of our black community.
2. We want full employment for our people.
3. We want an end to robbery by the white man of our black community.
4. We want decent homes, for shelter of human beings.
5. We want education for our people that exposes the true nature of this decadent American society. We want education that teaches us our true history and our role in the present day society.
6. We want all black men to be exempt from military service.
7. We want an immediate end to *police brutality* and *murder* of black people.
8. We want freedom for all black men held in federal state, county, and city prisons and jails.
9. We want all black people when brought to a trial to be tried in court by a jury of their peer group or people from their black communities, as defined by the Constitution of the United States.
10. We want land, bread, housing, education, clothing, justice and peace.[13]

With its firearms, black berets, and menacing Black Panther emblem, the new party (which organized armed patrols to protect the black community of East Oakland against police attacks) spread rapidly across the country, and appeared to be a direct threat to 'law and order'. In fact, the Panthers were initially reformist rather than revolutionary. In 1967 they initiated a free breakfast programme for black children, and offered medical advice to ghetto residents. By the end of the decade the Panthers had become a Marxist-Leninist party, advocating the revolutionary overthrow of capitalist America. But as a consequence of police and FBI infiltration and harassment, the party's leaders, by the early 1970s, were dead, imprisoned, or, as in the case of Eldridge Cleaver, the Panther's 'Minister of Information', in exile abroad.

The fundamentalist Nation of Islam also underwent significant changes in the 1970s. After the death of Elijah Muhammad in 1975, his son, Wallace D. Muhammad, assumed leadership of the sect, and began to modify (or to 'Malcolmize') its tenets. Re-named the World Community of Al-Islam in the West, it embraced the orthodox teachings of Islam, and began to direct its efforts toward the establishment of a collectivist capitalism, and whites were invited to join the movement which had earlier castigated them as 'devils'. Even before Elijah Muhammad's death, the Nation had begun to assume a Third World (as opposed to a traditional black nationalist) stance. It supported such disparate movements as Pan-Islam, Pan-Africanism, Puerto Rican nationalism and international socialism. The notion of a 'homeland' for Afro-Americans was considerably played down in favour of a more conventional form of Pan-Islamism. In 1976 Wallace Muhammad received $16 million from the United Arab Emirates, to build a new mosque and educational institution, and also obtained a contract to package food and supplies for the United States Army. However, not all black Muslims accepted these innovations. In 1981 Minister Louis Farrakhan announced his intention to return the Nation to the precepts and practices of Elijah Muhammad, hastening the fragmentation and decline of the black nationalist sect.

A year before his assassination, Malcolm X remarked that the legal victories achieved by the civil rights movement in the 1960s were making black Americans more politically conscious and assertive. During the 1970s and 1980s, many blacks appeared to believe that political activity and political power were the most effective means to realize further racial advancement. Accordingly, the strategies employed by black leaders turned increasingly away from demonstrations, confrontations and boycotts towards greater use of the ballot gained by the 1965 Voting Rights Act. In 1966 there were 6 black members in the United States Congress and 97 Negroes serving in state legislatures; by 1973, there were 16 blacks in Congress, and over 200 in 37 state legislatures. In 1979, blacks held 4,607 elected offices – 66 per cent of which were in the South – and there were 191 black mayors and 313 state legislators. The Democratic party responded to this upsurge in political activity by significantly increasing the number of black delegates to the party's 1972 National Convention, where black Congresswoman Shirley Chisholm campaigned (unsuccessfully) for the Democratic presidential nomination. In the 1976 presidential election, over 90 per cent of black voters supported the Democrat's nominee, Jimmy Carter. As president, Carter appointed some blacks to high office – most notably, Andrew Young, as US Ambassador to the United Nations, Patricia Harris as Cabinet secretary of housing and urban development, and John Reinhardt to the International Communications Agency. Willie Dennis, the black speaker of the California legislature, observed in 1981 that 'black leadership' had become more diffuse:

> Now the politicians who are black are providing one aspect of black leadership, the religious community another, and the professional organization another. This adds up to even greater international change than could ever have been brought about by a Martin Luther King rally or a Roy Wilkins boycott.[14]

Yet even by the early 1980s, elected black officials constituted less than 1 per cent of all elected officials nationally, and one forecast estimated that at this rate of change, blacks would only hold 3 per cent of all elective offices by the year 2000. Again, blacks had gained 'power' in large urban centres precisely when the continued migration of impoverished ethnic groups to metro-politan areas, and the ongoing exodus of affluent whites to the suburbs and (increasingly) to the 'sunbelt' states made the inner cities politically less significant than they had been in the past. A 1974 study found that in 23 out of 26 cities with black mayors, 16 ranked in the top third of all American cities based on their rates of poverty. Despite the growth of the black middle class – as measured by education, income and occupation – black unemploy-ment rates were at least double those of whites, life expectancy for blacks was shorter than that for whites, black infant mortality rates were greater, and many poor black families (nearly 70 per cent of the total) were headed by women.

Carter's successor, the Republican Ronald Reagan, had little sympathy for minority groups or civil rights. In its first six months in office, the Reagan administration only filed five law suits relating to racial discrimination with the Civil Rights Division at the Justice Department (as compared with twenty-four suits under Richard Nixon and seventeen under Carter during their first six months' tenure). Reagan insisted that enforcement of civil rights should be left to the individual states, curtailed laws against housing discrimination, and reduced the numbers of those eligible for such social welfare programmes as unemployment compensation, Medicaid, food stamps and Aid to Families with Dependent Children. Only after intense pressure from the Congressional Black Caucus, other members of Congress and civil rights sympathizers, did Reagan agree to sign the bill which commemorated Martin Luther King's birthday (15 January) as a national holiday. At a White House ceremony on 2 November 1983, Reagan (in the presence of the King family) declared that: 'traces of bigotry still mar America. So each year on Martin Luther King day, let us not only recall Dr. King, but rededicate ourselves to the commandments he believed in and sought to live everyday'.[15] If Reagan (unconvincingly) on this occasion, appeared to endorse King's precepts and practices, an aspiring black leader had already laid claims to being his true successor.

JESSE JACKSON: FROM A & T TO PUSH

Jesse Louis Jackson was born in Greensville, South Carolina in 1941, the illegitimate son of an Alabama sharecropper. A promising student and a natural athlete, Jackson later typified the Jim Crow system he was exposed to in the South Carolina of his youth as one of 'Humiliation':

...go to the back of the bus even though you pay the same fare. Humiliation: no public parks or libraries you can use even though you pay taxes. Humiliation: upstairs in movies. Back doors in hotels and cafes....Humiliation: all-white police with no police warrants who were so absolute in their power until they were called 'the law'. Humiliation: a dual school system. Black teachers and white teachers working the same hours, only the Black teachers taught more students and taught double shifts and received less pay....We used books exactly three years after white students used them. We used desks exactly four years after whites used them. There were no Black school boardmembers....We were rewarded for docility and punished for expressing manhood. Men were called boys. Women called girls. We called white children 'Master' and 'Missy'.[16]

Jackson won an athletic scholarship to the University of Illinois in 1959, but because of his colour was not allowed to play as a football quarterback and resented his exclusion from social events. He transferred to the all-black North Carolina Agricultural and Technical State University, where he became involved in the Greenboro student sit-in movement directed against segregated lunch counters. A. Knighton Stanley, a young black minister serving the A & T campus, and William Thomas, a CORE student activist, recognized that Jackson, flamboyant, dynamic, a football star and president of the Student Council, would be a valuable addition to the protests. Stanley later recalled:

> We needed Jesse as a football player the girls loved....We woke him up one day and told him to protest with us and he has been protesting ever since.[17]

Recruited to act as a marshal for downtown marches, Jackson soon became identified as a sit-in leader. On one occasion, he led seven hundred demonstrators to the City Hall in Greensboro, and in a reference to the SCLC's Birmingham, Alabama campaign, declared that, in a similar fashion, local blacks would 'take over the city of Greensboro'. When Jackson was arrested and put in jail, leaflets were printed with the headline 'Your great leader has been arrested'.[18]

After graduation, Jackson enrolled at the Chicago Theological Seminary, and, in 1963, joined the SCLC, and earned a reputation for his organizing abilities in rallying the city's black clergy behind Martin Luther King. In 1963 Jackson joined the SCLC campaign in Selma, and in 1966 helped to unite the SCLC and the Chicago Coordinating Council of Community Organizations into the Chicago Freedom Movement, which pressed for open housing and school integration. Appointed by King to head the SCLC's Operation Breadbasket, Jackson led protests for non-discriminatory hiring practices by Chicago businesses. Within twelve months, Jackson had helped to obtain 2,200 jobs for blacks in white-owned Chicago firms. Despite (or because of) his rapid ascendancy within the SCLC, Jackson was regarded by many of his colleagues as an upstart and a self-promoter. King himself shared some of these reservations about Jackson, and also questioned his failure to appreciate the need for a wholesale restructuring of the American economy. Andrew Young remembered that King, despite being impressed with Jackson's performance in Chicago and Cleveland with Operation Breadbasket:

> was quite rough on Jesse because he (King) said that...Breadbasket would not solve the problem...that jobs would finally have to be provided by the public sector rather than the private sector, and that Breadbasket was essentially a private sector programme.[19]

On another occasion, King remarked in exasperation:

> Jesse Jackson's so independent, I either want him in SCLC or out...he's a part of SCLC or he's not a part of SCLC.

William A. Rutherford, a black Chicago businessman who joined the SCLC in 1967, believed that King's displeasure with Jackson was more than a disagreement over ideology and recalled:

> He didn't trust Jesse, he didn't even like Jesse....If you ask me if there was any suspicion about Jesse's motives and even devotion to the movement, I would say categorically yes, there was – considerable. And we talked about it.

(Another SCLC executive remembered that King used to say 'Jesse, you have no love'.)[20]

Jackson was with King in Memphis when he was assassinated in April 1968, and aroused further bitterness (and disbelief) within SCLC by appearing on national television in Chicago, the same night, claiming to have King's blood on his shirt and to have been the last person to speak with him.

When SCLC, after King's death, decided to stage the Poor People's Campaign, Jackson appeared as the 'mayor' of 'Resurrection City' – the tent and plywood encampment set up near the Washington Monument. (Resurrection City was poorly organized and quickly became a liability to the SCLC, which was presented with a bill of $71,000 by the National Parks Service for damage caused, while blacks in the capital virtually ignored the protest.) Within SCLC itself, there was an opposition to Ralph Abernathy's assumption of leadership, and Jackson (already receiving national publicity for his Operation Breadbasket project) resigned from the organization in 1971. The occasion of the break came when Abernathy suspended Jackson for sixty days after he had staged a fair called 'Black Expo' under a separate organization, rather than under the aegis of SCLC, but the causes went back further. In April 1970 Jackson had appeared on the cover of *Time* magazine in an issue devoted to 'Black America 1970'. Characterized by *Time* as 'one leader among many', Jackson was, nevertheless, given an extensive profile:

> Tall and sensuously attractive, Jackson is the kind of leader who suggests both a dignity of bearing in his brooding dedication to his cause and a sense of brotherly warmth in his casual Levi's, boots and open sports shirts. He possesses what he himself matter-of-factly accepts as charisma, and he inspires devotion among a wide range of followers....At 28, he effectively bridges the widening gulf between the young activists and the old-style moralistic preachers. His strength is his use of evangelistic fervor to achieve pragmatic ends....He feels that many blacks have common economic grievances with poor whites....Jackson expounds his opinions forcefully in public. He does not arouse a crowd as readily as King did, but he employs cadence, sweeping hand gestures, a penetrating gaze and abrupt changes in volume to command attention. He deliberately mangles grammar and throws in mild profanity to develop rapport with audiences. He is hopelessly addicted to preacherly metaphors....He has a host of adoring admirers as well as caustic critics. But he is still too young to assume a black leadership role on a national scale.[21]

During the decade of the 1970s Jackson engaged in a carefully-planned campaign of self-advertisement, addressed over 500 civic and professional groups, including the National Conference of Mayors and the United Negro College Fund, and became a columnist with the *Los Angeles Times* syndicate. After his break with the SCLC in 1971, Jackson (who had been ordained as a Baptist minister in 1968) founded Operation PUSH (People United to Save Humanity) – later changed to People United to *Serve* Humanity – with its headquarters in Chicago. The organization grew rapidly to consist of seventy chapters with over 80,000 members. As the head of PUSH, Jackson threatened boycotts of selected companies if they did not offer parity for blacks. With distinct echoes of Booker T. Washington's ideas concerning the promotion of black capitalism, Jackson stated in 1974 that 'When we organized Operation PUSH, our stated objective was to help effect and direct a transformation of the Human Rights Movement from emphasis on Civil Rights to one on Civil Economics'.[22]

In August 1981 the Coca-Cola Company signed an agreement with PUSH to spend $14 million with minority vendors (a goal it soon surpassed by more than 22 per cent), and pledged to increase its management staffing from 5 to 12.5 per cent. Similar agreements were concluded with Burger King, Anheuser-Busch, the Southland Corporation and Kentucky Fried Chicken. In 1982 PUSH persuaded the Seven Up Corporation to sign a $61 million agreement to invest capital in black enterprises. PUSH also purchased shares in General

Motors, Ford, Chrysler and American Motors. (The Reagan administration, responding to Jackson's attacks on its policies on Central America and South Africa, launched an investigation on Operation PUSH's finances, and claimed that it had 'misused' over $1.7 million in government contracts.) Project PUSH EXCEL, initiated in 1975, was designed to promote parent/teacher cooperation and to motivate black students. Initially successful in gaining donations from private foundations, the federal government and even the Arab League, PUSH EXCEL was to encounter criticism in 1984 for its failure to make acceptable financial reports as required by state and federal laws.

At the twentieth anniversary of the March on Washington, Jackson alerted blacks to their as yet unrealized political power with reference to the outcome of the 1980 presidential election.

> Reagan won Alabama by 17,500 votes, but there were 272,000 unregistered blacks. He won Arkansas by 5,000 votes, with 85,000 unregistered blacks. He won Kentucky by 17,800 votes, with 62,000 unregistered blacks...the numbers show that Reagan won through a perverse coalition of the rich and the registered. But this is a new day. Hands that picked cotton in 1884 will pick the president in 1984.[23]

He repeated the same message across the country, and it became clear that Jackson himself would be a contender for the Democratic party's presidential nomination in 1984. Despite the criticisms of some black leaders like Benjamin Hooks of the NAACP, and John Jacob of the NUL, and Coretta Scott King herself that a black candidacy would split the Democratic vote, and produce a white backlash at the polls, Jackson declared:

> Part of our problem now is that some of our leaders do not seize opportunities. I was trained by Martin to be an opportunist.[24]

In lectures and speeches throughout the country, Jackson reiterated his basic contention:

> Blacks have their backs against the wall and are increasingly distressed by the erosion of past gains and the rapidly deteriorating conditions within the Black and poor communities. As black leaders have attempted to remedy these problems through the Democratic party...too often have they been ignored or treated with disrespect.... A black candidacy could use an 18-million eligible Black-voter base to put together a 'coalition of the rejected', including appealing to six million Hispanics, women, more than 500,000 Native Americans, twenty to forty million poor whites, and an appeal to the moral decency and enlightened economic self-interest of millions of rejected white moderates, liberals and others.... A black candidacy would alter the essentially negative and defensive option of the 'lesser of

two...evils', to the positive and offensive alternative of a 'live' option. An increase in voter-registration and political participation would have a profound impact upon the *status quo* of the Democratic party.... Never again should blacks live and operate below their political privilege and rights.[25]

PRESIDENTIAL CONTENDER

Eliciting and responding to his audiences' shouts of 'Run, Jesse, Run', Jackson, from the summer of 1983, began to campaign for the Democratic nomination. One of his announced goals was to increase voter registration among members of the 'Rainbow Coalition' which he hoped would invigorate the Democratic party. Jackson's appeal to minority groups was considerable. In the New York state primary election, he won 34 per cent of the Puerto Rican vote, and was the only candidate for the Democratic nomination to address the National Congress of American Indians. (One Indian journalist wrote that Jackson was 'a national minority leader who has captured the imagination of people of colour, other than blacks'.)[26] Among white voters, Jackson, in 1984, found support among left-wing activists, liberals, the unemployed, and blue collar workers. Blacks also responded to Jackson's campaign, which according to one estimate, was endorsed by over 90 per cent of the black clergy within two months of his announced candidacy. As Adam Fairclough observes, black support for Jackson in the 1984 presidential primaries 'represented a logical response to the political circumstances' in which they found themselves. 'The Jackson vote was a considered protest against the conservatism of the other Democratic contenders and the failure of white Democrats to reciprocate black support on an equal base.'[27]

In the area of foreign policy Jackson called for a reduction of the American and Soviet armoury, the removal of Cruise missiles from Europe, normalized diplomatic relations with Cuba, and an end to United States intervention in Central America. In a daring and dramatic move, Jackson went to Syria in December 1983 to ask President Hafez al-Hassad for the release of a young black navigator, Lt Robert Goodman, whose reconnaissance plane had been shot down, killing the pilot and with Goodman taken as a prisoner. After some discussion, President Hassad released Goodman to Jackson's custody, and the two men were given heroes' welcomes by President Reagan at the White House. Critics, however, argued that Jackson was interfering in the conduct of American foreign policy. (In 1979 Jackson had alienated many Jewish Americans when he met with Yasir Arafat, head of the Palestine Liberation Organization, on a visit to the Middle East.)

More serious criticism resulted from Jackson's off-the-record reference to a reporter from the *Washington Post* to New York City as 'Hymie Town'. Although Jackson insisted that no anti-Semitic slur was intended, the remark, together with his refusal to reject the support of Black Muslim Minister Louis Farrakhan after he had called Judaism 'a gutter religion', offended many American Jews and white liberals, already disturbed by the connections of PUSH with Arab groups. At the Democratic National Convention in San Francisco in July 1984 Jackson had gained approximately 300 delegates, but the Democratic front runner, Walter Mondale, had 200 black delegates, and Jackson's bargaining power was severely circumscribed. In the event, Mondale and Geraldine Ferraro gained the party's presidential and vice-presidential nominations, with Jackson becoming an unenthusiastic supporter of the Democratic ticket which went down to a crushing defeat with the re-election of Ronald Reagan. But Jackson's candidacy in 1984 undoubtedly contributed to a large black voter turnout. An estimated 3.05 million blacks voted in the Democratic primaries, and over ten million – 89 per cent of whom supported Mondale – participated in the November elections. In 1988 Jackson again attempted to gain the Democratic nomination, and emerged as the most 'radical' of all candidates. June Jordan, the distinguished black political commentator (and a Jackson supporter) observes that not only did he support such controversial causes as gay and women's rights but was also:

> the first presidential candidate in 1988 repeatedly to plead the plight of 650,000 American farmers who had lost their farms within the eight years of Reagan's reign...the first to identify drugs as the number one menace to domestic security...the first and only contender...to demand that South Africa be designated a terrorist state and treated accordingly...the first and only candidate to call for self-determination and statehood for Palestine...the first and only candidate, Republican or Democratic, to propose an international minimum wage.[28]

Despite impressive performances in the presidential primaries (in Michigan in March 1988 he received 55 per cent of the votes and then proceeded to win in Wisconsin – a state with less than a 4 per cent black population), Jackson lacked the support of the Democratic National Party, and failed to carry New York State (although he gained nearly all of New York City's black votes and an estimated 60 per cent of its Hispanic vote). Michael Dukakis gained the Democratic nomination but lost the November election to George Bush, Reagan's former vice-president.

To his admirers, Jackson, in 1988, had again demonstrated his ability to appeal to a 'Rainbow Coalition' of the American electorate – he gained three times as many white votes in the 1988 primaries than he had in 1984 – and remains the Democrats' most progressive, if not radical, figure, almost certain to continue as a serious contender for the party's presidential nomination in 1992. To his detractors, Jackson, in 1988, as earlier, projected confusing and contradictory images: a self-declared successor of Martin Luther King and a political opportunist, a colour-blind Populist and a confirmed anti-Semite, a preacher and a demagogue, an idealist and a 'hustler', a champion of the poor, and an ardent black capitalist. It is obviously too premature to offer an 'assessment' of Jesse Jackson's claim to be considered as a 'black leader' (a typification which he rejects anyway) of comparable stature to Booker T. Washington, W. E. B. Du Bois, Marcus Garvey, Martin Luther King or Malcolm X. But, as Gary Wills observes, Jackson was:

> the only nationally active and visible black leader in the late 1970s and 1980s, the one a whole new generation of blacks watched as they grew into adulthood....Many of the charges made against Jackson – that he is going outside his role as a civil rights leader, that he encourages a cult of personality, that he is risking prior gains by taking on new issues – were made against Dr. King in his day.[29]

And, Wills might have added, these and similar charges were also made against Booker T. Washington, W. E. B. Du Bois, Marcus Garvey and Malcolm X in theirs. Certainly the responses which Jackson (like Martin Luther King), has consistently evoked from his audiences – black and white – brings to mind John Dollard's personal observation, made in 1937, that:

> No more exhilarating form of leadership of human beings exists than that possible between the Negro preacher and his congregation.[30]

Whether Jackson's continued political preaching to a national 'congregation' will result in his becoming the first 'black leader' to occupy rather than simply visit the White House, remains to be seen. That he was in South Africa in 1990 to greet – and be photographed with – the released African National Congress leader

Nelson Mandela suggests Jackson's continuing ability to be in the right place at the right time.

REFERENCES

1. Jackson, J., quoted in the *Washington Post*, 14 March 1976.
2. Reed, A. L., Jr, *The Jesse Jackson Phenomenon: The Crisis of Purpose in Afro-American Politics* (Yale University Press, 1986), p.106.
3. Viorst, M., *Fire in the Streets: America in the 1960's* (New York, 1979), p.345.
4. Garrow, D. J., in C. W. Eagles (ed.), *The Civil Rights Movement in America* (University Press of Mississippi, 1986), p.62.
5. Lincoln, C. E., *The Black Muslims in America* (Rev. edn, Boston, 1973), p.212.
6. Viorst, *Fire in the Streets*, op. cit., p.374.
7. Lester, J., *Look Out Whitey! Black Power's Gon' Get Your Mama!* (New York, 1968), pp.100, 104.
8. Carmichael, S. and C. V. Hamilton, *Black Power: The Politics of Liberation in America* (Penguin Books, Harmondsworth, 1969), p.54.
9. Ibid., p.95.
10. *Report of the National Advisory Commission on Civil Disorders* (New York, 1968), p.235.
11. Marable, M., *Race, Reform and Rebellion: The Second Reconstruction in Black America*, 1945–1982 (London, 1984), pp.108–9.
12. Draper, T., *The Rediscovery of Black Nationalism* (New York, 1970), p.125.
13. Bracey, J. H., A. Meier and E. Rudwick, *Black Nationalism in America* (New York, 1970), pp.531–2.
14. *Time*, 21 September 1981.
15. Franklin, J. H. and A. A. Moss, Jr, *From Slavery to Freedom: A History of Negro Americans* (New York, 1988), p.477.
16. Marable, M., *Black American Politics: From the Washington Marches to Jesse Jackson* (London, 1985), p.258.
17. Chafe, W. H., *Civilities and Civil Rights: Greensboro, North Carolina and the Black Struggle for Freedom* (Oxford University Press, New York, 1980), p.125.
18. Ibid., pp.142–3.
19. Fairclough, A., *To Redeem the Soul of America: The Southern Christian Leadership Conference and Martin Luther King, Jr*, (London, 1987), pp.353–4.

20. Garrow, D. J., *Bearing the Cross: Martin Luther King, Jr.,and the Southern Christian Leadership Conference* (New York, 1986), pp.585–6.
21. Time, 6 April 1970, pp.11–13.
22. Marable, M., *Black American Politics*, op. cit., p.262.
23. Franklin, J. H., and A. A. Moss, *From Slavery to Freedom*, op. cit., p.478.
24. *Time*, 22 August, 1983, p.36.
25. Marable, M., *Black American Politics*, op. cit., p.257.
26. Ibid., p.275.
27. Fairclough, A., 'What Makes Jesse Run?', *Journal of American Studies*, 22 (1988), p.84.
28. Jordan, J., 'Next Time the Rainbow', *New Statesman and Society*, 6 January 1989, pp.32–3.
29. Wills, G., 'New Votuhs', *New York Review of Books*, 18 August 1988, p.4.
30. Dollard, J., *Caste and Class in the Southern Town* (3rd edn, Anchor Books, New York, 1957), p.243.

Conclusion

From colonial times to the present, black leaders in America have developed and utilized their distinctive personal qualities in attempts to improve (or eliminate) the inferior caste status of African-Americans. Their shared concern has been to improve the condition of blacks through economic, educational, political, and psychological progress. Whatever their differences on such issues as segregation and integration, 'accommodation' or protest, alliances with or rejection of whites, all have displayed and sought to build on a sense of racial pride and identity among their followers.

Lines of ideological continuity also link the leaders discussed: Booker T. Washington, the towering Southern black figure of the late nineteenth and early twentieth centuries, was a professed admirer of Frederick Douglass's ideas on 'industrial education' for Negroes. W. E. B. Du Bois, on several occasions, conceded that given the circumstances of his time and place, Washington had articulated and implemented a realistic (if incomplete) programme of racial advancement. Moreover, before the publication of *The Souls of Black Folk*, Du Bois and Washington shared some basic convictions. Both endorsed the white middle-class virtues of thrift, sobriety, education and capital accumulation, placed economic advancement before political rights, and were willing to accept suffrage restrictions based upon education or property qualifications. Marcus Garvey acknowledged Washington as the inspiration for his own racial and economic philosophy, as he also castigated Du Bois' integrationism and concern with the 'Talented Tenth'. Ironically, Du Bois came to agree with both Washington and Garvey on the necessity for a 'black economy', and also shared with Garvey a conviction that Afro-Americans needed to understand and acknowledge their African antecedents and culture.

Martin Luther King, Jr, recognized the achievements, even as he deplored the limitations of Washington, Du Bois and Garvey, and displayed at least a grudging respect for his contemporary rival, Malcolm X, who, in turn, expressed admiration for Garvey's racial vision. Jesse Jackson, currently the most visible black leader in America, has consistently presented himself as the spiritual disciple of Martin Luther King.

In assessing the achievements and contributions of black American leaders to their respective causes, a historical perspective reveals the shifting connotations of such key concepts as 'integration', 'segregation', 'separatism' and 'civil rights'. It also suggests that the adjectives 'radical' and 'conservative' when applied to black leaders and the policies they espoused, reflect particular conditions and 'limited options'. To his contemporary critics, Booker T. Washington's (public) deprecation of political action and support for the social separation of the races, smacked of supine surrender to white supremacy. It may well have been a shrewd and calculated recognition of the fearful penalties which would have attended any displays of Southern black militancy in the era of Jim Crow. From the end of Reconstruction to World War II, Southern black leadership was forced to operate within the 'separate but [un]equal' confines of a system predicated on and pledged to the maintenance of white supremacy. Whatever influence Southern black leaders possessed was exercised through white intermediaries, who were prepared only to make limited concessions within the framework of segregation. In the post-war period, however, a younger generation of Southern black men and women began to demand changes which ran directly counter to prevailing customs and mores. As Myrdal observed, next to racial intermarriage, the South's 'rank order of discriminations' encompassed:

> ...dancing, bathing, eating, drinking together and social intercourse generally...segregations and discriminations in the use of public facilities such as schools, churches and means of conveyance...discriminations in law courts, by the police, and other public servants. Finally came the discriminations in securing land, credit, relief and other social welfare facilities.[1]

From the 1950s onwards, and starting at the grass roots with local protests, black Southerners began to challenge this traditional list of racial proscriptions. The civil rights movement, which brought into prominence Martin Luther King, Jr, also owed its dynamic to the continued efforts of thousands of activists, black and white, male and female. It also came to provide training, membership and leadership for the protest and reform movements which followed: the anti-war movement, the student movement, and the campaigns for minority rights. Paradoxically, the civil rights movement, like earlier black protests, drew much of its strength from the sense of racial identity which segregation had (inadvertently) fostered. The NAACP, which institutionalized black opposition to Washington and the Tuskegee Machine, was at its inception a 'radical' organization, pledged to securing both black political participation and racial integration. Given the tradition of black protest which existed in the Northern states, such a response was feasible and timely. But the increasing shift of black Americans from the rural South to the industrialized urban centres of the North, also gave rise to conditions which fostered intense black separatist feelings, which, in turn, were capitalized upon by such leaders as Marcus Garvey, Elijah Muhammad and Malcolm X.

With the advent of the Nation of Islam, and the rise of the Black Power slogan in the 1960s, racial separatism was viewed as a 'radical' response to appalling socio-economic conditions, and a younger generation of black 'militants' rejected the integrationism of the NAACP, NUL and SCLC as 'assimilationism'. Instead, they advocated a form of cultural pluralism – 'a Negro nation within a nation' – without sufficient awareness of its historic antecedents and precedents. At the end of their respective careers, W. E. B. Du Bois, Martin Luther King, Jr, and Malcolm X, had moved beyond an exclusive concern with civil rights to formulate 'radical' critiques of capitalist society, colonialism, and militarism. Most recently, Jesse Jackson has attempted to project his social democratic concept of a 'Rainbow Coalition' of the disadvantaged and unrepresented into American politics.

The fundamental aspiration of the Afro-American, to which all black leaders have responded, was best expressed by W. E. B. Du Bois in *The Souls of Black Folk*:

> He simply wishes to make it possible for a man to be both a Negro and an American, without being cursed and spit upon by his fellows, without having the doors of Opportunity closed roughly in his face...to be a co-worker in the kingdom of culture, to escape both death and isolation, to husband and use his best power and his latent genius....Merely a concrete test for the underlying principles of the great republic is the Negro Problem, and the spiritual striving of the freedmen's sons is the travail of souls whose burden is almost beyond the measure of their strength, but who bear it in the name of an historic race, in the name of this the land of their father's fathers, and in the name of human opportunity.[2]

Writing in 1967, Alice Walker observed of the civil rights movement in America:

It gave some of us bread, some of us shelter, some of us knowledge and pride, all of us comfort. It gave us our children, our husbands, our brothers, our fathers, as men reborn and with a purpose for living. It broke the pattern of black servitude....It gave us history and men far greater than Presidents....It gave us heroes, selfless men of courage and strength, for our little boys and girls to follow. It gave us hope for tomorrow.[3]

REFERENCES

1. Myrdal, G., *An American Dilemma* (New York, 1944), p.61.
2. Du Bois, W. E. B., 'Of Our Spiritual Strivings', in *The Souls of Black Folk* (New York, 1961), pp.17–22.
3. Walker, A., *In Search of Our Mother's Gardens: Womanist Prose* (New York, 1984), pp.128–9.

Bibliographical Essay

ABBREVIATIONS FOR JOURNALS CITED:

AAS	*Afro-American Studies*
AHR	*American Historical Review*
AJS	*American Journal of Sociology*
AL	*American Literature*
AQ	*American Quarterly*
CWH	*Civil War History*
HWJ	*History Workshop Journal*
JAH	*Journal of American History*
JAS	*Journal of American Studies*
JHI	*Journal of the History of Ideas*
JNH	*Journal of Negro History*
JSH	*Journal of Southern History*
MassR	*Massachusetts Review*
PSQ	*Political Science Quarterly*
SAQ	*South Atlantic Quarterly*

INTRODUCTORY AND GENERAL STUDIES

The following texts contain useful and pertinent information on Afro-American history: Rayford W. Logan, *The Betrayal of the Negro: From Rutherford B. Hayes to Woodrow Wilson* (London, 1965); John Hope Franklin and Alfred A. Moss, Jr, *From Slavery to Freedom: A History of Negro Americans* (6th edn, New York,

1988); August Meier and Elliot Rudwick, *Along the Colour Line* (Urbana, Illinois, 1976); Robert H. Brisbane, *The Black Vanguard: Origins of the Negro Social Revolution 1900–1960* (Valley Forge, Pennsylvania, 1970); Mary Ellison, *The Black Experience: American Blacks Since 1865* (London, 1974); Mary F. Berry and John Blassingame, *Long Memory: The Black Experience in America* (New York, 1982). John Hope Franklin and August Meier (eds), *Black Leaders of the Twentieth Century* (University of Illinois Press, 1982), has valuable essays on Booker T. Washington, Du Bois, Garvey, Martin Luther King and Malcolm X, and also contains profiles of Ida B. Wells-Barnett, A. Philip Randolph, Mary McLeod Bethun, Mable K. Staupers, and Adam Clayton Powell, Jr, among others. See also: Howard N. Rabinowitz (ed.), *Southern Black Leaders of the Reconstruction Era* (University of Illinois Press, 1982), which contains an excellent section on collective biography. There are many editions of documentary materials, two of the best are: August Meier, Elliott Rudwick and Francis L. Broderick (eds), *Black Protest Thought in the Twentieth Century* (2nd edn, New York, 1971), and John H. Bracey, August Meier and Elliott Rudwick (eds), *Black Nationalism in America* (New York, 1970). See also the revealing conversations in Kenneth B. Clark, *The Negro Protest: James Baldwin, Malcolm X and Martin Luther King Talk With Kenneth B. Clark* (Boston, 1963). For the influence of Africa on the emergence of black nationalism in America, and the attractiveness (or otherwise) of Du Bois and Garvey to black Americans, see Harold R. Isaacs, *The New World of Negro Americans* (London, 1964).

The classic work on the black experience up to the New Deal remains the late Gunnar Myrdal's *An American Dilemma* (New York, 1944 and 1964), the most influential study of American race relations ever published. It contains some penetrating insights into the problems faced by black leaders. See also David W. Southern's assessment, *Gunnar Myrdal and Black–White Relations: The Use and Abuse of An American Dilemma* (Louisiana State University Press, 1987). His argument is partly summarized in 'An American Dilemma Revisited: Myrdalism and White Southern Liberals', SAQ, 75 (1976), pp.182–97. See also Ralph Ellison's 1944 critique of *An American Dilemma* in his stimulating collection of essays on black life, music and art: *Shadow and Act* (New York, 1972).

The following articles treat black leadership in chronological order: Frederick Cooper, 'Elevating the Race: The Social Thought of Black Leaders, 1827–50', AQ, 24 (1972), pp. 604–25; Guy B

Johnson, 'Negro Racial Movements and Leadership in the United State', AJS, 43 (1937–38), pp. 55–71; Wilson Record, 'Negro Intellectuals and Negro Movements in Historical Perspective', AQ, 8 (1956), pp. 3–20; Leslie H. Fishel, Jr, 'Repercussions of Reconstruction: The Northern Negro, 1870–1883', CWH, 14 (1968), pp. 325–45. Three excellent studies of black leadership are: Daniel C. Thompson,*The Negro Leadership Class* (Englewood Cliffs, New Jersey, 1963), which traces the social origins of black leaders in New Orleans from 1940 to 1960; M. Elaine Burgess, *Negro Leadership in a Southern City* (University of North Carolina Press, 1960), which also focuses on New Orleans, and Raymond Gavins, *The Perils and Prospects of Black Leadership: Gordon Blaine Hancock, 1874–1970* (Duke University Press, 1970), which describes the career of the Virginia–based educator, clergyman, journalist and theorist, who synthesized the contending philosophies of his two great contemporaries, Washington and Du Bois. For summaries of black protest within the wider perspective of minority group activities, see Alec Barbrook and Christine Bolt, *Power and Protest in American Life* (Oxford, 1980), and John Higham (ed.), *Ethnic Leadership in America* (Johns Hopkins University Press, 1978). In the autobiographical *Black Boy: A Record of Childhood and Youth* (London, 1947), the novelist Richard Wright (1908-1960) provides a moving and often harrowing account of his early life in Mississippi and Tennessee. The posthumously published *American Hunger* (New York, 1977), is an equally revealing record of Wright's experiences in Chicago during the 1930s.

John Dollard's famous study, *Caste and Class in a Southern Town* (3rd edn, New York, 1957), originally appeared in 1937. It is a pioneering appraisal by a social psychologist of the relations between blacks and whites in a Southern community – Indianola, Mississippi, and has been described as 'a sociological *Gulliver's Travels*'. See also, Allison Davis and John Dollard, *Children of Bondage: The Personality Development of Negro Youth in the Urban South* (New York, 1940 and 1964), a series of Negro life histories which complements *Caste and Class in a Southern Town* and the work of Allison Davis, Burleigh B. Gardner and Mary R. Gardner, *Deep South: A Social Anthropological Study of Caste and Class* (University of Chicago Press, 1941 and 1965). Two recent books which treat black life in Mississippi are: Douglas L. Conner with John F. Marszalek, *A Black Physician's Story: Bringing Hope To Mississippi* (University Press of Mississippi, 1985), a moving account of a black doctor who took on the self-imposed task of 'providing leadership for black people within the context of a segregated society', and Neil R. McMillen's graphic study, *Dark Journey: Black Mississippians in the Age of Jim Crow* (University of Illinois Press, 1989), an examination of black–white relations in perhaps the most repressive Southern state ('the land of the tree and the home of the grave') between 1890 and 1930. The responses of Southern white businessmen to the civil rights movement in the 1950s and 1960s are treated in a valuable collection of essays edited by Elizabeth Jacoway and David R. Colburn, *Southern Businessmen and Desegregation* (Louisiana State University Press, 1982). As the editors state, collectively these essays 'suggest that the response of the southern [white] leadership to the desegregation challenge was an accommodation to what was perceived as inevitable change...although they did not modify their racial attitudes, they did allow racial considerations to slip from the dominant position in their hierarchy of values.' See also A. J. Badger's review essay, 'Segregation and the Southern Business Elite', JAS, 18 (1984), pp.105–9. The noted black writer Alice Walker was born in rural Georgia; *In Search of Our Mother's Gardens: Womanist Prose* (New York, 1984), contains her reflections on 'The Black Writer and the Southern Experience,' and trenchant essays about the civil rights movement, Martin Luther King, Coretta King, and the tenth anniversary of the 1963 March on Washington.

Black protest movements and leaders from the late nineteenth century to recent years are treated in: E. L. Thornbrough, 'The National Afro-American League, 1887–1908', JSH, 27 (1961), pp.494–512; A. Meier and E. M. Rudwick, 'The Boycott Movement Against Jim Crow Street Cars in the South, 1900–1916', JAH, 55 (1969), pp.756–76; E. M. Rudwick, 'The Niagara Movement', JNH, 42 (1957), pp.177–200; Langston Hughes, *Fight For Freedom: The Story of the NAACP* (New York, 1962); Charles F. Kellog, *NAACP: A History of the National Association for the Advancement of Coloured People*, Vol. I, *1909–1920* (Baltimore, Maryland, 1967); B. Joyce Ross, *J. E. Spingarn and the Rise of the NAACP*, 1911–1939 (New York, 1972), and Mark V. Tushnet, *The NAACP's Legal Strategy Against Segregated Education, 1925–1950* (University of North Carolina Press, 1987). The National Urban League's first three decades are given comprehensive and judicious treatment in Nancy J. Weiss, *The National Urban League: 1910–1940* (Oxford University Press, New York, 1974). A more closely focused study is provided by Arvarh E. Strickland, *History of the Chicago Urban League* (University of Illinois Press, 1966), which covers the period

1915–1964, and concludes that because of the city's indifference to its black population, 'the agency has never been able to reach its full potential.'

On black Americans during the progressive era, see: D. W. Grantham, 'The Progressive Movement and the Negro', SAQ, 54 (1955), pp. 461–77; Gilbert Osofsky, 'Progressivism and the Negro', AQ, 16 (1964), pp.153–68; Thomas G. Dyer, *Theodore Roosevelt and the Idea of Race* (Louisiana State University Press, 1980); Nancy J. Weiss, 'The New Negro and the New Freedom: Fighting Wilsonian Segregation', PSQ, 84 (1968), pp.61–79; Katherine L. Wolgemuth, 'Woodrow Wilson's Appointment Policy and the Negro', JSH, 24 (1958), pp.450–71; Henry Blumenthal, 'Woodrow Wilson and the Race Question', JNH, 48 (1963), pp.1–21. Ray Stannard Baker's graphic 'eye-witness' account of American race relations (first published in 1908), is *Following the Colour Line: American Negro Citizenship in the Progressive Era* (New York, 1964), a prime (and primary) source of information.

Black attitudes to World War I are discussed in Theodore Kornweibel, Jr, 'Apathy and Dissent: Black America's Negative Responses to World War I', SAQ, 80 (1981), pp.322–38. Raymond Wolters, *The New Negro on Campus: Black College Rebellions of the 1920s* (Princeton University Press, 1975), is a detailed study of expressions of discontent against paternalism (black and whites) at such black colleges as Fisk, Howard, Tuskegee, Hampton and Wilberforce.

Black responses to the Depression and New Deal are included in the section of Du Bois (below), but see also, J. A. Harrel, 'Negro Leadership in the Election Year 1936', JSH, 34 (1968), pp.546–65, and Nancy J. Weiss, *Farewell to the Party of Lincoln: Black Politics in the Age of FDR* (Princeton University Press, 1983), which demonstrates conclusively that 'blacks became Democrats in response to the economic benefits of the New Deal...in spite of the New Deal's lack of a substantive record on race'. Father Divine's Peace Mission Movement is treated in Sara Harris, *Father Divine: Holy Husband* (New York, 1953), and Robert Weisbrot, *Father Divine and the Struggle of Racial Equality* (University of Illinois Press, 1983). Weisbrot argues convincingly that the Peace Mission Movement 'was easily among the most impressive examples of cooperative enterprise' during the Depression years, and suggests that Divine's appeal lay 'in part because he seemed the ultimate role model for many poor, uneducated blacks seeking evidence that they could improve their lot'. For the ambivalent relations between the Communist Party of the United States (CPUSA) and black Americans see especially two books by Wilson Record: *The Negro and the Communist Party* (University of North Carolina Press, Chapel Hills, 1951), and *Race Relations and Radicalism: The NAACP and the Communist Party in Conflict* (Ithaca, New York, 1964). Also valuable are William Nolan, *Communism Versus the Negro* (University of Chicago Press, 1951); V. D. Bornet, 'Historical Scholarship, Communism and the Negro,' JNH, 37 (1952), pp.304-24 and Harvey Klehr and William Tompson, 'Self-Determination in the Black Belt: Origins of a Communist Policy, *Labor History*, 30 (Summer, 1989), pp.354–66.

Black responses to World War II have been extensively treated. See especially, Neil A. Wynn, *The Afro-American and the Second World War* (London, 1976); A. Russell Buchanan, *Black Americans in World War II* (Oxford, 1977), and Philip McGuire, *Taps for a Jim Crow Army: Letters from Black Soldiers in World War II* (Oxford, 1983). Four distinctive interpretations of Afro-American protest activities during the war are to be found in: Richard M. Dalfiume, 'The Forgotten Years of the Negro Revolution', JAH, LV (1968), pp.90–106; N. A. Wynn, 'Black Attitudes Towards Participation in the American War Effort, 1941–1945', AAS, 3 (1972), pp.13–19; Harvard Sitkoff, 'Racial Militancy and Interracial Violence in the Second World War', JAH LVIII (1971), pp.661–8; Lee Finkle, 'The Conservative Aims of Militant Rhetoric: Black Protest During World War II', JAH, LX (1973), pp.692–713. See also: K. T. Anderson, 'Last Hired, First Fired: Black Women Workers During World War II', JAH, LXIX (1982), pp.82–97, and C. R. Koppes and G. D. Black, 'Blacks, Loyalty and Motion Picture Propaganda in World War II', JAH, 73 (1986), pp.383–406. The distinguished career of the first black federal judge, adviser to the War Department and reforming governor of the Virgin Islands is treated in Gilbert Ware's biography, *William Hastie: Grace Under Pressure* (New York, Oxford University Press, 1985).

The civil rights movement after the World War II has been extensively covered. See especially: Robert Kostad and Nelson Lichenstein, 'Opportunities Found and Lost: Labour, Radicals and the Early Civil Rights Movement', JAH, 75 (1988), pp.786–811; August Meier and Elliot Rudwick, *CORE: A Study in the Civil Rights Movement, 1952–1968* (New York, 1973); Howard Zinn, *SNCC: The New Abolitionists* (Boston, 1965); Clayborne Carson, *In Struggle: SNCC and the Black Awakening of the 1960s* (London, 1981); William Chafe, *Civilities and Civil Rights: Greensboro,*

North Carolina, and the Black Struggle for Freedom (Oxford University Press, New York, 1980); Harvard Sitkoff, *The Struggle for Black Equality, 1954–1980* (New York, 1981); Benjamin Muse, *The American Negro Revolution: From Civil Rights to Black Power* (Bloomington, Indiana, 1968). Charles W. Eagles (ed.), *The Civil Rights Movement in America* (University Press of Mississippi, 1986), contains insightful essays by David L. Lewis, Clayborne Carson, Nancy J. Weiss and William H. Chafe. The roles of women and the rank-and-file participants in the civil rights movement have recently begun to receive (overdue) attention. See particularly: Sheyann Webb and Rachel West Nelson, *Selma, Lord, Selma: Childhood Memories of the Civil-Rights Days as told to Frank Sikora* (University of Alabama Press, 1980); David J Garrow (ed.), *The Montgomery Bus Boycott and the Women Who Started It: The Memoir of Jo Ann Gibson Robinson* (University of Tennessee Press, 1987); Cynthia Stokes Brown (ed.), *Ready From Within: Septima Clark and the Civil Rights Movement* (Navarro, California, 1986), and Anne Moody, *Coming of Age in Mississippi* (New York, 1968). Close analysis of the competition and strategies of the civil rights coalition are offered by: Allen J. Matusow, 'From Civil Rights to Black Power: The Case of SNCC, 1960–1966,' in Barton J. Bernstein and Allen J. Matusow (eds), *Twentieth Century America: Recent Interpretations* (New York, 1969); Herbert H. Haines, *Black Radicals and the Civil Rights Mainstream, 1954–1970* (University of Tennessee Press, 1988); Jack M. Bloom, *Class, Race, and the Civil Rights Movement* (Indiana University Press, 1987), and Richard H. King, 'Citizenship and Self-Respect: Experience of Politics in the Civil Rights Movement', JAS, 22(1988), pp.7–24. Sociological treatments of the civil rights movement are to be found in Doug McAdam, *Political Process and the Development of Black Insurgency, 1930–1970* (University of Chicago Press, 1982), and Aldon D. Morris, *The Origins of the Civil Rights Movement: Black Communities Organize for Change* (New York, 1984). Manning Marable provides a black Marxist analysis in *Race, Reform and Rebellion: The Second Reconstruction in Black America, 1945–1982* (London, 1984), and *Black American Politics from the Washington Marches to Jesse Jackson* (London, 1985). Stephen J. Whitfield, *A Death in the Delta: The Story of Emmett Till* (New York and London, 1988), offers a detailed account of the episode, and suggests that 'the viciousness of the murder of Emmett Till spurred efforts to accelerate the tempo of civil rights advances for Southern blacks'. Taylor Branch, *Parting the Waters: America in the King Years*

1954–63 (London, 1989), is an epic (and highly readable) treatment of the classic phase of the civil rights movement, and devotes considerable attention to Martin Luther King and the SCLC. It is complemented by Juan Williams, *Eyes on the Prize: America's Civil Rights Years, 1954–1965* (Penguin Books, New York, 1988), the companion volume to the American Public Broadcasting TV series. Milton Viorst's *Fire In the Streets: America in the 1960s* (New York, 1979), offers some penetrating observations on the rifts that developed in the civil rights movement. The late Robert Penn Warren's collection of taped interviews with black protest leaders, *Who Speaks for the Negro?* (New York, 1965), is still a useful collection, but should be supplemented by Howard Raines, *My Soul is Rested: Movement Days in the Deep South Remembered* (Penguin Books, New York, 1983), an outstanding compilation of oral history. The epochal Brown decision of 1954 is given detailed examination in Richard Kluger, *Simple Justice: The History of Brown v. Board of Education and Black America's Struggle for Equality* (2 vols, New York, 1975), but see also Robert F. Burk, *The Eisenhower Administration and Black Civil Rights* (University of Tennessee Press, 1984), and Michael S. Mayer's article, 'With Much Deliberation and Some Speed: Eisenhower and the Brown Decision', JSH, LII (1986), pp.43–74. Catherine A. Barnes, *Journey from Jim Crow: Desegregation of Southern Transit* (Columbia University Press, 1983), provides a case study of the desegregation process in the South, and demonstrates that 'federal action came in response to black protest and pressure'. The following articles provide useful information: Harvard Sitkoff, 'Harry Truman and the Election of 1948: The Coming of Age of Civil Rights in American Politics', JSH, 37 (1971), pp.597–616; Monroe Billington, 'Civil Rights, President Truman and the South', JNH, 58 (1973), pp.127–39; William H. Chafe, 'The Civil Rights Revolution, 1945–60: The Gods Bring Threads to Webs Begun', in Robert H. Bremner and Gary W. Reichard (eds), *Reshaping America: Society and Institutions* (Ohio State University Press, 1982), pp.68–100; John Hart, 'Kennedy, Congress and Civil Rights', JAS, 13 (1979), pp.165–78; Monroe Billington, 'Lyndon B. Johnson and the Blacks: The Early Years', JNH, 61 (1977), pp.26–42; John Runcie, 'The Black Culture Movement and the Black Community', JAS, 10 (1976), pp.185–214, and John White, 'American Minorities: The Non-Melting Pot', in Henry S. Commager and Marcus Cunliffe (eds), *The American Destiny: An Illustrated Bicentennial History of the United States, Vol. 19 The Unquiet Years* (New York, 1976), pp.50–64. The urban racial disturbances of the 1960s are summarised and assessed in the Report of the *National Advisory Commission on Civil Disorders* (New York, 1968), the body appointed by President Lyndon Johnson under the chairmanship of Governor Otto Kerner of Illinois.

BLACK PROTEST AND ACCOMMODATION 1800–1877

There is an enormous literature on slave life, culture, adaptation and 'resistance'. For a sampling of this work see especially: Eugene D. Genovese, *Roll, Jordan, Roll: The World the Slaves Made* (New York, 1974); Elizabeth Fox-Genovese, *Within the Plantation Household: Black and White Women of the Old South* (University of North Carolina Press, 1988); John W. Blassingame, *The Slave Community: Plantation Life in the Antebellum South* (New York, 1972), and Lawrence W. Levine, *Black Culture and Black Consciousness: Afro-American Folk Thought from Slavery to Freedom* (Oxford University Press, New York, 1977). Eugene D. Genovese, *In Red and Black: Marxian Explorations in Southern and Afro-American History* (New York, 1971), includes provocative and stimulating analyses of slave resistance, black nationalism and Black Power.

The standard work on free blacks in the Old South is Ira Berlin, *Slaves Without Masters: The Free Negro in the Antebellum South* (New York, 1974). For the Southern black experience immediately after the Civil War, see Leon F. Litwack's excellent study, *Been In the Storm So Long: The Aftermath of Slavery* (New York, 1972). C. Vann Woodward's celebrated thesis concerning the emergence of Southern segregation appears in *The Strange Career of Jim Crow* (3rd rev. edn, New York, 1974). The 'Woodward Thesis' is convincingly modified in Howard N. Rabinowitz, *Race Relations in the Urban South, 1865–1890* (Oxford University Press, 1978), which suggests that urban segregation replaced earlier practices of the almost total 'exclusion' of blacks from public accommodations and welfare facilities.

The activities of Northern free blacks before the Civil War are surveyed in Leon F. Litwack, *North of Slavery: The Negro in the Free States, 1790–1860* (University of Chicago Press, 1961); Robert C. Dick, *Black Protest: Issues and Tactics* (London, 1974); Floyd J. Miller, *The Search for a Black Nationality: Black Emigration and Colonization, 1787–1863* (Urbana, Illinois, 1975); Jane H. and William H. Pease, *They Who Would Be Free: Blacks' Search For Freedom, 1830–1861* (New York, 1975), and Benjamin Quarles, *Black Abolitionists* (New York, 1964). Quarles has also written an excellent brief biography, *Frederick Douglass* (Washington, DC, 1984), but see also Waldo E. Martin, Jr, *The Mind of Frederick Douglass* (University of North Carolina Press, 1984, and Philip S. Foner (ed.), *Life and Writings of Frederick Douglass*, 4 vols, New York, 1950–1955). Booker T. Washington, *Frederick Douglass* (London, 1906), is as informative about the author as his subject.

There have been several notable interpretive studies of American Negro thought. Particularly recommended are: Benjamin E. Mays, *The Negro's God as Reflected in His Literature* (New York, 1938), August Meier, *Negro Thought in America, 1880–1915* (University of Michigan Press, 1963); Harold Cruse, *The Crisis of the Negro Intellectual: From Its Origins To The Present* (New York, 1967); Frank Hercules, *American Society and Black Revolution* (New York, 1972); Alfred A. Moss, *The American Negro Academy: Voice of the Talented Tenth* (London, 1981); Vincent P. Franklin, *Black Self-Determination: A Cultural History of the Faith of the Fathers* (Westport, Connecticut, 1984); David G. Nielson, *Black Ethos: Northern Urban Negro Life and Thought, 1890–1930* (London, 1977); William Toll, *The Resurgence Of Race: Black Social Theory from Reconstruction to the Pan-African Conferences* (University of Pennsylvania Press, 1979); Adam Lively, 'Continuity and Radicalism in American Black Nationalist Thought, 1914–1929', JAS, 18 (1984), pp.207–35, and two books by William J. Moses: *The Golden Age of Black Nationalism, 1850–1925* (Hamden, Connecticut, 1978), and *Black Messiahs and Uncle Toms: Social and Literary Manipulations of a Religious Myth* (Pennsylvania State University Press, 1982). Sterling Stuckey's *Slave Culture: Nationalist Theory and the Foundations of Black America* (Oxford University Press, New York, 1978), is a densely written and repetitious collection of essays, but offers some interesting observations on the black nationalist ideas of David Walker, Henry Highland Garnet, W. E. B. Du Bois and Paul Robeson.

BOOKER T. WASHINGTON

The outstanding authority on Washington's life is Louis R. Harlan.

His two-volume biography, *Booker T. Washington: The Making of a Black Leader, 1865–1901* (Oxford University Press, New York, 1972), and *Booker T. Washington: The Wizard of Tuskegee, 1901–1915* (Oxford University Press, New York, 1983), is a meticulously-researched and well-written account of Washington as a race leader and educator, but tends to judge him by the standards of present-day white liberalism. Harlan is also one of the editors of *The Booker T. Washington Papers*, 15 volumes plus a *Cumulative Index* (University of Illinois Press, 1972–1989). Individually indexed, with cross-references and informative notes, these volumes can be mined to extract material on every aspect of Washington's activities and interests. Volume I contains Washington's major autobiographical writings, *Up From Slavery, The Story of My Life and Work,* and extracts from *The Story of the Negro* and *My Larger Education,* together with shorter pieces. Professor Harlan has also written several informative articles on Washington: 'Booker T. Washington and the White Man's Burden', AHR, 71 (1965–66), pp.441–67; 'Booker T. Washington in Biographical Perspective', AHR, 75 (1970), pp.1581–99; 'The Secret Life of Booker T. Washington', JSH, 37 (1971), pp.393–416, and 'Booker T. Washington and the "Voice of the Negro"', JSH, 45 (1979), pp.45–62.

Older but still recommended biographies of Washington are: Basil Mathews, *Booker T. Washington: Educator and Inter-Racial Interpreter* (London, 1949); Samuel J. Spencer, *Booker T. Washington and the Negro's Place in American Life* (Boston, 1955), and Bernard Weisberger, *Booker T. Washington* (New York, 1972). Hugh Hawkins has edited an interesting collection of essays on Washington by his contemporaries and later commentators: *Booker T. Washington and his Critics* (2nd ed, Boston, 1974). Emma L. Thornbrough (ed.), *Booker T. Washington* (Englewood Cliffs, New Jersey, 1969), a volume in the 'Great Lives Observed' series, includes autobiographical extracts from Washington's writings, the views of his contemporaries and modern evaluations of his leadership and influence. Washington's White House dinner is mentioned in Seth M. Scheiner, 'President Theodore Roosevelt and the Negro, 1901–1908', JNH, 47 (1962), pp.169–82. Judith Stein, '"Of Mr Booker T. Washington and Others": The Political Economy of Racism in the United States', *Science and Society*, 38 (1974–75), pp.422–63, surveys race relations and politics in the South from 1877–1910, with particular reference to Washington, Populism and black disfranchisement. Other recommended articles are: August Meier, 'Booker T. Washington and the Negro Press', JNH, 38

(1953), pp.67–90; Daniel Walden, 'The Contemporary Opposition to the Political and Educational Ideas of Booker T. Washington', JNH, 45 (1960), pp.103–15, (see also Philip S. Foner's reprints of two early expressions of opposition to Washington by blacks: 'Is Booker T. Washington's Idea Correct?', and 'Washington and Douglass', JNH, 55, 1970, pp.343–7); Donald J. Calista, 'Booker T. Washington: Another Look', JNH, 49 (1964), pp.240–55; John P. Flynn, 'Booker T. Washington: Uncle Tom or Wooden Horse?', JNH, 54 (1969), pp.262–74; Emma Lou Thornbrough, 'More Light on Booker T. Washington and the *New York Age*', JNH, 43 (1958), pp.34–49, and 'Booker T. Washington As Seen By His White Contemporaries', JNH, 53 (1968), pp.161–82; and Lawrence J. Friedman, 'Life in the Lion's Mouth: Another Look at Booker T. Washington', JNH, 59 (1974), pp.337–51. J. R. Pole's essay 'Of Mr Booker T. Washington and Others', in his *Paths to the American Past* (Oxford University Press, 1979), offers some refreshing comments on Washington historiography. Literary textual analyses of *Up From Slavery* can be found in Robert B. Steptoe, *From Behind the Veil: A Study of Afro-American Narrative* (University of Illinois Press, 1979), pp.32–51, Houston A. Baker, Jr, *Long Black Song: Essays in Black American Literature and Culture* (University Press of Virginia, 1972), pp.84–95, and David Littlejohn, *Black on White: A Critical Survey of Writing By American Negroes* (New York, 1966).

On one of Washington's fiercest black critics see Charles W. Puttkammer and Ruth Worth, 'William Monroe Trotter, 1872–1934', JNH, 43 (1958), pp.298–316, and Yvonne Williams, 'William Monroe Trotter: Race Man, 1872–1934', AAS, 1 (1971), pp.243–51. Emma L. Thornbrough's *T. Thomas Fortune: Militant Journalist* (London, 1972), includes a careful account of his ambivalent relationship with Washington, and later association with Garvey as editor of the *Negro World*. Charles F. Kellog's *NAACP*, already cited, contains a detailed discussion of Washington's dealings with that organization up to his death in 1915. Tuskegee's most famous black teacher is accorded a succinct and balanced evaluation in Linda O. McMurray, *George Washington Carver: Scientist and Symbol* (Oxford University Press, New York, 1981). It can be read in connection with A. W. Jones' article, 'The Role Of Tuskegee Institute in the Education of Black Farmers', JNH, LX (1975), pp.252–67. That Washington's empire collapsed with his death is made clear in Carl S. Mathews' article, 'The Decline of the Tuskegee Machine, 1915–1925: The Abdication of Political Power', SAQ,

75 (1976), pp.460–69. See also Robert J. Norrell's excellent study, *Reaping the Whirlwind: The Civil Rights Movement In Tuskegee* (New York, 1985), which traces race relations in Tuskegee, Alabama from the 1870s to the 1960s. Norrell's provocative and persuasive thesis is that 'Washington's experiment, which promised that blacks would realize full equality once they had made themselves useful to society, ultimately succeeded in Tuskegee. Well-educated, economically secure Institute professors successfully challenged white conservative control of Tuskegee after Washington's hands-off policy toward politics was forsaken in the late 1930s.' Booker T. Washington's 'accommodationism' is placed firmly in its Southern context in C. Vann Woodward's celebrated *Origins of the New South* (Louisiana State University Press, Baton Rouge, 1951), and Paul M. Gaston's illuminating essay *The New South Creed: A Study in Southern Mythmaking* (Louisiana State University Press, Baton Rouge, 1970).

W. E. B. DU BOIS

Du Bois has been well-served by biographers. The four best studies are: Francis L. Broderick, *W. E. B. Du Bois: Negro Leader in a Time of Crisis* (Stanford, California, 1959); Elliott Rudwick, *W. E. B. Du Bois: Propagandist of the Negro Protest* (New York, 1969); Arnold Rampersad, *The Art and Imagination of W. E. B. Du Bois* (London, 1976), and Manning Marable, *W. E. B. Du Bois: Black Radical Democrat* (Boston, 1986). Rudwick is primarily concerned with Du Bois' conflicts with his contemporaries, from his opposition to Washington down to his resignation from the NAACP in 1934. Broderick covers much of the same ground, but takes Du Bois' career to 1952, when he had become increasingly involved in peace and socialist movements. Rampersad's biography stresses Du Bois' 'essentially poetic vision of human experience', and examines in detail his major writings, including novels and poetry. Rampersad concludes that Du Bois 'lived at least a double life, continually compelled to respond to the challenge of reconciling opposites'. Marable offers 'a general revisionist interpretation' of Du Bois's life and thought, and emphasizes his 'profound sense of morality and black prophetic Christianity'. Less convincingly, Marable argues that Du Bois was not a 'paradoxical' thinker, but concludes, more satisfactorily, that his 'greatest virtue was his committed empathy with all the oppressed and his divine dissatisfaction with all forms of injustice'. For shorter but judicious evaluations see: Jack B. Moore, *W. E. B. Du Bois* (Boston, 1981), and Joseph P. DeMarco, *The Social Thought of W. E. B. Du Bois* (London, 1983).

Rayford W. Logan has edited an uneven collection of essays which treat Du Bois' multiple careers as propagandist, historian, race leader and Pan-Africanist: *W. E. B. Du Bois: A Profile* (New York, 1971), which includes extracts from the Rudwick and Broderick studies. Julius Lester has collected and edited a representative selection of Du Bois' work: *The Seventh Son: The Thought and Writings of W. E. B. Du Bois*, 2 vols, (New York, 1971.) See also, John Henrik Clark *et al.*, *Black Titan: W. E. B. Du Bois, An Anthology by the Editors of Freedomways* (Boston, 1970), and Herbert Aptheker (ed.), *W. E. B. Du Bois, Against Racism: Unpublished Essays, Papers, Addresses, 1887–1961* (University of Massachusetts Press, 1985), and Philips S. Foner (ed), *W. E. B. Du Bois Speaks: Speeches and Addresses, 1890–1919* (New York, 1970). The following articles offer good summaries of significant aspects of Du Bois' life and preoccupations: E. M. Rudwick, 'W. E. B. Du Bois in the Role of *Crisis* Editor', JNH, 43 (1958), pp. 214–40; Mary Law Chafee, 'W. E. B. Du Bois' Concept of the Racial Problem in the United States', JNH, 41 (1956) pp. 241–58; Ben F. Rodgers, 'W. E. B. Du Bois, Marcus Garvey and Pan-Africa', JNH, 40 (1955) pp. 154–65; Wilson J. Moses, 'The Politics of Ethiopianism: W. E. B. Du Bois and Literary Black Nationalism,' AL, XLVII (1975), pp. 411–26; Clarence G. Contee, 'W. E. B. Du Bois, the NAACP and the Pan-African Congress of 1919', JNH, 57 (1972), pp. 13–28, and 'The Emergence of W. E. B. Du Bois as an African Nationalist', JNH, 54 (1969), pp. 48–60; Jean Fagan Yellin, 'Du Bois' Crisis and Women's Suffrage', MassR, 14 (1973), PP. 365–75; C. H. Wesley, 'W. E. B. Du Bois: The Historian', JNH, 50 (1965), pp. 147–62, and Katherine M. Glazer, 'W. E. B. Du Bois' Impressions of Woodrow Wilson', JNH, 58 (1973), pp. 452–9.

For Du Bois' responses to the Depression and New Deal, see in addition to the biographies cited: Raymond Wolters, *Negroes and the Great Depression: The Problem of Economic Recovery* (Westport, Connecticut, 1970); John B. Kirby, *Black Americans in the Roosevelt Era* (Knoxville, Tennessee, 1980), and Harvard Sitkoff, *A New Deal for Blacks: The Emergence of Civil Rights as a National Issue*, Vol. 1, *The Depression Decade* (Oxford University Press,

New York, 1978).

Du Bois' major writings, available in several editions include *Dusk of Dawn* (1940), which he described as 'not so much my autobiography as the autobiography of a concept of race', and *The Autobiography of W. E. B. Du Bois* (1968), edited by Herbert Aptheker. Du Bois' major historical and sociological works (all of which are currently in print) include: *The Suppression of the African Slave Trade to the U.S.A., 1638–1870* (1896); *The Philadelphia Negro* (1899); *The Souls of Black Folk* (1903 and 1968); *The Negro* (1915); *Darkwater: Voices From Within the Veil* (1920 and 1969); *Black Reconstruction in America* (1935), *Colour and Democracy* (1945), and *The World and Africa* (1947).

MARCUS GARVEY

Garvey's biographers have reached very differing conclusions about their subject and the movement he led. Edmund David Cronon's *Black Moses: The Story of Marcus Garvey and the Universal Negro Improvement Association* (Madison, Wisconsin, 1962), offers a mixed verdict. On the one hand, Cronon found Garvey to have been an inept leader with such serious deficiencies that they 'overbalanced the sounder aspects of his programme'. On the other, Cronon conceded that Garvey was essentially honest, was harassed by his black and white critics, but yet managed to make a permanent contribution to the precepts and practice of black nationalism in America. Theodore G Vincent's *Black Power and the Garvey Movement* (San Francisco, California, 1972), depicts Garvey as the inspiration of the later leaders of independent African states, and the UNIA as a heterogeneous body, some of whose members were concerned with securing racial equality in America. Vincent argues that Cronon displayed a 'negative attitude' toward the UNIA, since he 'could not visualise a black nationalism that was neither reactionary nor demagogic'. Vincent sees Garvey as the leading ideological forerunner of the black separatist theorists of the 1960s. In *Race First: The Ideological and Organizational Struggles of Marcus Garvey and the UNIA* (Westport, Connecticut, 1976), Tony Martin claims that Garvey was 'the greatest black figure in the twentieth century'. Martin's over-long study ignores factionalism within the UNIA, and asserts unconvincingly that

Garvey was a 'revolutionary' nationalist. But the DuBois–Garvey feud receives the fullest documentation in Martin's book. Garvey's wider American influence and appeal is examined in Emory J. Tolbert, *The UNIA and Black Los Angeles: Ideology and Community in the Garvey Movement* (Los Angeles: UCLA's Centre for Afro-American Studies 1980). Tolbert demonstrates that a large percentage of Garveyites in Los Angeles were homeowners and experienced activists; unlike New York Garveyites, they did not 'engage in open ideological warfare' that characterized relations between the UNIA and the NAACP in Harlem. In *Garveyism as a Religious Movement: The Institutionalization of a Black Religion* (Metuchen, New Jersey and London, 1978), Randall K. Burkett examines the implicitly and explicitly religious language, symbols and rituals of the UNIA, and concludes convincingly that 'the religious ethos of the UNIA was pervasive, embracing nearly every facet of its organizational life'. Judith Stein, *The World of Marcus Garvey: Race and Class in Modern Society* (Louisiana State University Press, 1986), emphasizes the petit bourgeois spirit of Garveyism, and examines Garvey's career from the comparative perspective of the class structure and divisions within the black community.

Professor Robert A. Hill has undertaken a formidable task – the assembly of 'a comprehensive survey of all the presently available historical manuscripts and records pertaining to the life and work of Marcus Mosiah Garvey, as well as the popular worldwide organization that he founded and led from its inception in 1914 until his death in 1940'. Six volumes (four have already appeared) will cover Garvey and the UNIA activities in the United States, two will plot the impact of Garveyism in Africa, and two final volumes will deal with the man and his movement in the Caribbean. On the evidence so far, *The Marcus Garvey and Universal Negro Improvement Association Papers* (University of California Press, 1979 to 1985, and continuing), promises to be the most significant undertaking in African-American historiography since the publication of the *Booker T. Washington Papers*. Informative footnotes identify Garvey's disciples and critics and each volume is handsomely produced. Less satisfactory, however, is the intended general introduction to Garvey and the UNIA offered in Volume 1. Defining Garveyism as symbolizing 'the historic encounter between two highly developed socioeconomic and political traditions: the social consciousness and drive for self-governance of the Caribbean peasantry and the racial consciousness and search for justice of the Afro-American community', with the UNIA, after 1920, as 'a black government in exile', Hill adopts a clumsy classification of Garvey's achievements under such headings as 'Garveyism as the Religion of Success', 'Confraternity and Self Cultures', and 'The Mirror of Nationalism' in a rambling and poorly-written essay. (He also fails to mention that Garvey never set foot in Africa.) But as source materials, the Garvey *Papers* are indispensable to the student of the period.

Briefer and generally sound assessments of Garvey's American years can be found in: Robert G. Weisbord, *Ebony Kinship: Africa, Africans, and the Afro-Americans* (Westport, Connecticut, 1973); Leonard E. Barrett, *Soul Force: African Heritage in Afro-American Religion* (New York, 1974); Alphonso Pinkney, *Red Black, and Green: Black Nationalism in the United States* (Cambridge University Press, 1976), and Theodore Draper, *The Rediscovery of Black Nationalism* (New York, 1970). The opposition of black American socialists to Garvey is treated in Theodore Kornweibel, Jr, *No Crystal Stair: Black Life and the Messenger, 1917–1928* (Westport, Connecticut, 1975). (For a brief account of A. Philip Randolph's career, see William H. Harris, 'A. Philip Randolph as a Charismatic Leader, 1925–1941', JNH, XLIV (1979), pp.301–15). On relations between black Americans and West Indians in *Harlem*, see David J. Hellwig, 'Black Meets Black: Afro-American Reactions to West Indian Immigrants in the 1920s', SAQ, 77 (1978), pp.206–24. Two important studies of Harlem are: Gilbert Osofsky, Harlem: *The Making of a Ghetto, 1880–1930* (New York, 1963), and Nathan I. Huggins, *Harlem Renaissance* (New York, 1971). John Runcie has written two excellent articles on neglected aspects of Garveyism: 'Marcus Garvey and the Harlem Renaissance', *Afro-Americans in New York Life and History* (July, 1986), pp 7–28, and 'Black Music and the Garvey Movement', *Afro-Americans in New York Life and History* (July, 1987), pp.7–23. See also Jervis Anderson , *Harlem: The Great Black Way, 1900–1950* (London, 1982), a vivid account by a black journalist of the culture and politics of the most famous black ghetto.

Of 'eyewitness' descriptions of Garvey and the UNIA in New York, the most graphic are by Claude McKay, *Harlem: Negro Metropolis* (New York, 1940, 1968); Roi Ottley, *'New World A-Coming'* (New York, 1943, 1969), Adam Clayton Powell, Sr, *Against the Tide: An Autobiography* (New York, 1938); James Weldon Johnson, *Black Manhattan* (New York, 1930, 1968). Richard Wright, the noted black novelist, describes his meetings with Garveyites in Chicago during the Depression in *American Hunger*

(New York, 1944, 1977).

Robert H. Brisbane, Jr, provides a concise account of Garvey's American activities in 'Some New Light on the Garvey Movement', JNH, 36 (1951), pp.53–62. Garvey's widow (and second wife), Amy-Jacques Garvey edited the valuable *Philosophy and Opinions of Marcus Garvey* (New York, 1969), the speeches and writings of Garvey before 1925. See also, her partisan but fascinating account, *Garvey and Garveyism* (Kingston, Jamaica, 1963), and E. U. Essien-Udom and Amy-Jacques Garvey (eds), *More Philosophy and Opinions of Marcus Garvey* (London, 1977). John Henrik Clark (ed.), *Marcus Garvey and the Vision of Africa* (New York, 1974), contains Garvey's important 1923 autobiographical piece, 'The Negro's Greatest Enemy', various speeches, and insightful essays by Richard B. Moore, Edwin S. Redkey and Marcus Garvey, Jr.

MARTIN LUTHER KING, JR

There are now several major studies of King and his role in the civil rights movement. David L. Lewis, *King: A Critical Biography* (London, 1970), charts the major stages of King's career, and has some pertinent comments on his personality, but is poorly written and adopts a patronizing tone. Stephen B. Oates, *Let The Trumpet Sound: The Life of Martin Luther King, Jr.*, (London, 1982), covers much the same ground, but avoids any serious analysis of King's stature as a black leader, and lapses frequently into purple prose. David J. Garrow has written three important books: *Protest at Selma: Martin Luther King, Jr. and the Voting Rights Act of 1965* (New Haven, 1978), is a close analysis of the SCLC campaign and its aftermath; *The FBI and Martin Luther King, Jr: From 'Solo' to Memphis* (London, 1981), argues convincingly that King was a real, rather than an imagined, threat to the established order, in that he had become, in the last years of his life, a radical figure; *Bearing the Cross: Martin Luther King, Jr., and the Southern Christian Leadership Conference* (New York, 1986), offers a massively detailed narrative account of the man and the movement. King's private life (and the FBI's interest in his extra-marital activities), tensions within the SCLC, the campaigns in Albany, Birmingham, Selma and Chicago all receive close attention. Garrow is particularly concerned to prove that King was primarily motivated more by a visionary religious faith than by his reading of Gandhi or Walter Rauschenbusch. Adam Fairclough's excellent account, *To Redeem the Soul of America: The Southern Christian Leadership Conference and Martin Luther King, Jr.*, (University of Georgia Press, London, 1987), stresses SCLC's achievements as an organized protest movement, and offers balanced assessments of King's strengths and weaknesses. Fairclough has also written four useful articles: 'The SCLC and the Second Reconstruction 1957–1963', SAQ, 80 (Spring, 1981), pp. 177–94; 'Was Martin Luther King a Marxist?', HWJ, 15 (Spring, 1983), pp. 117–25; 'Martin Luther King, Jr., and the War in Vietnam', Phylon, XLV (March, 1984), pp. 19–39, and 'The Preachers and the People: The Origins and Early Years of the SCLC, 1955–1959', JSH, L11 (August, 1986), pp.403–40. James A. Colaiaco, *Martin Luther King, Jr.: Apostle of Militant Nonviolence* (New York, 1988), is a short but informative biography. Colaiaco stresses that King was 'among the first black American leaders to shift his focus from civil rights to human rights', and towards the end of his life had begun to formulate 'a radical critique of American institutions and foreign policy'. Like other recent commentators, Colaiaco believes that King sympathized with Black Power and Marxist critiques of American capitalism and militarism.

King's intellectual and spiritual development receive considered attention in Hanes Walton, Jr, *The Political Philosophy of Martin Luther King, Jr.* (Westport, Connecticut, 1971), and in John G. Ansbro, *Martin Luther King, Jr,: The Making of a Mind* (New York, 1983), which is particularly informative on King's attitudes to American involvement in Vietnam. See also the following articles: John E. Rathbun, 'Martin Luther King: The Theology of Social Action', AQ, 20 (1968), pp. 38–53; Warren E. Steinkraus, 'Martin Luther King's Personalism and Nonviolence', JHI, 34 (1973), pp. 97–111, and Mohan Lal Sharma, 'Martin Luther King: Modern America's Greatest Theologian of Social Action', JNH, 53 (1968), pp. 257–63.

August Meier's influential essay of 1965, 'On the Role of Martin Luther King', is reprinted in John Bracey, August Meier, and Elliott Rudwick's anthology, *Conflict and Competition: Studies in the Recent Black Protest Movement* (Belmont, California, 1971), David J. Garrow, Clayborne Carson, James H. Cone, Vincent G. Harding and Nathan I. Huggins are the contributors to a valuable symposium: 'A Round Table: Martin Luther King, Jr.', JAH, 74 (1987), pp. 436–81. Clayborne Carson has also written perceptively on King's relationship with young black militants: *In Struggle: SNCC and the Black Awakening of the 1960's* (cited above). C. Eric Lincoln edited a good collection of essays, *Martin Luther King Jr.: A Profile* (New York, 1970), with contributions from James Baldwin, Ralph Abernathy and August Meier. The best account and analysis of the Montgomery boycott is provided by J. Mills Thornton III, 'Challenge and response in the Montgomery Bus Boycott of 1955–1956,' reprinted in Sarah W. Wiggins (ed.), *From Civil War to Civil Rights: Alabama 1860-1960, An Anthology from the Alabama Review* (University of Alabama Press, 1987), pp.463–519. On the Memphis strike see Davis M. Tucker's essay, 'Rev. James M. Lawson, Jr., and the Garbage Strike', in his study, *Black Pastors and Leaders: Memphis 1819-1972* (Memphis State University Press, 1975).

For a personal account of King's life and work, see Coretta Scott King, *My Life With Martin Luther King, Jr.* (New York, 1970).

King's major writings are: *Stride Toward Freedom: The Montgomery Story* (New York, 1958); *Why We Can't Wait* (New York, 1964); *Where Do We Go From Here: Chaos or Community?* (New York, 1967) and the *Triumph of Conscience* (New York, 1968).

MALCOLM X

Any study of Malcolm X must begin with *The Autobiography of Malcolm X* (New York, 1965), now available in several paperback editions. The British Penguin edition (1980) contains a useful index. Written in collaboration with Alex Haley (later the author of the phenomenal best seller and TV series, *Roots*) it is, on every count, a remarkable document. Haley's 'foreword' is also essential for an understanding of the genesis of the book, and for its insights into Malcolm's personality, style and intellectual development. The *Autobiography of Malcolm X* has been subjected to rigorous scholarly interpretation and exegesis. See especially: Barrett J. Mandell, 'The Didactic Achievement of Malcolm X's Autobiography', AAS, 2 (1972), pp.269–74; Frederick D. Harper, 'A Reconstruction of Malcolm X's Personality', AAS, 3 (1972), pp.1–6; Cedric J. Robinson, 'Malcolm Little as Charismatic Leader', AAS, 4 (1972), pp.81–96; Samuel J. Weiss, 'The Ordeal of Malcolm X', SAQ, 67 (1968), pp. 53–63; Carol Ohman, 'The Autobiography of Malcolm X: A Revolutionary Use of the Franklin Tradition', AQ, 22 (1970), pp.131–49, and Eugene Victor Wolfenstein's essay, 'The Autobiography of Malcolm X', in his perceptive but difficult study, *The Victims of Democracy: Malcolm X and the Black Revolution* (University of California Press, 1981), pp.284–92.

Peter Goldman, a senior editor of *Newsweek* magazine, examines Malcolm's later years in *The Death and Life of Malcolm X* (London, 1974), an overblown but sympathetic biography. See also Goldman's shorter essay: 'Malcolm X: Witness for the Prosecution', in Franklin and Meier (eds), *Black Leaders of the Twentieth Century* (cited above).

Favourable assessments of Malcolm are to be found in Thomas L. Blair, *Retreat to the Ghetto: The End of a Dream?* (London, 1977), and Alphonso Pinkney, *Red, Black, and Green: Black Nationalism in the United States* (cited above). Archie Epps, editor of the *Speeches of Malcolm X at Harvard* (New York, 1969), also provides an informative analytical and descriptive essay, 'The Paradoxes of Malcolm X'. John Henrik Clark (ed.), *Malcolm X: The Man and His Times* (Toronto, 1969), is a collection of black estimates (all of them eulogistic) of Malcolm, together with a selection of his speeches and interviews. George Breitman has also collected statements by Malcolm in *By Any Means Necessary: Speeches, Interviews, and a Letter By Malcolm X* (New York, 1970), and *Malcolm X Speaks* (New York, 1965). In *The Last Year of Malcolm X* (New York, 1967) Breitman claims that he was 'one of the most slandered and misunderstood Americans of our time', and offers 'what is missing or muted in *The Autobiography*' as a corrective to the view that it represents a full record of Malcolm's political development, arguing (unconvincingly) that he became a revolutionary socialist. Also valuable for the insights they afford into Malcolm's views are: *Malcolm X: The Last Speeches*, edited by Bruce Perry (Pathfinder Press: New York, 1989), which includes six previously unpublished addresses and interviews, and *Malcolm X on Afro-American History: Expanded and Illustrated Edition* (Pathfinder Press, New York, 1970 and 1988), with an introduction by George Breitman, which contains selections from Malcolm's *Autobiography*, the text of an address to the Organization of Afro-American Unity, 24 January, 1965, and short discourses on such topics as 'The House Negro and the Field Negro' and 'Africa and Self-Hate'.

On the origins and growth of The Nation of Islam, see: C. Eric Lincoln, *The Black Muslims in America* (rev. ed, Boston, 1973), and his article 'The Black Muslims Revisited or the State of the Black Nation of Islam', AAS, 3 (1972), pp.175–86; E. U. Essien-Udom, *Black Nationalism: The Rise of the Black Muslims in the U.S.A.* (Penguin Books, Harmondsworth, 1966), and Louis E. Lomax, *When the Word is Given: A Report on Elijah Muhammad and the Black Muslim World* (New York, 1964).

A critical estimate of Malcolm is provided by Tom Kahn and Bayard Rustin, 'The Ambiguous Legacy of Malcolm X', *Dissent*, 12 (1965), pp.188–92. For more favourable verdicts see: Le Roi Jones, 'The Legacy of Malcolm X and the Coming of the Black Nation', in his collected pieces *Home: Social Essays* (New York, 1966), and the late I. F. Stone's thoughtful essay, 'The Pilgrimage of Malcolm X', from *In a Time of Torment* (New York, 1967), pp.110–21. Wilson J. Moses in *Black Messiahs and Uncle Toms* (cited above), suggests plausibly that Malcolm X might be regarded as 'a sort of "apostle to the gentiles", because he expended an appreciable amount of energy during his last years addressing predominantly white audiences'.

In *One Day When I Was Lost* (London, 1974) James Baldwin created an intriguing 'scenario' based on Malcolm's *Autobiography*, dictated in part by 'the legal complexities created by Malcolm's rupture with the Nation of Islam Movement'. It is a sensitive evocation of the 'much-maligned, groping and very moving character of a man known as Malcolm X'. Maya Angelou recounts her meetings with Malcolm in *The Heart of a Woman* (London, 1986), and *All God's Children Need Travelling Shoes* (London, 1987). See also Eldridge Cleaver's tribute, 'Initial Reactions on the Assassination of Malcolm X', in *Soul on Ice* (London, 1969). Two spirited expositions of Black Power are to be found in Julius Lester, *Look Out Whitey! Black Power's Gon' Get Your Mama!* (New York, 1968), and Stokely Carmichael and Charles V. Hamilton, *Black Power: The Politics of Liberation in America* (Penguin Books, Harmondsworth, 1969).

JESSE JACKSON

There is no satisfactory biography of Jackson, but see: Barbara A. Reynolds, *Jesse Jackson: The Man, The Movement, The Myth* (Chicago, 1975). Adolph L. Reed, Jr, *The Jesse Jackson Phenomenon: The Crisis of Purpose in Afro-American Politics* (New Haven and

London, 1986) is a highly critical evaluation, which criticizes Jackson for engaging in 'symbolic politics' and unconvincingly insists that he is not a significant figure in American politics. Adam Fairclough's Review Essay, 'What Makes Jesse Run?', JAS, 22 (April, 1988), pp.77–86, and Manning Marable, *Black American Politics: From The Washington Marches to Jesse Jackson* (cited above), offer more positive assessments of Jackson as a black leader. See also the black political commentator June Jordan's essay, 'Next Time the Rainbow', an analysis of Jackson's 1988 presidential campaign, in the *New Statesman and Society* (6 January 1989), pp.31–5.

For an influential statement of the view that 'many important features of black and white relations in America are not captured when the issue is defined as majority versus minority and that a preoccupation with race and racial conflict obscures fundamental problems that derive from the intersection of race and class', see William Julius Wilson, *The Declining Significance of Race: Blacks and Changing American Institutions* (2nd edn, University of Chicago Press, 1980). Wilson's views are partially refuted in Alphonso Pinkney's *The Myth of Black Progress* (Cambridge University Press, 1984), which offers a sober (and sobering) assessment of the black American condition in the 1980s. His concern is with the continuing erosion of a 'commitment to racial equality, and a general shift to the right on matters pertaining to race and poverty' – symbolized by Reagan's victories in 1980 and 1984.

Index